11/11/74

Best wishes

Fred

Coming to Terms
with Death

Coming to Terms with

Death: *how to face*

the inevitable
with wisdom and dignity

Fred Cutter, Ph.D.

Nelson-Hall Company 𝗻𝗵 Chicago

Library of Congress Cataloging in Publication Data

Cutter, Fred, 1924-
    Coming to terms with death.

    Bibliography: p.
    1. Death—Psychology.   I. Title.
BF789.D4C87   155.9'37   74-8397
ISBN 0-911012-29-X

                    ISBN: 0-911012-29-X

        Manufactured in the United States of America

To Gregory Bateson, who taught me about the differences that make a difference, and to Frank Johnson, who died with dignity because he knew the difference.

Contents

Preface

Recently, I tried to help a close friend die. He believed in God, immortality of the soul, and was thoughtful about his daily behavior. Like the rest of us, he suffered from the conventional fear and avoidance of death. His wife knew he was dying and had accepted the inevitable, but was distressed by his avoiding the subject. Her inability to discuss his imminent death eventually loomed as a monstrous barrier between them during their last days together. One of their children began to suffer from night-mares, but these disappeared as soon as the mother shared her burden with the children. Even more upsetting, her husband acted with obvious displeasure at her daily visits. He acted as though he didn't want to see her anymore.

When I visited him in the hospital, he grasped my hand passionately. He grasped my hand again when I left; this time in farewell and as a gesture of enduring friendship. In between he avoided any direct confirmation of his impending death, yet he did acknowledge that the pain, suffering, and impairment were inherently lonely. "No one can do this for me," he said.

During the previous six months of his illness, I had listened to him and accepted his great concern for his family as natural. His concern deepened as the illness lingered. He wanted most of all for his family to continue the way of life they had established. Most of all he was afraid of becoming a burden to them.

Earlier in his illness I had suggested a "business as usual" philosophy, since this would induce the least change in the family's way of life. As the illness continued and his disability increased, my friend finally accepted the prospect of death and tried to minimize any demands on his family. Essentially he wrote himself off as a lost cause, expendable, in effect already dead. In his relations to most people, he acted as if nothing were wrong. It wasn't that he pretended to be well, but rather he made believe he was not dying in the same way some people make believe or pretend that a person isn't crippled or disfigured when they are. More relevantly, all of us make believe that terminally-ill people are neither dead nor alive. By doing so, we ignore the most essential aspect of their existence, the fatal illness that afflicts them.

The ailing man's wife and I discussed this aspect and together we realized that his avoidance behaviors were his unique ways of coping with the final encounter. We both tried to shift our gears accordingly. His wife now visited him casually, almost on-the-run, apparently just dropping in for fifteen minutes or so while taking care of other matters. This helped a lot. She also began to bring colorful objects like fresh flowers and green plants, posters, the children's school constructions, to brighten up the drab hospital environment that enveloped him. She also began to include the children, one at a time, to share with their father the daily achievements they brought home. In that way, they were able to participate in the final moments rather than remaining sheltered from the truth. My friend was able to derive some comfort from his family while giving them a chance to prepare for his loss. His children would later remember these important experiences in their adult years.

My friend was setting an example in the ways he accepted his own eventual death. He was using as a model the death of his own father, who suffered from a heart failure while driving home from work. His father had somehow managed to park his car alongside the curb, opened his wallet with his identification showing, and quietly waited. When he was found, he was dead. My friend had told me this story on eight different occasions over a five-year period. To him it had represented an admirable way to face death. From this precedent he was able to shape an ideal way to face his own end and he did so with quiet courage.

He died quickly, one week after he had grasped my hand in farewell. I think his last days were somewhat more pleasant and the final encounters with his family were meaningful to all of them. His dying affected me in many ways that even today, nearly four years later, are not entirely clear. We were very close, first as colleagues, later as friends. We had worked together and were about the same age. We had similar interests. During his illness, however, our roles shifted. In the beginning I was the helper, trying to explain and put into perspective the events which befell him. Towards the end, when death was near, he tried to offer me a perspective by his example. In hindsight, I respect and admire the way he faced his own cessation, and hope I can do as well. The larger value of his final visits with me were moments of truth; he had died the way he had lived and believed. In doing so, he provided me with an opportunity to reciprocate. I did, but now *he* was the comforter while I struggled with the prospect of loss.

In large measure, his passing and my bereavement inspired this book. Such losses represent extreme changes for those who remain. Some are noticed and simply called differences. Certain differences are more important than others, of course, but the ultimate change is cessation of awareness entirely. Yet, imminent death is almost always publicly ignored. Even in private, there is a corresponding reluctance to examine the impact on remaining life created by the prospect of death. It simply isn't faced.

Pathetically, though, it is that very absence of human awareness that robs the dying person of a dignified death. Prolonged dying becomes macabre when the identity of the patient is no longer visible. As long as he can continue his human role, the survivors can try to respond with their complementary self-expectations. But when the dying person slips into the role of nonperson, object, or terminal patient, prolonged existence lacks dignity in the eyes of his survivors.

The loss of this identity comes on gradually, usually precipitated by the loss of vitality associated with fatal illness.

However, the prior default of self-examination, and preparation for this eventuality, accelerates the transition of the
dying into the role of a nonperson.

This book hopefully will provide readers with help in how
to prepare for the death of others and to help the dying retain
dignity.

1

Last Encounters and Survival Gaps

Everybody is a survivor. Sooner or later each person suffers from the loss of a close relative, friend, and in lesser degrees of acquaintances. Nobody in this culture is given systematic preparation for loss and bereavement except a lucky few who can look to their elders for examples. No other universal experience is given less preparation, more avoidance, or greater distress. Survivors face tremendously difficult choices before, during, and after a death. They need help in coping with informed consent for inevitable choices.

All survivors are potential victims who must also prepare for their own deaths by making each day count while still alive. Survivors can help to shape the dying process, to make it a more positive encounter with the people for whom they care deeply. One needs to pay sufficient attention to the inevitability of death, and make a personal preparation for it.

As grim as the subject of death may appear, its problems are only made worse by avoiding reality. Because of this almost universal denial, death always seems to come as a surprise. Then comes the crisis. Suddenly there is an urgent need for quick decisions at a time when the survivors are least able to cope. Even worse, survivors may discover that only unpleasant alternatives are available. In hindsight, they may realize that better choices were possible earlier but "only if they knew before what they know now." Many of the suggestions offered here are derived from the errors and unnecessary grief suffered by survivors. Perhaps greater insight can minimize some of those hazards for you.

There are several recurring themes that might as well be explicitly stated at the start. First is the Socratic notion that the unexamined life is not worth living. The second theme is that all life is a rehearsal for death. This apparently morbid and enigmatic phrasing is a simplified formulation of the meaning a unique person can assign to his own death. A third theme is the universal denial of death which erects taboos about the subject. These barriers block inquiry and the achievement of consensus. The most extreme example is the avoidance by the mass media of topics publicizing fatal diseases that are so commonplace while overemphasizing violent or rare forms of death.

A corollary is the universality of death, but a failure to accept fatal diseases. Birth and death are inevitable and expected, but one is considered normal, and the other is always regarded as pathological.

A fourth theme is the inherent value of knowledge. No one can leave death to the last minute without distressing consequences. Preparation should be life-long, or at least several years before termination becomes imminent. To default on last things produces the same degree of catastrophe as failure to prepare for other eventualities—birth, health care, job, marriage, retirement, fire, crime, and more recently, drug abuse.

A fifth theme is the wish to die. Everyone encounters this feeling at some point in their lives. In some degree, it is always present as a potential motive for a variety of self-injurious or accidental behaviors. The circumstances under which it increases are generally overlooked, as well as the variety of deaths motivated.

A sixth theme is the total absence in the American ethos of a positive definition for appropriate death. The one offered here is the readiness of the victim to accept cessation in which he neither seeks nor avoids the possibility of termination; more significantly, he does not display excessive efforts for either extreme.

These themes and the behavior they elicit permit a person

to develop a liberated approach to the death of those close, and eventually to his or her own. Coming to terms with the inevitability of death frees the individual to give his daily life the best value he can. All of these themes can be demonstrated in the basic encounters people experience.

An "encounter" refers to what people do in contrast to what they say they do. Since much of human interaction is verbal, it is often difficult to test statements or evaluate behavior. Strong emotions such as crying, rage, laughter are authentic reactions to a particular encounter and reflect a corresponding moment of truth for the participants. In more subtle ways the acts, gestures, and deeds people do are their responses to encounters, no matter what they say. Sometimes they are merely being polite, but more often there is a deliberate deception present. Occasionally, the individuals are deceiving themselves.

Final encounters are events in which important last things occur to survivors as they respond to one in the role of a dying person. Additionally, this someone is a person bearing a special connection; typically a relative, parent, child, spouse. Quite often the relation is that of friend, colleague, boss, employee. What survivors do in the last interactions with a dying person are expressive of the special relation between them. It is a moment of truth in which the unique history of the pair limits their respective choices. Each is compelled to do his own thing and be true to the relation shared. In deciding what to do, the past is prologue; the earlier is a rehearsal for the later; and the individual dies in the way he lived. Each person prepares for the last encounter by the habits, choices, and approaches developed over a lifetime. When a victim is able to accept his cessation, his death becomes appropriate, natural, or even desirable, no matter what the biological cause of termination. The shock of bereavement is minimized if the survivor can recognize this readiness to cease.

Pathetically, the usual circumstances of dying impede victims from accepting their own cessation and survivors from either helping or recognizing the kind of death that is occurring. The overwhelming majority of adult deaths each year come ignominiously in sterile, ugly places with the victim isolated and bereft in his final moments. There is no necessity for a victim of terminal disease to pass his or her last weeks or months in drab or depressing settings. The ones who work there don't usually notice and the ones who do see have no license to act. The atmosphere is unnecessarily bad because of default and lack of attention. It is within the survivors' power to specify the settings, furnishings, circumstances and other special requests. It only takes planning and preparation. The real problem is, why the avoidance of and failure to accept the obvious? The American way of dying is not only expensive, but traumatic to all parties.

Dying has become a problem in recent years because of medical success in postponing biological termination and in reversing clinical expiration. Today, the moment of death is impossible to define, and requires twenty-four-hour observation periods. Simultaneously, the American public expects physicians to delay death indefinitely. Everyone regards it fearfully; as something to be avoided, denied, and as representing the ultimate absurdity. The current orientation towards dying in America is phobic, the subject totally unfit for polite conversation. The subject of death is even more of a taboo than sex once was.

Where death is considered an abnormal event, most people react to it by simple avoidance, or lip service to traditional explanations. For those who devoutly believe in heaven and hell, and who base their convictions on careful examination, the religious position is certainly valid. But the majority seem to give only superficial attention to religion as well as death. A smaller group, typically young, prefers to believe in reincarnation. The more intellectual persons lean toward science-fiction solutions, that old age is a curable disease. Another subgroup regards freezing and indefinite storage as a means of bypassing death entirely, since they expect to be revived eventually. No one can fully reject such optimism concerning death and the continuation of the individual. But, for those who do accept the inevitability of death, the purpose here is to offer positive suggestions for adequate preparation. To do so requires information about effective decision-making and an orientation to the variety of ways of securing knowledge.

In effect, everyone goes about pursuing "happiness" with the resources and abilities they find available. While scientific achievements and resulting technology have increased the range of choices, these discoveries have also changed the accepted or customary ways of getting things done. Most people have adapted almost without noticing. The recent interest in ecological consequences as a by-product of technology is a belated recognition of how changes influence the way people live.

The majority of our daily choices are made on the basis of whimsical or conventional motives. There's no reason for doing or choosing something except that it's available or because others are doing it. More thoughtful and rational decisions are made by everybody, but in relatively small areas of their lives. To try for independence or autonomy requires greater effort than most persons are willing to make. Most people take the easy way out, conserve energy, and make the majority of daily choices on some superficial basis. The use of scientific methods, rational criteria, or philosophical premises is rare. Individuals tend to fall back on the same habits, look to their neighbors, or leave it to chance. Regardless of why, each choice remains an expression of personal preference even though these are often conventional or whimsical. Psychologists call these values.

The source of values is really not obscure. In most individuals and in most of their values, they simply express uncritically what they have accumulated from parents, siblings, peers, and others, and more recently from television or movies. This is a general description of how people develop important preferences that reflect underlying values. One value is that life is better than death, or at least that death is worse than life. Many of the old values are gone. Youth of today have demonstrated that dying for God, country, and family is no longer the heroic ideal previously admired.

Now, the emphasis is on hedonistic experiences. Enjoy the moment because tomorrow you may die. Death makes an absurdity out of any value, other than more survival, or continuing pleasure.

The professionals who prepare television commercials

use themes that penetrate deeply into the most powerful motives in human beings, whom they view as potential consumers. Every product is advertised as making existence more pleasurable, safer, healthier, or longer. Nowhere does the viewer ever hear about products which will make death pleasant, timely, or seemly. Even funeral establishments are reluctant to advertise.

The American way of dying has incorporated within it an implicit existentialism. In this point of view, death is the ultimate absurdity in a meaningless existence, because death comes to the good as well as the bad. Human life is limited to the interval between birth and death, so that none of the values of immortality, the soul, or posterity are believed in by existentialists.

Neither scientists nor physicians pay much attention to death and certainly not to the problems of its aftermath—continuation into heaven, hell, limbo, or reincarnation. Medicine is preoccupied with postponing death, keeping patients alive, and hopefully curing them or easing their pain. There is evidence that attending physicians spend less time with terminally ill patients than others, visit them less frequently, and are more attentive to symptoms than to the person involved. Recent medical success in postponing the moment of death has been labeled as prolonging of dying rather than the extension of life because the net effect does so little for the quality of existence given to the patient. Such procedures have been criticized as robbing the patient of a dignified death, imposing burdens on the survivors, and wasting socially valuable resources.

Neither science nor medicine offers a choice when it comes to preparation for death. However, it is possible to cultivate the notion that death can be appropriate. One can conceive of death as natural: as normal within a certain stage of life, and under some circumstances even optimal for the victim. Still, the position taken in the media—television, radio, newspapers, and magazines—is that death is always a tragedy, ignoring the fact that death is a natural phenomenon. The acceptance of death by means of a personal readiness to die is resisted and often interpreted as the wish to die. The latter is quickly equated with suicide, the ultimate negation of all the values that this society holds dear.

Americans suffer accelerating hazards to life and pleasure as they try to accumulate seniority in the social system. The earliest dangers are sexual, but by the age of three or four, the game of life makes children forget them until puberty. The rules of the social game demand kids to act as if neither sex nor death is real, lest their behavior remind parents of problems still unsolved. In time children discover answers to sexual questions. Conversely, death was once a more natural phenomenon that was accepted as inevitable. Nowadays, children never see anybody keel over and die in their living room, on their front porch, or in bed. Instead, they are told "so-and-so passed away," or is "going to heaven," or has achieved eternal rest. All a kid can see is that "he ain't there no more," with everybody pretending that he never was. This deception helps everyone get along until a child talks about it. He or she, in turn, is made to feel like a freak for bringing up a forbidden topic.

There are a variety of discrepancies in our American attitudes about death that make us victims of social contradiction. These mutually exclusive expectations are identified as survival gaps because they threaten the equanimity of the recently bereaved.

Superficial Mourning Rites

Every survivor encounters conflicts between what he feels and that which is expected of him. That person suffers conflicts in attempting to cope with grief. Regardless of the relation the survivor had with the deceased, intimate feelings always appear to be wrong and certainly inappropriate when expressed in public. However, mourning does require some public ritual. The survivors often find that they must ignore their unique feelings and pretend the stereotyped emotions.

The correct posture at most funerals involves some superficial allusion to the immortality of the deceased. Many mourners find their personal convictions incompatible with such a stereotype and blocked from public expression. The memorial service leaves them alienated from other mourners and deprived of an adequate opportunity to express their grief.

Birth as well as death in our society further illustrates how group-accepted notions of appropriate behavior impose limitations on intimate feelings. Today the birth of a baby is viewed as a natural and happy experience even when it is undesirable or impractical. But death is always considered pathological regardless of how appropriate. Joy and congratulations are the expected behavior even when a pregnancy is unwanted. It makes no difference how deprived the subsequent childhood may become. Yet death always requires some expression of sorrow even though the deceased might have enjoyed a complete life and faced only a grim existence if dying were prolonged.

These conventional expectations block an individual from expressing his unique reactions to these personal but otherwise universal events. A sixteen-year-old high school girl delivers a baby. She deserves condolences, not congratulations. She has closed most of her future options for a career, lost her freedom to develop as a woman, and has no time even to become an adequate mother. Negatively, she has brought into the world an unneeded child, one who will be a burden to herself, her husband or other persons, and their parents, if not the community as a whole. In American society, couples under twenty-five are usually economically immature and need financial support.

A child in this family situation is automatically deprived. The parents will also suffer hardships, at least by the standards of what their contemporaries have in the way of choices. Where the girl is unwed, alone, and the parents unable to assist, the child and its mother face a very difficult and insecure future. Is such a birth cause for joy? Unfortunately, it appears to be easier for everybody to pretend all is well and sweep the ugly possibilities out of sight.

Another situation is equally grotesque. An elderly man

suffers a series of debilitating strokes. He is retired, his friends are gone, his waking day is spent in efforts to keep himself fed, clean, medicated and comfortable. Actually his death should be celebrated as a release for everybody. While his passing should be regretted and his memory mourned, *his death is not a tragedy.* It should be experienced as a relief, and survivors may even feel some joy at his escape from continuing misery. In an older time, the death of the aged would have been called "God's will" or natural.

Psychologically, the stroke victim may have died much earlier in the debilitating process. But these contradictions place survivors in various conflicts, so that their real feelings almost always emerge inappropriately. Individuals faced with these situations are forced to deny their actual feelings. The parents of the pregnant girl must suppress their horror and pretend joy. The children of the elderly man must evidence symptoms of grief when all they can honestly feel is relief. Birth and death, in an increasingly wider range of situations, demand stereotyped reactions, forcing individuals to repress their natural emotions.

The same conflict between repressed emotions and the expected feelings occurs when an individual must comply with the stereotype—speak no evil of the dead. Genuine emotions in any relation almost always include negative, hostile, or other publicly unacceptable responses. Yet in bereavement, the survivor has no place to go and no one to accept his or her feelings about the disrupted relation. Despite strong individual feelings, this person finds only tolerance and later exhortations to forget, be brave, and carry on. The complications from this peculiar survival gap will be described more fully in a later chapter.

Real Feelings Denied

Repression of actual feelings creates a secondary survival gap. In order to cope with the primary one of proper versus improper behavior, many survivors deny their real feelings to a point where psychological repression occurs, and the unacceptable impulses are forgotten so completely that awareness of the whole experience is narrowed. The survivor becomes unable to remember those events in which the unacceptable memories or emotions were experienced.

This type of conflict was first identified in the area of sexual phenomena with the recognition that forgetting unacceptable impulses was a common, but ineffectual way of resolving discrepancies between proper and improper expectations. During the Victorian era, the various sexual prohibitions induced a large degree of repression. The basic deficiency of this psychological defense is that the forgotten impulses return in the form of irrational symptoms, inappropriate emotion, hypochondriacal complaints, hysterical paralysis, phobias about neutral objects, and more commonly in the form of nightmares, fantasies, or preoccupations.

With the liberation of sexual behavior from the excessive restrictions, younger Americans function with fewer sexual conflicts. However, the increasing avoidance of death in the same generation produces similar psychological hazards. Ideas about death have become progressively more distasteful in public. Privately, individuals also avoid talking about dying. The net effect is to pressure survivors into repressing their grief or relief.

Grief is considered improper if it continues too long or assumes unconventional forms. Both of these judgments are arbitrary. Even so, there is a prevailing expectation that grief should subside sooner rather than later. The survivor is expected to forget and carry on. To succeed he must act as if death had not occurred but that that person is merely away, asleep, or worse, never existed in the first place. Forgetting can only be accomplished by repression of memories. This creates another survival gap that tends to block adequate mourning, catharsis, and the right to grieve.

Excessive avoidance of death can be countered. No one needs to suffer irrational symptoms because of a lack of sufficient outlets for grief. The crippling effects of this secondary survival gap predispose towards future difficulties in coping with other deaths and, worst of all, eventually in preparing for one's own. Most Americans encounter bereavement the first time with no or minimal preparation. This failure to anticipate the problems created by the primary and secondary survival gaps comes from barriers created by a third.

A Different Kind of Death

A shift has occurred in the nature of dying over the last twenty or thirty years, but not in the corresponding expectations Americans conventionally hold. Every year about 90 percent of adult deaths occur because of fatal diseases, such as heart, cancer and stroke. These illnesses progress slowly from onset to termination. Where death used to arrive relatively fast, it now comes slowly.

During the last thirty years, the quality of dying has also changed. Death has become something other than an impersonal event. Dying is now a final encounter. This permits the victim to shape the quality of his or her dying by performing the kinds of acts that express unique values or lifestyles. But, for the most part, the last encounters are more unpleasant than they need be because of the failure to shift expectations appropriately.

Traditional ideas in Western civilization about the significance of human life were derived from the institutions of God, king, and family. Existence was divided around service to all three. Each promoted the notion that the individuals received meaning in piety, obedience and mutual labor, respectively. Devotion to God in the form of prayer, ritual, and sacrifice yielded a conviction of grace, explanation for the inexplicable, and a direction for one's own life. Obedience to the king gave one a legitimate place in society. The family had always been an economic unit with a division of labor appropriate to age and sex, both of which determined daily activities. All the practices gave meaning to life and accumulated traditional sentiment. In time, these intense commitments with corresponding values were considered as manifestations of either virtue or vice. Since most people assumed immortality of the soul. death had a certain meaning, a transition into the next world where rewards would be given according to one's earthly works.

In nineteenth-century America, pioneer necessities, and especially the possibilities for changing status by movement or individual endeavors, influenced accepted attitudes about life and death. The individual judged and was judged by his efforts during his lifetime. The man who produced was more acceptable and could earn a place of respect wherever he went. Titles of nobility and knowing one's special place became less important. The struggle for survival and the opportunity for economic advancement produced special meanings and different values. Individual achievement was the measure of success. Social and economic mobility were early characteristics of American lifestyle. And they continue to be.

Success on earth was one sign of being a chosen person, one who would surely go to heaven. That was part of what came to be known as the Puritan ethic. Achievement meant virtue and was the act of a good man.

In recent times because of increasing American affluence, leisure time, and concentration on consumption, the meaning of life is often construed as the pursuit of pleasure. Death announces the end, and is increasingly seen as the ultimate absurdity. There has also been increased secularization of organized religion. Even individuals who retain church membership and believe in the continuation of the soul after death often manifest a partial seduction by hedonism. While the atheists perceive termination as the absolute end of pleasure, religious believers see death as a transition, one in which earthly satisfactions are replaced by heavenly ones. Death has become a total negation of life while at the same time the capacity to shape the circumstances of dying has increased. The survivor is caught between an inevitable event that must be anticipated and a definition of it as something to be totally avoided. Constructive suggestions are offered for this survival gap in Chapter Nine, "Readiness to Die."

Avoidance of Death

A fourth survival gap follows directly from the third. Familiarity with death has declined dramatically. It has been removed as a natural corollary to living. Death occurs in impersonal situations and within institutions. Professional assistance in preparing Americans for death—their own and that of others—is noticeably absent. Traditionally, religion provided a rationale and solace, both of which worked as long as the participants had faith. But increasing agnosticism, atheism, and emphasis on hedonism have diluted and diminished the effectiveness of organized religion. Philosophy offers intellectual alternatives, but the modern compartmentalization of education restricts the study of philosophy as an option; it has become an intellectual diversion rather than a statement of the relevance of life and death. Modern medicine concentrates on curing illness and prolonging life by technology. Psychology focuses on the emotions and on helping people avoid distress. The general effect, if not the intent, of both is to eliminate death as a subject of inquiry or as a topic for informal conversation.

Each person is left to his or her own devices when it comes to coping with the problems created by death. Because of almost universal avoidance, death most always comes as a surprise to the survivors, even in an aged, terminal patient. Suddenly, on the heels of the sad news comes the need for decisions about last things. What to do with his body? Embalm, cremate, or nothing? Which mortician? Which cemetery? What kind of casket, shroud, hearse? Then there are the kinds of memorial services, and the costs of each. Under the usual circumstances, no survivor can ever adequately comparative-shop for these items. Yet they constitute one of the largest expenditures any family will ever have. Nowhere can a survivor find immediate, simple, and inexpensive assistance with all the practical problems he must handle.

Instruction for death is even more of a taboo than that for sex or drug abuse. Even the relatively straightforward mechanics of death, burial, memorials, and wills are difficult to perform under emotional stress or an absence of resources. Additional complications result with special problems of permission to perform autopsy, donate organs, or even to choose life-prolonging treatment for a person who is approaching termination. Yet the relatively long dying period is typically left to chance or the whims of others. For any one adult contemplating his or her own prospective death, it is highly probable that termination will come slowly. Whether in a hospital, extended care facility, or private home, the circumstances under which dying occurs require detailed preparation. The potential victim must assert preferences or suffer unnecessary consequences.

Would a prospective bride leave the choice of the wedding service, church, dinner, or flowers to strangers? Would a potential home buyer leave choice of site, house, furniture, and landscaping to just anybody? Would a diner in a gourmet restaurant take any entree, dessert, or beverage offered by the waiter? Probably not. Yet survivors approaching death often default on the details of where, on what, and how an individual's last days will be spent.

The Ultimate Absurdity

A fifth survival gap occurs in knowing that in the death of another, one's own personal future is also limited. Traditional answers are no longer effective. The majority of mourners experience some threat to the prospect of their personal continuation. They sense something distressing, but attribute it to grief, or the impossibility of better answers. They shrug their shoulders and attempt to avoid the whole unpleasant topic as soon as possible.

Today, the prospect of termination represents the ultimate future shock, against which there appears to be no defense. Given this attitude, any suggestion of death becomes a psychological equivalent for the real event. Just as sexual symbols reminded Victorians of feelings they had repressed, ideas about death are a threat to the current denial systems of its existence. The shift in the quality of death and the increasing taboos associated with it, make the imminence of death loom as a nightmare over daily life. It provokes even more extreme avoidance efforts.

This threatening situation has become universal in the

United States. The causes can be traced. The major factors are technological and medical success in postponing death; American affluence and its culture of instant gratification. These produce a shared conviction that death is the final absurdity. From this perspective, existentialism flourished as a philosophy of life. The net effect is to reject death as a relevant possibility. Daily life continues with the same old choices.

Any effort to change present attitudes must first examine the contemporary meaning of life and implicitly the meaning of death. Existence in America today assumes certain universal notions. These shape the ideas that individuals can legitimately adopt, even when they attempt to act on their most unique impulses. The ways people could feel about death reflect these prevailing expectations. Currently, however, the range of acceptable reactions has diminished in the context of death or dying.

What about the recent demands for a more dignified death? These refer to circumstances whereby physicians treating the terminally ill are left with the final decision of whether to support or abort life. Medical technology can sustain physiological functioning for extended periods even though psychological life has effectively ceased. The result is a state of limbo in which the patient is neither alive nor dead. Yet when an individual calls for cessation, his efforts are blocked by public fears and taboos associated with suicide or euthanasia.

Readiness to accept death, however, does not necessarily or automatically lead to any kind of action. On the contrary, the sense of an appropriate time to die permits a survivor to develop informed consent when it comes to making decisions involving medical care, nursing homes, settlement of estates, travel options, and hosts of other mundane alternatives. All of these decisions require some personal evaluation of psychological cost-benefits to and for the patient. Such options affect the quality of life remaining and should be taken with reference to personal values. Especially relevant in this context is the decision to apply any of the medical procedures to postpone death, where the net effect is to prolong the dying process. Even when medical interventions do extend existence, some evaluation of the extra life given to the patient must be attempted. Optimally this judgment should be done by the person himself, but granting his or her inability under the circumstances, survivors would need to be aware of the conditions under which death would be preferable to the victim.

Death is Taboo

A survival gap occurs in the conspiracy of silence that surrounds any taboo, but in America this occurs especially with death.

The prevalence of taboos is especially effective in block-prohibitions as if they had always been present and will always continue. A similar phenomenon took place in modern history concerning sexual prohibitions. Even writing about sexual themes in the past was far more difficult than many contemporaries recognize. D. H. Lawrence, Henry Hiller, and other writers risked public censure and economic penalties for daring to explore intimate emotions about sex. Today it is equally difficult to write about death themes, expecially in the context of natural termination. The obstacles are not so much threats and sanctions as polite censorship—few publications, poor sales, and little attention or recognition.

This spontaneous and collective avoidance of death themes gave rise to the conspiracy of silence around all deaths but especially terminal diseases. In contrast, violent death receives excessive attention in all media. As long as the reader or viewer has no personal involvement, sudden death continues as a fascinating topic. However, the survivors of individuals who are victims of violent death have mixed feelings. They suffer conflicts in discussing this disrupted relationship. Loyalty to the memory conflicts with the actual feelings generated by the previous relationship and its sudden end. The presence of a conspiracy of silence around potential suicide victims impedes efforts to prevent self-injury while the victim is still alive. Similar obstacles occur in the context of accident and homicide prevention. This topic will be pursued in Chapter Four, "The Youthful Way."

Attempts to study suicide and its prevention provide many examples of impeding effects attributable to death taboos. Simply gathering information about people who attempt to kill themselves becomes prohibitive. It is extremely arduous to track down an incomplete suicide over a period of several years, if only to determine whether or not he or she is still alive. The problems of follow-up are made more difficult by the stigmas associated with suicide.

Today certain researchers of suicide prevention are currently trying to identify future deaths. However, this research is pious since long-range prevention is almost totally lacking. The certainty that someone would try to kill himself within six months or a year would not materially help to prevent his or her death. Contemporary research indicates the current rate of identification is a mere 2 percent of all potential future suicides. Yet this information is not used to prevent death. Instead, police, doctors, and hospitals make an excessive response only *after* the self-injury. If the patient survives, he or she is often locked up and heavily medicated. Later when the patient reassures the experts that he is no longer a danger to himself, everyone ignores the risk of future self-injuries.

Management of formerly suicidal patients is similar to to the dangers of new suicidal attempts. Actual data document the fact that mental patients have the highest suicide rates of any identified group. Casual inquiry shows that close to half of the hospitalized mental patients have histories of prior self-injuries or excessive suicidal preoccupations. Two-thirds of the subsequent deaths by suicide occur within a period of twelve to twenty-four months after returning to the community.

In the period when a patient begins to manifest genuine symptoms of recovery from the distress that led to self-injury, his or her acute wish to die diminishes. Paradoxically, this marks the onset of a high-risk interval. As the depression begins to lift, as progress occurs in psychotherapy, as staff begins to relax its vigilance—that is when the risk of recurrence also begins to increase. The failure to attend to the high-risk person in between suicidal attempts is a fault of the system within the institution of care. Overloaded staff members are distracted by other crises and often are unable to give extra attention when it is most needed. Nor is the system alone in its default of high-risk patients. Considering the frequency of medical malpractice suits, it is unusual that survivors of a suicide victim do not likewise seek redress. The apparent assumption is that self-destructive behavior cannot be blamed on the quality of institutional care given. But that is exactly where much of the burden lies. A California court recognized this when an alcoholic patient with a history of suicidal behavior killed himself thirty-six hours after being released from a state hospital. The family contended that private psychiatrists had recommended long-term care. They charged the staff with negligence in the care, treatment, and release of the man which resulted in his premature death. The physicians serving the state institution argued that they had released the patient because he had improved. However, they based their legal defense on the unpredictability of suicidal behavior in a paranoid, schizophrenic personality. The jury awarded $125,000 to the family after deliberating only two hours.

The evidence is that psychiatric patients with histories of prior self-injuries are approximately ten times more likely to kill themselves than other psychiatric patients; these, in turn, are ten times more likely to commit suicide than people in the general population. For the medical profession to ignore this risk factor constitutes negligence.

Limitations on effective research and prevention of suicide occur because taboos surrounding all deaths block understanding and decision-making. Hospital practices have never fully incorporated the little that is known about suicide because it appears to be similar to the top of an iceberg. The remainder is the whole business of dying which in America is effectively tabooed. Except for television and movie titillation of the public with themes of violent death, there is no systematic access to information about natural death. Accident, homicide, and suicide prevention will never be possible until the American orientation toward dying becomes natural again.

The survival gaps described above are hazards to every survivor who is a victim of loss, and facing inevitable death himself. This book attempts to provide some answers and redress to the current avoidance phenomena. This writer's training, experience, and talents have permitted these necessarily personal answers. However, like the "Emperor's New Clothes," the concepts presented may free the reader to accept his own feelings and perceptions of the real ties surrounding modern death.

2

Common Denials of Death

Birth and death punctuate personal existence, but no one is ever fully satisfied with the current average life-span of seventy years. Instead we all wish and search for alternatives that promise more. In the past, immortality of the soul within the context of Christianity was the most acceptable answer. Today this is less satisfying. Instead other ideas flourish. Reincarnation, magic, spirits, spooks, and ghosts are increasingly believable to the young. Those over thirty anticipate longer life expectancies and healthier existences than were possible before. Some look to science and medicine to provide a means to postpone death indefinitely. Others simplistically regard the signs of aging as curable diseases. There are still others who look to the day when clinical death will be forestalled by freezing, storage, and revival. Any form of continuation is seductive to those unable to accept the inevitability of death. This chapter will describe some of the common denials prevalent today and their limitations. All of them create survival gaps for the individual by permitting him or her to ignore the limited time available for the pursuit of personal goals. Instead of making each day count, people act as if they have forever. Termination always comes as a surprise and with associated crises.

Denial of death's inevitability is built into the person at an early age and it continues throughout life. In time a person develops a self-awareness and cannot think of himself as another object. He can perceive the death of other people, but he can only imagine his own death as an object of his fantasy. He can experience sexual intercourse, the eating of food, getting drunk, fighting, pain, but he can only imagine death. In such fantasies about one's own death, the individual goes on imagining what will happen after the point of death, and begins to imagine existence as a soul in the after-life. A person is emotionally unable to imagine the world without himself in it.

To consider the prospect of one's own death is to take a self-conscious point of view in which intellectual or imaginary processes substitute for the actual event. We cannot experience death before we die. We can never reach a point in our existence where we can say "Ah! so this is how death feels" or "Now I am dead." Movies and television always portray the after-life in this sort of format, thereby reinforcing such notions in the popular expectation. Anyone who contemplates his death must always imagine his cessation before it happens. In so doing the very process of imagination continues past the point at which the subject perceives himself dead; conveying thereby a sense of further continuation and confirmation of personal immortality. The individual can conceive of himself as an object who like others will die, but he continues as a subject who imagines the whole event.

There are few if any psychological events that prepare a human for his own cessation. Narrow escapes from accident, homicide, or even suicide sometimes have the net effect of causing a chain reaction that leads to sensitivity and eventual acceptance of death's inevitability. Aside from these exceptional experiences, the whole evolution of personal awareness predisposes a belief in survival after death. Despite interruptions of awareness in daily life by sleep, intoxication, accidental trauma, or occasional anesthesia, the individual builds up a sense of his or her history and its continuity through a sequence of events. The subject always recovers the thread of his awareness on reviving. Life simply induces the expectation of more life. From perceptual habit, limitations of psychological process, and, more simply, fear of death, an individual is handicapped from taking his own termination seriously. Daily behavior implies that most people expect to be around for a long time, if not actually forever.

This personal incapacity to experience death is augmented by a similar phenomenon at the group or social level. Collectively, Americans portrayed in the mass media are unable to accept or even acknowledge the fact that death may also terminate the identity of the person. Instead, mass-media references to life after death are made in some affirmative sense, religious or secular. There is a strange absence of dialogue concerning after-life. Believers in reincarnation, ghosts, and extrasensory perception rarely encounter the existentialists or the religiously faithful and their conception of immortality of the soul. Each group asserts its separate belief, secure in the faith that all others are not only wrong, but that they will eventually be converted to the opposite belief. Each is apparently oblivious of the other. The absence of dialogue about death is most peculiar.

The net effect of the media's vacuum on this topic is to eliminate a potential psychological experience that would challenge the avoidance of personal death. The individual is left to human accidents in developing awareness of the hazards associated with dying. The inability to experience death and the absence of social challenges to this vacuum mean that any one belief about survival after death cannot be tested. The individual is left to his own devices, and tends to take his cues from what he observes in others.

Life After Death

The typical acceptable behavior observed in funeral and memorial services contains some reference to continuation of life after death. The eulogies usually refer to the "departed," "eternal sleep," "rest in peace," and other assertions about his or her continuation in some way. Even the nonreligious gathering after a cremation will include conversation about the deceased, as if that person's spirit were still present. All of these phenomena reflect a continuing habit, if not an outright faith, in the immortality of spiritual or psychological self, and socially confirm the same belief.

Archaeological evidence of prehistorical peoples documents their expectations that the dead person would return, carry-on, or in some way use the various artifacts provided in his tomb for his after-life. In the pre-Christian era, the notions about the dead were rationalized into a repetitive cycle of infinite birth, death. and rebirth of the soul much like reincarnation. Modern Christianity continues this faith in its familiar litany of death, burial, limbo, heaven, hell and, resurrection.

The current secular position about life after death is negative. Human awareness is confined to the life-cycle of biological functioning. Birth or conception is the beginning and death is the end. The assumption is simply that human awareness ceases at death because there is no scientific evidence to document any form of continuation. The weakness in this admittedly limited position is an arbitrary value of science. Data is only admissible if it is tangible and can be quantified. Eyewitness, group-consensus, or psychological experiences are not fully credible to scientists. This position slams the door on other kinds of information such as extrasensory perception experiences, hypnotic regression, automatic writing, or the use of acknowledged sensitives or mediums. All of these are limited and not fully reliable, but so too are all scientific methods.

In every society, "true" stories occur which circulate affirming events that imply an action or the existence of the deceased. The scientific reaction is that these perceptions are coincidences or frauds. There are indeed a number of incidents, documented by eyewitnesses, or investigated scrupulously by competent psychic researchers which imply that certain individuals have managed, at least temporarily, to survive past the point of biological death. Without necessarily accepting them, scientists can no longer write these off. The incidents may be explainable by natural phenomena, but pompous denials merely reflect a prejudice toward an unac-

ceptable notion. Parenthetically, the dogmatic pronounce-
ments of academic establishments against notions of reincarnation nourish a growing credibility gap among all young
people with respect to academics. Assertions about the nature
of truth, knowledge, virtue and, even health, are often made
dogmatically so as to invite doubt, especially by the young.
Where an individual can detect a discrepancy between what
has been experienced and what is asserted about that experience, the dogmatic statement is rejected. An example of this
process occurred recently with the "drug abuse" scare.

The various dire warnings about the use of marijuana
first by the federal law enforcers, and later exaggerated by
local, parental, and federal groups were seen as ludicrous by
the kids. The warnings were half-truths motivated by fear or
cynicism. This created a boomerang effect, because kids
discovered that many of these warnings were not true. Marijuana did *not* produce addiction, sin, or even debilitation.
The kids went on to try other drugs, often more potent. To
their sorrow some discovered there was indeed a grain of
truth in some of the warnings.

A similar phenomenon occurred with respect to mastur-
bation. In the past, parents had always warned that this practice was a mortal sin and would induce insanity, "grow hair"
on their palms, and have other dire consequences. The evidence is that almost all youngsters masturbate. The damage?
Many kids suffered unnecessary guilt and distress while others
escaped conflict by becoming cynical of parental warnings
about most things. Kids throw out the baby with the wash
when they discover the discrepancy between a warning and
their own experiences.

Literal heaven or hell is no longer fully credible to young
people, but the finality of death is also inconceivable to
them. The gap is bridged by a relative increase in preoccupation with life-after-death phenomena in the thoughts and
conversation of the young. Their concern creates a spreading
out or ripple effect that touches the rest of American society.

A visible but not immediately obvious example is the
recent popularity of astrology. The date of a person's birth can

be translated into a known sign of the zodiac which together with the relative positions of moon and planets at that particular time provide a means of explaining or anticipating the behavior of the individual. From these random birth dates and known configurations of moon, planets, and sun comes a horoscope. Whether prepared by experts for one unique individual or for many, assertions are made about the near and distant future. Like other efforts to predict the future, most people usually remember only the successes. Two or three anticipations deemed accurate validate the system. Indeed there may well be a self-fulfilling prophecy in this as well as other notions about future events. Any expectations, especially about other humans, tend to invite acceptance of the first expectation. Avoiding decisions on an astrologically bad day will certainly eliminate failures. It may just as well eliminate successes. Making decisions on a "good" day will yield more successes than failures because of personal confidence. Like any philosophy of life, these notions facilitate human existence as long as the individual has faith in them. There is no harm done by the current interest in astrology, but it does encourage faith in a nonreligious higher, or other power and predispose for beliefs in extrasensory perception, ghosts, or reincarnation.

Reincarnation implies a belief in the immortality of the spirit. In brief, it is the assertion that there is an infinite cycle of birth, death, and rebirth in which a recognizable identity continues for eternity without beginning or end. In this philosophy of life, birth and death are analogous to day and night. Individuals retain a sense of their identity even though there is an interruption of their awareness by each rebirth, much like sleep temporarily interrupts continuity. As with dreaming, the reincarnated individual tends to forget prior existences. Just as fragments of some dreams are recollected, so aspects of prior lives are recalled, recognized, or somehow identified.

In Hinduism and Buddhism, the present life is determined by the karma or action and deeds of a previous existence, which can only be changed by behavior in the present life to influence the subsequent existence. Each succeeding existence is a step towards improvement and eventual destiny known as Atma. When this is achieved, the individual will have attained insight into the world spirit or Brahma. Buddhism does not include Atma. Instead an individual is reborn again and again until he has extinguished craving, and desire for pleasure. At this stage he has achieved the state of nirvana, a state of bliss, and need not be reborn, but continues to develop as a conscious being.

The idea of reincarnation predates Christianity not only in Eastern but also in Western thought. The Greeks and early Christians accepted the idea of reincarnation, including the existence of the soul before birth. By the time of the second council of Constantinople, Christians repudiated the metaphysical belief that the pre-existing soul returned at the birth of a child. Even so, Eastern and Western philosophers at subsequent times and places, and currently, have written favorably about reincarnation.

David Hume, a Scottish philosopher from the Age of Enlightenment, distrusted speculation about life after death. Hume assumed a vigorous agnosticism. He neither believed nor disbelieved the supernatural. In his writings he questioned the tenets of the Christian argument that the human soul was immortal. He accepted the physical evidence of death as cessation of the soul as well.

Immanuel Kant, a German philosopher, wrote in his Critique of Pure Reason that the life of the human spirit is not necessarily subject to the changes of time. He described the limits of human knowledge differently from Hume. He believed that one could have knowledge about what has not been experienced as well as what had already been experienced.

Arthur Schopenhauer, another German philosopher, wrote in his The World as Will and Idea a chapter about death and its relationship to the indestructibility of true nature. Schopenhauer postulated that human will is eternal and will appear again and again through new births. Schopenhauer's ideas reflect the influence of Hinduism and Buddhism.

James Ward, an English philosopher-psychologist, tried

to meet the various objections raised by philosophers against the doctrine of transmigration of the soul. While not really proving the case for reincarnation, he concluded that its validity would demand a continuity through eternity of the individual awareness. Granting this, then death is indeed like sleep, only longer, dividing life from life as night divides the day. The latter idea is a common conception about death, especially in explanations parents offer their children. Implicitly, many Americans also accept the possibility of the dead being "awakened" some day. A fuller discussion about the evidence for survival after death is written by C. J. Ducasse, a professor of philosophy, emeritus, at Brown University. See the list of Recommended Reading in this book.

Some Americans have dealt with their needs for immortality in ways other than a belief in reincarnation. Along with an abiding faith in the scientific-technological institutions, they have gradually taken some of their prevailing notions from "health" literature and science-fiction ideas. With daily reminders of each new medical breakthrough, it is very easy to develop the expectation that adults will live longer, healthier lives. This reasonable notion gets generalized into a hope that the life span really is much longer, and that only the exceptional die young. There is an implicit notion that symptoms of the aging process are really the results of some disease. They unconsciously believe that soon cures will be available for wrinkling, sensory losses, feebleness, memory failures, brittle bones, lack of agility, sexual incapacity, and so forth. There is enough scientific and medical confirmation of these cures to support their hope. This helps them deny the inevitability of death.

Cryogenics and Cryonics

One of the more dramatic scientific innovations is cryogenics, whereby a body part is frozen, stored indefinitely, and later implanted in a living human. Residual problems of these procedures are the rejection phenomenon and the psychological aftermath the patient suffers in adapting to the new organ.

Both kinds of distress will no doubt eventually be solved. The patient equipped with a transplant is often saved from death, but the quality of his existence is dramatically impaired. Enough complications have been observed to raise moral controversy about general use of these experimental interventions in otherwise fatal diseases. The general public tends to ignore these consequences and continues to entertain notions of personal, never-ending existence in their present form.

It is rather a simple extension logically from cryogenics to cryonics, the freezing of human bodies for cold storage, and later revival. While it is technically feasible to freeze mammals for periods of time without tissue damage, life has never been restored after freezing. What encourages many cryonic advocates are examples of revival in people who were clinically dead by drowning, heart failure, or unknown causes. Typically, the short period of suspension involved, minutes or hours, implies unusual medical competence or just plain luck in restoring the individual to life. There is neither a miracle nor a mystery about these clinical returns from death. But often the public misunderstands how "death" is defined. Cessation of the heart beat or respiration is no longer the criterion of death, since these can now be stopped or started by competent physicians and equipment. Low temperatures also tend to retard dying processes associated with heart stoppage. All of these reinforce the notion that death can be avoided or postponed indefinitely. Cryonics seems to offer the most explicit support.

Cryonic suspension is an attractive alternative to existential or sectarian notions of finite human life. R. W. Ettinger is generally acknowledged as the first proponent of this idea in his book, The Prospect of Immortality, published in 1964. His rationale is really quite simple: it is technically feasible to freeze mammals with little or no deterioration, even if stored for hundreds of years. Because Ettinger anticipates that the solution to the problem of revival will be discovered before 1980, he argues that it is appropriate to freeze the dead now in anticipation of future restoration. The proposal itself smacks

of science fiction but is no more incredible than earlier scoff-
ing at the possibility of interplanetary rocket travel. Ettinger
is clearly an enthusiastic person having an almost messianic
optimism. Even so, he is generally accurate and knowledgeable
with respect to his subject. Modern technology seems to have
no limits in achieving mechanical goals; getting from here to
there, replacing human labor, or even in the relaying of simple
messages from one machine to another. As heart transplants
offer the prospect of extending human existence, so, too, does
cryonics promise indefinite storage by freezing. The door is
open to the possibility of later clinical revival, by some technical means not now fully understood nor anticipated. Rather
than dismissing this prospect as impossible, the author is
more disturbed by its possibility and the consequences which
might ensue. The whole notion could be dropped if earlier scientific achievement had not been so devilishly successful with
previously "impossible" endeavors.

R. W. Ettinger tends to be overly optimistic in his discussion of successful revival. In the first edition of his book he
regards the psychological problem of readjustment as if it
were merely a matter of updating an unused computer. In
1964 he suggested the use of taped information, presumably
in a sleep-learning format. Later he added the concept of
restoration centers designed to help the revivees adapt to their
extended life. Given the perennial misbehavior of humans,
Ettinger also anticipates many legal and moral problems. As
an example, he talks about the widower who remarries while
waiting for his wife to be revived. Is this bigamy? If she is
restored would he need to reject one of them? Then there
would ensue the complicated questions of property rights.
Each revivee would generate litigation in seeking to recover
his former place, property, and relationships. If death could be
undone, what about estate taxes? Could the Internal Revenue
Service legitimately take these if a person is merely frozen?

In the revisions of his book, Ettinger recognizes that
revival would need to be selective. Only those whose terminal
illness could be arrested or cured would be eligible for
defrosting. Borderline cases might occur with debilitating or

crippling illness where the victim could be restored to life as an invalid. Clearly, younger people whose bodies were in better shape at death would be more restorable than the elderly.

The basic error Ettinger may be making is his premise that indefinite life is desirable both for society and for the individual. Naturally, he is hoping to continue in his present way of life and wants very much to be restored to this same condition should he die. However, everything changes and both his health and way of life may alter so much that, on second thought, existence may be less desirable even to him. There are also many people whose wish to live disappears altogether. These are the ones who seek cessation through self-injury behavior, while otherwise being in good physical health. The majority of victims who die by self-injury are not necessarily insane or depressed. Aside from suicide, there are many people in senior-citizen age groups who may not want revival after death. Some of these may be objecting on philosophical grounds and others on the basis of fear. One very practical obstacle is the deteriorating body to which the revivee would presumably be restored. Additional life in a frail, crippled body is not very tempting.

Ettinger goes on to suggest that restoration should be further restricted to those whose bodies can be rejuvenated to some acceptable level. Assuming further that the day will eventually come when this is technically possible, what would happen to people revived from cryonic suspension and restored to life with the health and vigor of adults in their forties? Would these people do more or less with their additional existence than before? Given such opportunities, prediction is impossible. However, extremes are apparent to any casual observer. Some people might use the additional life in constructive directions. Others might not. The latter might use restoration as proof that immortality was possible, and therefore a license for total hedonism. The more likely outcome for the majority might be a continuation of the past existence, with its errors and its virtues.

Ettinger's rebuttal takes the form of even more optimism

in that the history of civilization can be written with examples of apparently impossible problems eventually solved by human ingenuity, and people's adaptation to changing conditions. Such optimism defies analysis! It must be admired but it also inspires skepticism. The initial gratitude and humility a revivee might give for an additional existence, perhaps in a healthier body, would soon dissipate. In time, the old habits would return. The majority of people restored to additional existence might tend towards further abuse of their opportunities. The prospect of freeze-wait-reanimate may be achievable eventually and might even be desirable for some individuals, but it will also bring inevitable abuses. This should neither deter the hope nor the effort, but does require attention to sort out the possible consequences.

Aside from the problems of emotional adjustment following revival, a medically feasible restoration following clinical death is seductive. In part this is due to the increasingly unsettled position on immortality so apparent in the secularization of organized religion, and the dilution of its impact on church members.

The alternative of cryonic suspension competes for the soul, mind, or personality. Instead of death, burial, and resurrection, the individual receives freezing, storage, and revival. The latter is more credible than the waning faith in a day of judgment. While both alternatives offer the prospect of eventual reawakening, the religious one is on some millennial day of reckoning, while the cryonic revival could conceivably occur within the next generation.

One possible advantage from the deep-freeze might occur on a more pedestrian basis. It represents a more efficient way of dealing with human remains than the traditional embalming and burial. Freezing will preserve the body at death more effectively and for longer periods. While it may cost more at this time, volume and technical improvements may eventually bring the charges down to a feasible if not competitive price.

As long as faith in the immortality of the soul was imbedded in a moral system, there were also restraints and reminders of eventual consequences. In an era of religious secularization with diminishing loyalty to country, family, and jobs, the fear of death may be the last external force for motivating moral examinations. In a more positive direction, a finite life makes the individual aware that each day should count. While the first reaction to the threat of eventual death may be some form of pleasure-seeking, hedonism is eventually self-defeating. It takes more and more to receive less and less pleasure. Eventually, the person starts making choices on the basis of values; he must prefer good over evil.

Ignoring the obvious complications, it is really quite remarkable that cryonic suspension has not swept this country as the hula-hoop did some years ago. The cost factor is certainly formidable enough to prevent impulse buying as well as to limit demand to the very few who have that amount of money available at death. Still, technical improvements and volume purchases could certainly reduce costs, if money were the only problem. The opposite is more the case. As a form of novel or high-class burial, cryonic suspension is already a reality and has been used by a dozen people at this writing. The consumer resistance stems from the ambivalence about dying. It derives from the irrational conflicts about death in American society. Everyone gives some kind of lip service to immortality of the soul or personality. In behavior, everyone acts as if he alone will live forever. This conflict occurs at the unconscious level much like the old sexual desires and prohibition once did. Americans are so afraid of death, they have repressed their awareness of it. Yet their behavior demonstrates the phobia. Before they could choose the revival after death alternative, they would need to admit that termination could really occur to them in the first place.

The denial of death takes many forms, even though everyone tends to verbalize statements about the inevitability of death. It turns out that no one really knows what death is by experience. They may have seen others die, they may verbalize imaginative notions about how it feels, or what occurs to the soul. Statements by individuals about the nature of death are assertions credible only to the degree that the person is himself believable. However, such ideas are not testable by currently known methods. Essentially then, everyone is an amateur when it comes to death and the survival of the individual afterwards. Furthermore almost any belief system is possible and potentially acceptable by people.

Among youth, many descriptions occur that seem to document belief in reincarnation. These range from recollections, dreams, déjà vu phenomena, and other extrasensory perceptions. The individuals use these to confirm some form of birth-death-rebirth. Very often these conclusions are embedded in an Eastern philosophy. The young believers are practically all drop-outs from Judeo-Christian religions. In rejecting the Judeo-Christian ethic, the young seek a replacement notion for immortality of the soul. Reincarnation beliefs serve this purpose. Since such assertions cannot be tested, an individual's right to hold them must be accepted, and given a legitimacy by group consensus. The popularity of this notion among the young gives it the same credibility as survival of the soul, true of other generations. While both systems deny the end of the individual, Christianity has the advantage of providing a set of ethics to live by, with a tradition of group expectations and sanctions. Reincarnation provides only a license.

The older groups tend to use other denial systems such as: "I won't die till I'm ready"; "I'm too young"; "I won't feel it when it comes," and so forth. These verbal denials have in common the effect of allaying anxiety, avoiding the necessity of planning for the eventuality of death. In the opposite direction is the philosophy of existentialism. Life itself is perceived as meaningless or absurd since death comes randomly to both the good and the evil. While death is acknowledged as the final end of the individual, there is no effort to prepare for that eventuality among existentialists. There is, I think, an implicit exhortation to "eat, drink, and be merry." Most believers in existentialism develop some form of instant pleasure-seeking, which adds to the absurdity of death by stopping all pleasure. In between these extreme positions, the majority of Americans develop less extreme, but multiple, ways of denying death.

The denials most often employed tend to be rational and socially acceptable in that there are elements of truth in each of them. For example, children, fame, achievements, philanthropy or intellectual success in science or the arts represent a form of immortality, and thus overcoming the mortality of the individual. While anyone can be a parent, make money, or achieve some kind of success, the symbolic mortality of a remembered name is not quite the same as living forever.

The more modern denial of death occurs in the faith that science, and especially medicine, can postpone death indefinitely.

The alternative to denial of death is acceptance and the examination of the balance of existence. Here the prospect of a finite life can only be handled by intellectual or substitute behavior, in which the individual thinks about the circumstances around dying before the need occurs. These ideas can be further developed and tested through discussion and debate with peers. Eventually, the candidate for an appropriate death develops a preferred expectation and the ability to arrange the personal conditions of dying to his satisfaction. Techniques will be described later.

3

The Unnatural Way

Natural death occupies a strange and vanishing wilderness in American culture. The phrase itself explains nothing, has little medical meaning, and enjoys the same social usage as normalcy in mental illness; undefined, unrecognizable in practice, and yet somehow applicable to everybody. Even though 90 percent of adult deaths in America every year are due to fatal diseases, most people expect to die from "old age," "natural causes," or in their sleep. If pressed further, they will go on to say they want to die quickly and without pain. Yet the majority can expect to die slowly, after a prolonged illness, and with gradually increasing impairments. The quality of death in America has changed dramatically since the World War II era, but without a parallel change in awareness by Americans. Because of this particular survival gap, old age and fatal illness are viewed with even greater horror than they used to inspire.

The "natural" mode of death is a legal term assigned by a coroner who uses a fourfold classification system—natural, accidental, suicide, homicide. The major usage of these terms is in law enforcement, property, and insurance settlements. In evaluating the cause for the natural mode of death, medical findings are always used, but expressed in pathological terms. In practice it turns out that every death from fatal illness is abnormal, medically speaking. While common sense blames old age for natural death, the whole event is experienced as unnatural. There is, in addition, an increasing tendency to view the symptoms of aging as a disease, and to hope for medical delay, if not outright cure. In the meantime, death from natural causes even among the elderly lacks a proper place in the daily life of Americans.

In other places and in earlier times, death from natural causes was highly visible in ordinary life, and custom accommodated the inevitability of dying. However, even folklore, myth, and religious ritual attributed death events to unnatural forces. Primitive cultures invoked supernatural explanations for the daily deaths they actually observed. The resulting mythology "explains" and incidentally justifies termination of life in man's natural condition. Typically some taboo was violated and death became a consequence of human errors. In Australian aboriginal tribes, women were supposed not to go near a tree where lived a bat. Once a woman broke this prohibition; a bat fluttered out, and that was the reason that men have died ever since. The Ningpo of China were banished from paradise and became mortal because someone bathed in taboo waters. In a Greek myth, men lived forever, and without disease, until Pandora's box was opened. In Genesis, the knowledge of good and evil caused death and precipitated man's fall from grace when Adam ate the forbidden fruit. Despite the universal occurrence of these explanations, no culture has ever fully accepted the total naturalness of death. Instead death has always been resisted, and alternatives always sought in a religious concept of immortality of the soul, the fountain of youth, and the philosopher's conundrum of the mind-body dilemma.

In recent years, science and medicine have engineered dramatic changes in the technology that affects the quality of the dying process. The most obvious outgrowth is a reduction of death rates, and the extension of life. Currently, the average life expectation for Americans is about seventy-five years. Life expectancy has increased significantly in modern times, and because of that there is a realistic basis for anticipating even greater longevity in the future.

The implication is that death can increasingly be postponed indefinitely with adequate research and medical care.

But while specific diseases can be studied and cures sought, there does appear to be a biological limit for both individuals and the human species.

Actually, adult life expectancy has changed little from Biblical days. The Bible speaks of three score, and of four score for the extraordinary. Present life expectancy even by favored categories such as white women is still less than eighty years. In 1900 white males from thirty to thirty-four years lived six fewer years than the same age group in 1968. The increase for those seventy-five to seventy-nine years old is only 1.3 years since 1900. These are averages, of course, and never apply equally to individuals. However, for those who wish to guess how much life remains or hope that things will get better in the next few years, the facts are only minimally encouraging.

The bulk of medical success with life expectancies and the reason for the increased probabilities of longer life reported in the press are due to reduction of infant mortality and the effective treatment of diseases striking youth and young adults. Yet even in 1968 three percent of all deaths due to fatal disease in any one year came to children under ten and six percent to people under thirty. Despite the very real progress in preventing death in the young, American society is not first among the nations of the world reporting vital statistics.

The devastating flu epidemics of World War I have disappeared, at least with respect to fatalities. Smallpox no longer kills and has become so rare that the compulsory vaccination has been made optional in the United States. Cures have been found for many other once fatal diseases and progress occurs daily with others. Antibiotics first used during World War II not only saved lives, but prevented serious infections from even gaining a foothold. Reviewing medical history, it is easy to conclude that natural death is less inevitable today than it used to be. It is, of course, self-evident that death takes no holiday, and still works a seven-day week. What has changed is the quality of death; the kinds of diseases that kill are different today than twenty years ago. The top ten killers are published every year by National Institutes of Health statisticians and are reproduced. The first three account for two-thirds

Estimated Death Rates for the 10 Leading Causes of Deaths in the U.S. 1972

Rank	Cause	Percent of all deaths	Rate/ 100,000
1.	Diseases of the heart	38.3	361.3
2.	Malignant neoplasms	17.7	166.6
3.	Cerebrovascular diseases	10.7	100.9
4.	Accidents	5.8	54.6
5.	Influenza and pneumonia	3.1	29.4
6.	Diabetes mellitus	2.0	18.8
7.	Certain causes of infant death	1.7	16.4
8.	Arteriosclerosis	1.7	15.8
9.	Cirrhosis of the liver	1.7	15.7
10.	Bronchitis, emphysema, & asthma	1.5	13.8
	All other causes including suicide and homicide	15.8	148.9

*Monthly Vital Statistics Report. HEW-PHS, Rockville, Md. 20852 Vol. 21, #13, Jun. 27, 1973

of all adult deaths every year. These are in rank order: heart disease, cancer, and stroke. In the last few years, the first has diminished while the second continues to increase. Recent successes in open heart surgery, pacemakers, and other techniques have permitted an effective reduction in the number of deaths from heart disease. While success is occurring in curbing various cancers, the rates are still rising.

Changing Death-Styles

These changing rates and corresponding practices illustrate how the quality of death in America is also changing. Since roughly the end of World War II (the introduction of antibiotics and other successful practices) dying, the coping with death, and consequent attitudes towards the subject have shifted remarkably; all the more since so little notice is taken of it. While writers like Jessica Mitford in *The American Way of Death,* and professional thanatologists have reacted, the mass media have not picked up this theme sufficiently to sensitize the culture.

The majority of the communications industry generally ignores the theme of natural death and the associated subject of fatal disease, implying that it is rare, uninteresting, and possibly offensive. Yet sudden and violent death is portrayed *universally* even though it accounts for less than 5 percent of adult deaths per year.

The most obvious way that dying and the causes of death have changed can be seen in the three diseases with the highest death rates. Heart disease, cancer, and stroke have in common the net effect of killing slowly, despite some dramatic exceptions. "Slowly" implies years, sometimes decades rather than days or weeks. Pathological processes develop slowly, even though they may manifest themselves suddenly with a symptom. After diagnosis, these diseases may run three to twelve months before the patient can be clinically impaired enough to be describable as terminal. For the majority of victims, fatal diseases typically require several years and often longer. The increasingly typical slowness of dying forces the victim to deal with others over a prolonged period, which permits an individual time to develop unique styles to dominate the ways in which he or she solves personal needs and copes with the medical circumstances. In a very contemporary sense, dying requires each patient to develop a style, especially in relation to the people who care for him. These patterns become human encounters in the same sense as the toreador meets a bull in the moment of truth. There is no pretending, even though human pretense may be attempted. In final encounters there come one or more moments when the dying individual must choose A over B; now rather than later; here better than there; and with you rather than not. These preferences accumulate and become expressions of habits, personal values, and lifestyles.

In this process, the individual participates in shaping the circumstances of his own termination. He has affected the quality of his dying. His final encounters permit a personal meaning to which he and all those who care for him, assign some value. The result is the ability to influence the quality of the dying, and the value of the life which ends. It is through this process that participants can give the patient a dignified death. The individual can seek an appropriate cessation, and everyone can come out of the dark age that shrouds dying in taboos, nameless dreads, or cynical practitioners of the death trades.

The ability of the victim to influence or cause his own death has always been known, yet this knowledge has never penetrated official, legal, or medical usage with an appropriate recognition. In the coroners' work, increasing technological competence permits more effective evaluation of death, but the fourfold classification ignores completely the role of the victim in precipitating death.

The victim contributes to the quality and timing by his or her habits, errors, and preferences. Exhortations to drive carefully, stay off dark streets at night, or call for help are clearly intended to motivate victims away from death. The reverse is not so easily noted. Accidents are known to be non-random events; they may be unexpected, but they occur to people with some known characteristics. For example, insurance premiums for males under twenty-five are set higher because of the actuarial data that they are indeed the ones most likely to have fatal accidents in motor vehicles. Victim-precipitated homicide has been described as a suicidal equivalent for some blacks in the Philadelphia area who believe that self-injury is effeminate. Suicide itself is the extreme example of victim-precipitation of death.

In fatal diseases, the patient himself maximizes some pathology and minimizes others by his habitual acts over a lifetime, but especially during terminal stages. The extreme cases are written off as uncooperative, neurotic, or suicidal. However, these labels do many patients an injustice. Anxiety, whether acute or customary, impairs judgment, and phobias about dying are universal. The net effect in the patient is a convergence between organ weakness, prior habits, and efforts to avoid distress, all of which can hasten or aggravate the terminal process.

Violent Death

In an earlier era, before the world wars, death used to come frequently, randomly and impersonally in the form of wars, plagues, and natural catastrophes. In the folklore of Americans, these past experiences are still vivid and induce the image of death—the grim reaper, the ultimate enemy. He is the killer, personified as an adversary who just happens to always win. Today death comes less often, is non-random with respect to cause and is experienced as a final encounter by the participants; an encounter that is influenced by the quality of the prior unique relationship existing between the victim and his survivors. Parenthetically, this involvement develops over the lifetime of the victim and during the years which the relation existed. This evolving interaction anticipates, and has meaning as a rehearsal for, the last encounters both will share when death comes to either. Despite the kinds of changes in dying suggested above, the old expectations persist untouched by the dramatic changes in medical fact or technology. One reason for this culture lag is the removal from daily experience of the phenomena of a dying process.

Where once death took place at home, work, or on the street, today dying occurs in specialized settings. While each person will experience one or more deaths of others in his own lifetime, there is no preparation for these experiences. Natural death has been effectively removed from its natural setting; children and the weak are protected and even the strong are sheltered from too much contact with the dying.

The 1970s will be known as a period when birth was natural, expected, and tolerated. But fatal illnesses were regarded as abnormal, even though humans always have, still do, and most probably will, continue to die from them. This discrepancy between expectation and fact creates a crunch when individuals seek care and receive less than the miraculous cures they anticipate. In such disappointments, the public accumulates a residual frustration that gets expressed in more realistic demands and objective criticisms. Malpractice suits are so common that no physician or hospital can dare to practice without insurance. One of the corollaries of this defensive medical attitude is leaning over backwards to avoid criticism in management of the dying process. Heroic interventions are prescribed and carried out, when there is no hope of saving life or even providing meaningful days of con-

tinuation. Quite often these are imposed over the feeble protests of the victims who ask only to be left alone and allowed
to die at their own rates. Such procedures have led to cries
for a dignified death and, implicitly, for euthanasia.

Such controversy represents a surfacing of long-standing
dissatisfaction with medical management in the context of
death. Recent medical "success" has made it possible to delay
termination but not necessarily to extend meaningful existence. Conversely, clinical death is frequently reversed or
prevented altogether, at least temporarily. These procedures
have created a medical no-man's land in which firm biological
criteria are absent. The patient and his survivors lose whatever informed consent they may have had and see no alternatives that offer a significant choice. Prolonged dying is
always justified as the safe, proper, and even hopeful thing to
do even when death is more appropriate. The medical experts
tend to pre-empt the decision because the victim and his
survivors default. Aside from fear of a law suit, the medical
preference is a natural reflex in a group that values the saving
of a life, is personally fearful of dying, and perceives death as
professional failure.

The whole trend in medicine now and for the indefinite
future will serve to widen the gap and increase the no-man's
land. In the interim, and perhaps optimally, social criteria
that determine when life is over may be more useful. Actually,
age, sex, social status, work history, income, race are all influ-
ential to some degree. Extraordinary efforts are lavished on
well-known personalities like Eisenhower or Churchill, and
probably should be. However, the opposite members of society
get short shrift. Even the nice old guy down the street gets
cavalier treatment in a terminal context. There is an acute
need for solutions in this area.

In the meantime, every individual must prepare for this
inevitable prospect by attempting to shape the kind of death
he would prefer. Not so much the mode or medical disease,
but rather the circumstances and final encounters he or she
would like to have. Most of all an individual must avoid default
in the decision-making process. Any personal decision is better

than those imposed by the professionals of death who will be motivated to prevent superficial criticism, make profit, and stay within conventional expectations.

In American culture today the whole subject of dying is offensive. Death is not a proper subject for consideration and discourse in daily life. Everybody acts as if termination could not possibly happen to him. Never now, always later. The current avoidance blocks communication and the development of greater awareness. Instead the choices are narrowed to stereotyped and "proper" protocols. These are enforced rigidly by social penalties such as embarrassment, criticism, or rejection.

In Western civilization, taboos have traditionally centered around sex and excretion, with corresponding rituals for seemly behavior, especially in a heterosexual context. The unseemly occurrence of sexual acts is called obscene and the reference is typically to social behavior between two or more people. There are words and gestures which cause shock, laughter, or awkwardness, even though these are not real copulation or excretion. Pornography, on the other hand, is a private experience with substitute materials. Literary, graphic, or sculptural symbols are most often used to portray the forbidden and generate substitute sources of satisfaction. Most often the motives are for gratification of universal sexual impulses.

The Victorian era with its taboo of sexual topics and its corollary pornographies occurred at a period when death was common and "natural." Subsequently, there has been a relaxation of the taboos against sex and an increase in those against death. Today there exists a relative reversal in the position of each. Death is an obscenity and stimulates the same distress, sniggering, or embarrassment that sexual topics used to provoke. Some writers such as Geoffrey Gorer, an English anthropologist, call the taboo the "pornography of death."

The absence of daily experience with any form of dying and the blocking of intellectual knowledge creates a state of deprivation which gets filled in by television or movie depiction of sudden death. The media's emphasis on suicide, homicide, or accidental death is a substitute for the private state of deprivation experienced by Americans with respect to the natural modes of dying.

When natural death was considered natural, death-bed scenes also frequently appeared in literature and in the theater. The removal of natural dying from daily life has been replaced by the quasi-experience of sudden death in the communication media. Violent death is a daily part of everyone's experience because of the greater vividness and immediacy of television, movies, or press. Violent death, of course, was an early characteristic of American culture.

The increased violence, with death and the threat of death always implied, has frequently been defended by the media as meeting the interests of the consumer. The viewers are indeed drawn to violence and sudden death more than to other themes. The usual explanation for the preference is the dramatic nature of sudden death. However, this interpretation ignores the factors which make the natural mode of dying less interesting. Unpredicted death has become more familiar and is therefore more suitable for further presentation and exploitation, all of which makes it even more familiar. Simultaneously, the far more universal natural modes of dying are portrayed less often because they are observed so rarely in daily life. All of which converges to make dying from natural modes an even less familiar, and unacceptable topic for the mass media.

The national radio and television networks themselves are also victims of this process even while contributing to its continuation. The rule can be given: the more rare and bizarre the incident of dying, the greater the publicity it will receive. While very few people would spontaneously acknowledge an interest in death events, the deprivation state motivates a fascination for the subject. Police are familiar with the morbid curiosity of crowds around the occasional "shoot-out" or brawls. The free-way gawker slowing to observe a vehicle accident is another example. A similar phenomenon is well-known with respect to television violence, programs with aggressive, combative content tend to be watched more than those without.

The substitution of violent death in the media for the real experiences with natural modes of dying is called pornographic by Geoffrey Gorer because a) the substitute materials are symbolic or dramatic representations for the real event, and b) are shared by the public through the media. Just as sexual prohibitions invited an explicit search for visual, dramatic or other images, so today the public phobia about dying invokes images of sudden death.

So strong is the taboo on natural dying that the traditional normal-abnormal relation tends to get reversed. Natural dying elicits complaints as too morbid and unseemly. Americans are more disturbed by accounts of prolonged dying than by sudden death.

So extreme is the taboo surrounding death, that even people who are presumed to be suffering from some terminal disease such as one of the cancers get treated as a non-person —neither dead nor alive.

A number of patients who have returned from surgery or cobalt treatment for a malignancy have described the shock and the avoidance they suffer when former co-workers, friends, even relatives can hardly wait to leave, or make-believe nothing ever happened. Conversely, the other side of the experience is equally distressing when an old friend suddenly returns from a long hospitalization in which the assumption is made that a terminal disease is the cause. There is an inherent ambiguity in the expectations towards one who is obviously still alive, but expected to die shortly. The distress is especially aggravated by doubts about proper behavior. Is it better to pretend nothing happened, or does one ask about the illness? Ordinarily yes, but what if the answer is some dread disease? How does one respond to the question about health if the answer is "Yes, I am dying"?

The youth culture would say "tell it like it is." The over-thirty group is squeamish. It's only partly the matter of discretion and not hurting others' feelings. The bigger issue is how would *you* wish to be treated? Unfortunately, most people would prefer to gloss over the subject with no reminders that death is imminent. From this personal fear comes a reluctance to ask others the question that distresses individuals the most.

Because of these taboos, and the lack of practice, the typical victim of natural dying passes slowly and in this passing suffers far more distress than is necessary. Pain and suffering can be endured. Modern medicine is relatively effective in minimizing somatic distress. The central tragedy is the loss of human comfort that only authentic last encounters can provide. Instead the victim is treated with massive denial and pretense. He is addressed as if only temporarily ill, and the most essential questions are ignored because everyone denies the imminence of death. Decisions about last things are approached surreptitiously. The victim must struggle with his awareness and feelings by himself since no one breaks the conspiracy of silence. The last encounters with the survivors become warped by the falseness imposed through the unspoken taboos.

All this derives from the removal of natural dying to secluded settings, and the systematic avoidance of dying as a seemly topic in public. In its stead is a substitute awareness of sudden death which titillates without enlightening the public. Each candidate for an appropriate death is left with a massive discrepancy between what he seeks and what seems to be available.

4

The Youthful Way

Homicide, suicide, and accidental death are modes of dying that occur rarely in America, despite the media's overemphasis. Less than five percent of all deaths each year are due to violence. While each of these sudden ways is unexpected, none is truly random. Predisposing factors can usually be found in every unpredicted death. The clearest aspects are the age and sex of the victims. Sudden death comes more often to men, and to the young more than to the old. The person marked for death by violence participates in shaping the circumstances of his own destiny. Some of these choices and conditions will be described now.

Accidental Death

Statistics document the fact that automobile fatalities occur most often to young men, while all other types of accidents tend to strike the older man. Accidental circumstances may appear to occur quite suddenly to the victim, but in hindsight at least, errors of omission or commission are always apparent within the situation. These function as predisposing conditions that provide underlying causes of fatal accidents. A man over fifty is much more vulnerable to nonvehicular accidents, such as falling down the stairs, slipping in the bathtub, forgetting to turn off the gas, or becoming disoriented and thereby falling into dangerous situations. These types of accidents are associated with aging and the conditions under which a person lives. Equally important are the physical conditions of the victim, especially in respect to his senses and the kind of judgment he can exercise.

Sex is another determining factor. Being a man automatically assures the individual of greater risk at every age. More men than women die at each yearly level. By the sixth decade of life, the surviving women far outnumber the men. In the context of accidental death, women manage to avoid this unexpected form of fatality more successfully than men do. Even though women may suffer the same debility and impairments, they get them later, have less severe consequences, or manage to adapt to the losses better than men.

The more decisive factor is the character of the victim. A willful, formerly successful man will have more difficulty accepting the consequences of hearing or vision impairment than one who has had earlier experience adjusting to illness or impairment. In fighting the symptoms of aging, the victim may resist help or will refuse to curtail his or her activities. In doing so he plays Russian roulette each time he attempts to maintain his former self-sufficiency. He predisposes himself for a fatal accident. Actually he is neither suicidal nor even accident-prone. The persistence of a formerly decisive and aggressive personality now becomes a handicap that increases the probability of an unexpected injury or death.

Insurance companies have long recognized the predictable elements of fatal automobile accidents. The higher insurance premiums for liability and property-damage policies are computed on the basis of age, sex, and prior driving experience, especially violations. It is well-documented that men under thirty, and more so under twenty-five, are drivers with highest risk factor. Among these, the ones with Driver Education behind them appear to be safer than those without. However, the more decisive factor is the prior driving history. Previous citations for speeding or other moving violations create an ominous foreshadowing. One or more accidents lengthen the shadow into a forecast of auto fatality. These are statistical kinds of predictions. At a personal level, everyone knows

individuals who drive in a risky manner, if not entirely hazardous. When these people die, their end may shock but rarely
surprise those who knew them best.

Recent publicity has focused on drunk-driving as the major
single cause of automobile fatalities. The excessive use of
alcohol is indeed a predisposing factor which increases the
probability of a fatal accident. The only way to be safe is not
to drink at all before driving. Unfortunately, this sensible conclusion is as useful as the abstinence method of birth control.
Driving under the influence of alcohol appears safe, and does
not inevitably lead to drunk driving. Therein occurs a seduction. Having driven home numerous times from parties or
cocktail luncheons, a male driver gets the illusion he can hold
his liquor or he only has one drink. Aside from the self-decep-
tion implied in this, there is also an element of reality in the
experience. What the unsuspecting driver overlooks is his
slower reflexes, reduced alertness, and diminishing judgment.
For the addicted problem-drinker, there are additional changes
that produce more extreme impairments.

Social drinking changes gradually into problem drinking
for some people. Regardless of why or who these may be, the
victims undergo a habituation which eventually becomes an
addiction. At the habit stage, there are still elements of choice
over when and where one drinks, but not whether. At the
addiction level, even these decreasing choices disappear.
There is also a progression of effects from the impairments of
social drinking to the irreversible deterioration of the addicted
alcoholic. Along the way, the social drinker is seduced into
addiction because the impairments are not apparent until
the last stages are reached. The damage accumulates imper-
ceptibly, but manifests suddenly in the form of bizarre judgment, instant drunkenness, damaged coordination, confusion,
or disorientation. All of these predispose to accidents, especially if the symptoms manifest themselves suddenly, as they
typically do in the later phases of alcohol addiction.

Similar hazards exist for those who become dependent on
prescription drugs such as tranquilizers, sedatives, pain-
killers, sleepers, or diet pills. The habituation and addiction

cycle is faster, but the mental impairments are similar to those in the alcohol sequence. The easy sense of well-being masks a slowing of reflexes; the euphoria facilitates flights of imagination and distractibility. The whole process predisposes an individual to accidents, especially when the car moves faster than the driver can think. Occurrence of automobile fatalities by drunk drivers is inflated because alcohol is more visible while the influence of drugs often goes undetected.

The preceding can be illustrated by an action-oriented, impulsive young man with good coordination. After two or three years of driving experience, he may develop sufficient skill to drive faster and resort to maneuvering rather than prudence. In time, his skill permits him to pay less attention to the road and more to his companions or daydreams. Given the distraction of a girl friend in the right front seat, a congenial couple in the rear, and the easy euphoria of a pleasant evening, excesses can occur. Add sudden changes in conditions of driving such as weather or road surfaces and the situation is ripe for a fatal accident. While this description applies to a very large portion of young and even older drivers, not all of them suffer fatalities every time they drive this way. Successful driving with such obstacles provides a kind of seduction to keep on driving the same way and the eventual emergence of dangerous habits. Drivers operating in this way can easily be described as accidents searching for a place to happen. Eventually, with an additional factor such as the unpredictable behavior of another motorist, fatigue, emotional stress, or physical illness, the final accident occurs. When it does, the victim is not randomly chosen. He is self-elected.

Prevention of accidental death requires a shift in thinking by the American public as expressed in the news media. The major modification needed is in the willingness to deal with the subject of death as openly as sexual content is now handled on television or movies. Simultaneously, the romantic or pornographic element in sudden death will also diminish. This reversal will reduce the scapegoating of certain villains or extremes as dangerous, while all the rest are merely nice people. Safe driving is everybody's responsibility, and the victim who needs the most safety is the driver who thinks accidents only happen to the other fellow. Under the right combination of habit, circumstance, and provocation anyone is vulnerable to fatality by accident. To really believe that last statement, the reader has to accept and believe that death can really come to him also, now rather than later, and here rather than there. This last statement is a reminder of the universal inability to imagine existence without the individual being there to observe the results of his own death.

Homicide

A similar line of reasoning is possible with murder, but some differences will be apparent. Clearly anyone who is killed must be given the full benefit of doubt and sympathy. However, victims are *not* randomly selected. The nature and variety of the qualities that characterize the victim will be described as each kind of homicide is discussed.

The recent calls for "law and order" have generally failed to account for the orderliness and variety of crime in America. Depending on how the data is analyzed, there are several ways to classify homicide. Judge David L. Bazelon, U. S. Court of Appeals, Washington, D. C., and clinical professor of socio-legal aspects of psychiatry at George Washington University, has suggested at least four kinds of crime. Judge Bazelon is also known for his precedent-setting Durham decision that justified diminished responsibility for criminal acts.

The first of Bazelon's categories is white-collar crime, a crime in which a respectable citizen or businessman will manufacture a substandard piece of equipment or service. This, in turn, endangers the lives of the users. Examples are automobile parts, military weapons, building structures, foods, medical service, drugs, resort equipment and so forth. Deaths from these are always called accidental or, more rarely, manslaughter. Their number is not known officially nor is it quite clear that the deaths are murder in the conventional sense. However, consider the degree of outrage against a defective car manufacturer versus the unintentional victim of drunk driving. The outrage against the drunk driver is absolutely justified, but it should be even more so against the white collar criminal.

The victims of white-collar crimes are randomly selected in the sense that they just happen to be users of certain products or services. Beyond that, they represent people whose income, taste, and way of life predispose them to use such goods. This logic can be called an impersonal kind of over-determinism.

The second kind of homicidal crime, using Judge Bazelon's four categories, is called organized crime. The reference here is to the murders committed by gang members in the course of conducting their illegitimate businesses. Among these are murder for hire, enforcement of gang business practices, or just plain inter-gang warfare. In each of these types of homicides, the person doing the killing and his victim have an impersonal relation. It's strictly gang business, nothing more. Just a man doing his job. By the same token, the victim is also carefully chosen for his value to the gang. He is a client of gang services for which he fails to pay; someone he knows has "purchased" his death, or, he is in the same business competing with the gang that accomplishes his death. The three possibilities do not occur to just anyone. The victims have placed themselves in the position to be killed by organized crime.

Gang murders can only occur if the community doesn't care. Publicity is the single most effective deterrent to organized crime, especially murder. An effective press coverage of organized crime is usually sufficient to generate enough heat to reduce temporarily illegal activities including homicide. However, crimes reappear as soon as attention lapses. Ironically, too much inter-gang rivalry usually commands publicity and eventually leads to reduced crime.

The third category of homicide is the crimes of passion. Murders among married couples account for approximately one-half of all the homicides in the United States. Clearly, the victim killed by a spouse is not selected at random. One can

almost say the condition of "love" over-determines who will
be killed in at least half of the murders every year. Additional
factors are the typical ways one of the partners expresses emotions, especially anger. These are circumstances under which
loss of control is encouraged as in drinking or during family
quarrels. Identifying marital homicide as the single largest
group of murders makes it clear that law enforcement has
little to offer in the way of prevention. Similarly, the deterrent
value of capital punishment is irrelevant. Anyone is vulnerable to a moment of passion—the young more than the old,
lovers more than strangers. The only protection possible is to
recommend the removal of potential weapons. The more lethal
the weapon, the more destructive the act of injury can be during the moment of emotion. Guns easily accessible in the home
invite the final act of passion. Simply making them difficult to
reach quickly or easily may be enough to prevent a murder.
Self-defense is too high a price to pay if it permits or precip-
itates murder.

These three kinds of homicide are well-known, account
for the majority of deaths, and are largely ignored with respect
to deterrence or prevention. The whole focus of public attention
in the media and law enforcement is directed toward crime on
the streets. Typically this refers to robbery and assault with
deadly weapons of citizens as they go about their daily business. Death is usually incidental to the crime, often described
as unprovoked, and generally serving no useful purpose to
either the victim or the murderer. An additional element is the
tendency of the criminal to choose a victim from the same
area or nearby his own neighborhood. A frequent by-product
of this proximity is the tendency for both to be members of a
minority or poverty group. By no stretch of the imagination
do poor people commit the majority of crimes, but impoverish-
ment encourages them in the same causal way that cigarette
smoking encourages cancer. Some crimes are a response to
need, most to frustration. Many blindly take an option because
it is there, with no real chance of even enjoying the money, let
alone changing the rut they are in. Ghetto criminals them-

selves lead such damaged lives that their acts of violence express the same fatality that has characterized much of their entire existence.

Typically, the victim of crime on the streets is a proprietor of a neighborhood store. The most popular seems to be the liquor store. These victims are indeed different because of their simple decision to open a store in a high-risk neighborhood. Theoretically, an individual has the right to run his business anywhere. Practically speaking, the owner who chooses a high-risk area incurs the risk of getting himself robbed or killed. Mobility and increasing frustration with American life has spread the risk to other neighborhoods.

Those store-owners who get robbed or assaulted assume a certain vulnerability by choosing to enter the business, operate in that kind of ghetto neighborhood, and by the kinds of precautions they develop. Most of the time they make some mental estimate of cost-benefit in accepting the dangers of the given business. Perhaps none of them considers the danger of homicide. Robbery, yes. Give the thief the money, and carry on. Unfortunately, there is always the danger of an unprovoked murder during the course of a robbery. Newspaper accounts typically describe such homicides as senseless, serving no useful purpose to anyone. The piece of information that is usually missing is the kind of person conducting the robbery. The crime is usually an impulsive or poorly planned affair carried out by a marginal or desperate personality. From any standard, these people are socially inadequate with respect to education, job skills, earning capacity, income, family stability, and marriage. The chaos of their home life is as crippling as the criminal life they lead. Going to jail is a period of respite, relief, and stability in the career of typical criminals of the streets. From a psychiatric perspective, these criminals often qualify as not-guilty by reason of insanity.

Parenthetically, when these individuals do get off, they usually serve longer periods in mental hospitals if found not guilty, than if sent to prison on a simple conviction. There is an unwritten practice such that a superior court judge will not declare an insane person restored to sanity if his period of detention appears too short. It should be noted that sanity is a legal concept that is applied by the courts rather than by psychiatrists, although the latter serve in an advisory or consultant capacity. Suffice it to say that when a criminally insane murderer is finally restored to society he tends to be burned-out, institutionalized, and passive. These ex-murderers are more likely to wind up as quiet menials in large companies, workers for live-in situations, or recipients of some form of organized charity. It should be noted that the usual age of these criminals when released after ten to twenty years of incarceration tends to be above fifty.

This picture helps to explain the "unprovoked" nature of homicide during crime-on-the-streets type of robbery. What can an owner do to minimize his risk of homicide during these robberies? The proprietor of a business is in a position similar to the captain of an airliner during a hijacking. They both serve the public and are vulnerable to instant death at the hands of a frustrated, inept member of some socially deprived, minority group. Psychological profiles of hijackers evidence a similarity with those who engage in street crime.

Hijacking has been significantly reduced in the United States by the use of a screening approach for all boarding passengers. Only desperation could justify this expensive and time-consuming investment. Yet, it has worked and appears to have been worth the trouble. In hindsight one can ask were there equally effective alternatives that were simpler and cheaper? There may well have been. The typical hijacker was engaged in a last gasp effort to "do something" that would change his life of repeated failures. Any systematic, all-airplane, all-passenger approach might have worked. The one suggested here is that of a public information campaign on the order of "hijack prevention is everyone's business." Along with that would go instructions to report all suspicious passengers immediately. Such advertising itself would have had a deterring effect on easily frightened hijackers. Fortunately, it is not really necessary to test this suggestion any more. However, it is mentioned now for reference in the context of robbery and prevention of unprovoked murder.

The owner of a store that carries a high-risk quotient for robbery would need to think in terms of a system of deterrence peculiar to his neighborhood and business. The rationale would be the same as with hijacking. Essentially some form of unanswerable threat would be needed. A relatively large crowd of people always present would be effective during store hours. The use of videotape cameras remotely controlled and electronic gadgetry are also potentially effective. Their presence needs to be well advertised and their fail-safe alarms clearly noted. Another dimension is the instant locking of large sums of money in such a way that no one on the premises can achieve access to the safe except when adequate police protection is available. All of these ideas represent some systematic notion that deters crime by its insolubility, and eliminates the majority of impulse or panic criminals.

Beyond the principle of deterrence, there remains the inevitable day when a victim is faced with a hold-up man. Maximum cooperation is still the basic way of preventing homicide. Unfortunately, this is not always enough, because of the frightened, inadequate person who commits robbery. A simple additional way of safeguarding life is to remember his fears as well. Any signal or word that indicates the victim's fear and cooperation will be reassuring to the gunman, who needs to know that his control is effective. His anxiety makes this perception difficult. The victim's most innocent gestures are easily misconstrued. When faced with a gunman, offer a word or phrase indicating surrender and cooperation. These signals will minimize the unprovoked homicide.

A somewhat different variation of crime in street-type murders is the "unprovoked" shooting of uniformed policemen. Typically, the officer is killed during the course of his routine duties by someone he hasn't even seen. The murder is usually senseless except as an attack on the establishment or policemen in general.

If the victim is struck down randomly, it seems reasonable to infer that the murderer is also striking out at a hated symbol. There's nothing personal about the encounter even though one person kills another. It almost suggests the impersonal act of a soldier killing an enemy. It is not like that of course.

These assailants are easily seduced and suggestible. As members of some minority or abused subgroup, they are frequently exposed to the largely verbal hate talk of their peer groups. Nobody intends for them to go out and kill, but the hatred and emotion are present. Some of these marginal individuals are seduced by their emotions into a readiness to act.

There are two kinds of phenomena that facilitate the random killing of police by hyper-suggestible individuals. First is a general loosening of social restraints. The fear of God, the law, the neighbors or even one's parents is largely absent. In its place are the search for kicks and the avoidance of pain. Inadequate people have few internal restraints, and are encouraged by the self-expression visible in people they admire. The second phenomenon lies within the nature of police work. Police are expected to implement the prevailing prejudices of the middle class who pay for this service, or for those who wield political power. The individual officer must keep "those people" in their place. In this fashion they are responding to what is expected of them by the nice people. But policemen have their reference group too, where their own ego ideals express a certain point of view, often emotional and hateful, toward adversaries—crooks, kooks, hippies, or drop-out kids. The young and suggestible cop gets a slant, learns a prejudice, or has it reinforced in much the same way that marginal members of any group get brainwashed in order to share the beliefs and prejudices of their specific reference group. The net effect is to increase the probabilities of a differential regard towards easily-identified target groups such as those people found in urban ghettos. The culture of policemen and the people they restrain form a symbiotic relationship. From this mutual competitiveness come the individual eruptions that strike down innocent victims on both sides of the law.

Gun Regulation

One of the most frequently voiced suggestions as a solution for reducing homicides is the regulation of guns. The physical removal of guns from the hands of the public would certainly reduce the number of homicides by married couples, accidental fatalities, and deliberate self-injury. The very efficiency of guns facilitates death when an emotional or impulsive decision is also present. Registration of guns is one form of control in the sense of identifying who sells, buys, or uses a gun. It is effective only with the law-abiding citizenry. In principle, ex-felons and mental patients are already ineligible to own guns. However, the former do not bother with legal channels, and the latter simply don't indicate their mental illness on applications. Mental patients learn quickly that telling the truth about their past is always held against them when it comes to jobs, apartments, credit. Why should they tell the truth when it comes to purchasing a gun, whether for legitimate or other usage? Even if law enforcement were tightened to exclude unpredictable people from owning guns, it still wouldn't help much because most of the homicides in this country are committed by "nice" people who use properly registered guns to kill someone they know intimately in the crime of passion. Approximately 75 percent of all homicides are committed by an assailant intimately involved with the victim.

Gun registration provides a deterring effect in that the time required to purchase and use a gun removes the impulsive element. Once in the possession of the owner, however, there is little or no protection from registration. Aside from the value of identifying a murder weapon through police records, registration provides no saving of lives.

Suicide

Despite the drama attached to violent murder in the United States it just does not approach the enormity of the suicide problem. The true number of suicides is not known, but is certainly in excess of 24,000 per year. There is an overall tendency of coroners to rule in favor of "accidental" or "natural" causes if there exists the slightest ambiguity about the reason of death. Coroners are elected or appointed officials who must be sensitive to social pressures that come from the families who seek to avoid shame and stigma. The victim generally does the same, by seeking to make his death appear accidental. Automobile fatalities are easily construed as accidents even though they may reflect a death wish on the driver's mind.

The single most effective suicide prevention approach possible is an accurate counting system. This would require objective and consistent standards for identifying a suicide by the use of a psychological autopsy procedure. Trained behavioral scientists would interview survivors, evaluate personal documents, and review the usual coroners' data to assess the role of the victim in facilitating his own death.

A good reporting system facilitates suicide prevention because it creates a dependable yardstick for judging the extent of the problem. To become really aware of the circumstances of any suicide is to experience a sense of obligation to deter future self-injuries.

It may startle some to discover that all modes of death vary by uncontrollable factors such as age, sex, race, marital status, and geographical location. These are called epidemiological variables, and public health diseases are known to be distributed on the basis of these. Thus, certain diseases and types of death occur more frequently to one sex than to the other; some to the younger people and others to specific racial groups. For example, cancer of the cervix only occurs with women; similarly with cancer of the breast or uterus. Older people are more likely to die from heart disease, cancer, or stroke. Birth traumas only come to infants.

This same logic applies to other epidemiological variables, but are not as obvious or easy to document. Suicide rates and race illustrate the difficulties. The reported suicide rate per 100,000 blacks is different than that for whites. The suicide rates for whites in all reporting areas, for both sexes, and marital status increase progressively with age. The older the white group, the higher the suicide rates observed. The black suicide rates reach a plateau in the twenties for both men and women. There is indeed evidence that supports the stereotype that blacks do not commit suicide as frequently as whites.

Herbert Hendin in his book entitled *Black Suicide* reports

on suicides in New York City between 1940 and 1960. He notes that suicide rates for black men and women level off after the age of twenty. White suicide rates climb more slowly, but reach higher levels after the age of fifty-five. Hendin calls attention to the higher frequencies of suicides among young blacks than among young whites. Between the ages of twenty to thirty-five, the black suicide rate for men in New York City is twice that of whites. Hendin also notes that these same ages provide the peak years for black homicide. Is this a coincidence? Hendin goes on to suggest that both external aggression and self-injury are expressions of the rage black young men and women feel as they attempt to cope with the frustrations they encounter because of race. Hendin argues that suicide victims provide a barometer of the pressures felt by different groups at different ages in American society.

Hendin's ideas are based upon in-depth interviews of blacks in New York City and other studies. It should also be noted that black suicide rates are more vulnerable because of poor reporting than those for whites. There is a greater tendency of white coroners to assign a murder mode to black victims when in fact a suicide has occurred.

Hendin's explanations may be relevant to the recent observations that suicide rates for young people in the Los Angeles area are climbing dramatically. Between 1961 and 1969, the rates for white males in their twenties more than doubled, but those for females more than quadrupled. This same direction is also apparent in the national rates for white men and women in their twenties. The frustration experienced by today's youth is observable everywhere, in terms of recent campus disorders, the Vietnam War and draft, unemployment rates, and the frantic drifting from coast to coast.

The correlation between the increasing rate of suicide and the presence of frustrating experiences in the young is consistent with traditional variation of suicides. However in wartime, the number of suicides usually declines. Actually, the rates of the older-age groups have declined somewhat, at the same time the rates of those under thirty have been rising. The recent halt of American fighting in Southeast Asia will reduce one set of frustrations for an identifiable group of Americans. The suicide rates of this group over the next few years will provide a test of Hendin's thesis that rage and frustration are a cause of suicide in the young. The same theory applied to black groups is more difficult to test because any improvements tend to raise the level of aspiration, which often increases their sense of frustration. Hopefully, some improvements in the socio-economic sphere will occur for blacks and the justification for their rage will diminish.

Another minority group with a history of persecution and excessive suicides is homosexuals. The recent emergence of gay liberation groups and the resulting redefinition of their problems have reduced much of the unnecessary distress these individuals encounter. A practicing homosexual with a consenting adult partner need no longer live a double life or suffer internal conflict. While hazards and discrimination still exist, the success of the Metropolitan Community Church Fellowship documents a constructive adaptation to a perennial problem. These churches located in nearly a dozen large American cities provide a context of Christian acceptance and brotherhood for homophile communities and their "straight friends." The general stereotype has always been offered that to practice homosexuality was to automatically become a highrisk for eventual self-injury and suicide. There are certainly hazards to the gay life, but evidence of increased suicide rates is absent or obscure.

A more paradoxical minority is women. Granting the lack of equal opportunity, or inequality of reward for achievement, female suicide rates are considerably lower than for males of all ages and races. At first glance this seems to support a male chauvinist notion that women thrive on abuse. However, a more careful evaluation suggests two relevant observations. Frustrated or competitive wives can play an insidiously debilitating role predisposing the husband for an act of self-injury that can end in death. In time, a chronically frustrated wife may develop a complaining, nagging, or competitive manner. These patterns may become critical in facilitating a final act of self-injury when the husband starts seeking death.

The second relevant observation is the frequency of wives as murderers. Earlier it was noted that about half of the annual homicides are committed by spouses. Since more men are murdered than women, the inference seems clear that wives kill their husbands more often than the reverse. In another situation a similar result is apparent. Fatal automobile accidents typically kill more men than women. While these men are usually under thirty, presumably single, they still drive with female companions. Girl friends and wives in male-chauvinist America ordinarily sit on the right side of the vehicle, a position generally resulting in more fatalities than behind the driver's wheel. Considering the equal opportunity a wife has to be murdered or killed in an auto accident, the prevalence of male deaths raises the same question as in suicide. Is there a role for wives and girl friends too, that facilitates the occurrence of homicide and fatal vehicular accidents by their male companions?

The implication here is that the mistreatment of women by systematic deprivation of equal opportunity and privileges is frustrating to this largest of all minority groups. The death rates for men from all violent modes is significantly greater than that for women. These two statements describe some kind of correlation. The two phenomena seem to vary equally. However, the increased death rates by violence of blacks, the young, homosexuals when observed, or other minority groups are usually explained in terms of cultural vicissitudes or deprivations. These additional hazards to life are construed as sufficient motivations to explain unpredicted death in members of frustrated or disadvantaged groups. Yet these same forces in women do not yield higher death rates. Indeed, the opposite occurs. Does mistreatment yield lesser death rates for women, or do they somehow contribute to the higher death rates of their men?

The question of why anyone kills himself is not answerable with any certainty. The effort to explain the collective suicide rates of any minority is doomed to speculation. However, the existing speculations tend to include prevailing prejudices such as those exhibited towards homosexuals, blacks, youth, and women. The reverse of this phenomenon occurs when a white, middle-class male commits suicide. Typically, his motives get analyzed as a psychiatric problem. The possibility that the majority group may also be suffering from cultural deprivations is rarely considered in clinical explanations.

There is apparent here a curious paradox—when victims of some specified minority group commit suicide, authorities usually accept as the basic or predisposing "cause" the stress of membership in that group. When a white, middle-class male commits suicide, the basic cause is presumed to be a defect of character. The paradox comes in the double standard used to explain suicide. There is a failure to look at the unique motivations in the minority group member and a failure to study group influences in the majority victims.

The paradox occurs because there is a lack of interest and attention to the whole subject of suicide. Theories, in turn, are either piecemeal or culture-bound to social classes. An illustration of what is needed as well as an example of a testable theory is offered next. It has the immediate advantage of plausibility and provides options for people who wish to act constructively.

Everybody has some notion of the circumstances under which he or she prefers to be dead. This criterion is usually elevated to heroic proportions as in the famous words of Patrick Henry, "Give me liberty or give me death." As the perception of ugly reality begins to approach this idealized standard, the individual becomes more tempted by the idea of death as a release. In this context, the wish to die tends to increase to a point where it may surpass the more typical wish to live. At some threshold level, the wish starts to motivate self-injurious behavior.

The death wish is a necessary, but insufficient condition for the occurrence of self-injurious actions. Suicide requires opportunities, precipitant situations, and rehearsals because the actual self-injury is predetermined by the previous habits and the experiences of the victim. Suicide prevention requires familiarity with the ways in which a certain individual will go about achieving his own death. The most direct source of information is the potential victim himself, who will ordinarily respond to all questions with complete candor. Every person has a preferred way of killing himself, and will describe this, if asked. Frequent reviews with the potential victim will indicate if there is a shift in method, with a consequent need to shift the corresponding prevention plan developed for a specific victim.

The survival of the victim following a self-injury is contingent upon three kinds of factors. First is the chance occurrence of rescue which often confounds the overt intention of the victim. Many die accidentally while attempting suicide or live in spite of their best efforts to die. Secondly, other people often tip the balance; increasing or diminishing the wish to die. In this way, they help to precipitate an act of self-injury or fail to initiate effective rescue behavior. A third category of factors is the victim's typical approach to all goal achievements. These will dominate how effectively he or she goes about the business of suicide.

Currently there is no medication or deterrent to self-injury in high-risk people, that is, those individuals who are in-between one or more suicide attempts. The majority of people who kill themselves in the United States do so when they have returned to live within the community, without known mental illness or clinical depression, who function just like the rest of us "normal" people. In short, fatal self-injury occurs in victims who are indistinguishable from the majority. Anyone of these individuals will tell under what circumstance he or she would prefer to be dead if asked, and the method of self-injury he or she would choose. The prevention problem is one of developing resources for potential victims. The direction suggested here is an educational effort to publicize the dangers of suicide, much as was done with drug abuse, venereal disease, and the need for appropriate contraceptives.

Of course, there is a general theory that the mentally ill are the most prone to acts of suicide, and among these, the greatest risk occurs with the clinically depressed. Statistically speaking this is true. However, in terms of the actual number of people dying from an act of self-injury, the opposite is usually the case. While depressed psychiatric patients have the highest suicide rates, they also represent only 13 percent of all mental patients. The largest number of deaths each year come to those diagnosed as schizophrenics. Hospitalized or recently discharged mental patients have the highest rates, but also represent a very small percentage of the total American population. The largest absolute number of suicidal deaths happen among people living in the community, conducting their affairs in the usual way at least in the eyes of their associates, neither depressed nor mentally ill.

To attempt to reduce the more than 24,000 suicidal deaths each year, there is an increasing necessity to come to grips with the whole business of dying in America. Natural as well as unnatural death modes must be restored to some proper dimension. This requires the removal of taboos about dying in general, and the morbid preoccupation with sudden death in particular. The mass media's glorification of the not quite suicidal deaths of Janis Joplin and Jimi Hendrix are examples. These young rock singers were popular idols whose premature deaths by accidental overdoses of heroin were given international attention. The publicity was unavoidable, but the emphasis seemed to be on the admirable example they set by their short, talented, and tragic lives.

Sylvia Plath is a less publicized example of the same phenomenon. Her suicidal death in 1963 didn't attract as much attention as the deaths of the two rock stars. But since then her only novel, *The Bell Jar*, was published in the United States. That and more especially her poetry, have won her a permanent place in the literary world and also among the young. Her current position is much like that of a latter-day Joan of Arc. Sylvia Plath's death by asphyxiation is construed by some as a sacrifice to her literary art by personal suffering. Her suicide has been romanticized as the inevitable, even desirable, consequence of creativity. But that was not so.

The sudden death of Sylvia Plath illustrates most of the fuzzy thinking evidenced by the mores of the young and among mental health professionals with respect to manage-

ment of the potentially suicidal. Sylvia Plath's actual preoccupations, previous self-injuries, and eventual death are
described vividly in two books. The first is in her own largely
autobiographical novel *The Bell Jar.* The second is *Savage
God* by A. Alvarez published in 1972. Dr. Alvarez' book represents an intelligent effort to analyze suicide among artists.
He begins his book with the recollections of Sylvia's last days
and death. Both books provide sufficient detail to illustrate
the accidental and compulsive factors in her tragic and totally
avoidable death.

Esther Greenwood, the heroine of *The Bell Jar,* almost dies
from a self-injury. The book's dialogue allows the reader to
trace Sylvia's perceptions of various social scenes through
the character who represented her alter ego. The events move
from great scholastic success at Smith College to the offices
of *Mademoiselle* magazine, to her home in the Boston suburbs,
and eventually to psychiatric treatment in a private mental
hospital. Along the way, the author provides much sensitive
detail in a stream-of-consciousness style that permits the
reader to formulate a personal opinion, and also, incidentally,
justifies self-injury behavior in those who might identify with
Esther Greenwood. The novel ends with the heroine's release
from the hospital. Knowing the author's eventual ending fore-
shadows a dire conclusion that is almost larger than life.

The novel's setting is circa 1954, before tranquilizers,
suicide-prevention centers, hot lines, or crisis intervention.
These are all emergency services for acutely suicidal people.
But they do little for patients over the longer, high-risk intervals between suicide attempts. The best single basis for prediction of future self-injurious behavior can be found in the
history of the individual's previous suicide attempts, no matter how superficial or manipulative they might have appeared
at the time. The next best substitute for an actual attempt is
the excessive and clinically observable preoccupation with
the consequences of suicide. Both of these behaviors are easily
elicited from suicidal individuals by simple questioning, once
rapport has been established. Neither one poses any potential

threat because a discussion is solicited. Therefore, there is little danger and many advantages in asking people about their previous suicide attempts. However, this option is rarely exercised in current suicide prevention procedures.

In *The Bell Jar*, Esther Greenwood is a bright, hard-working, twenty-year-old winner of a trip to New York City as a guest college editor of *Mademoiselle*. The novel describes her adventures, conflicts, surrenders, depression, increasing preoccupation with death wishes, and efforts to injure herself. She is an acute observer of human behavior and can sense how others feel. These perceptions stir her own complementary emotions. However, she lacks the control to handle these and becomes overwhelmed by them.

The novel goes on to show how Esther eventually becomes a psychiatric patient. During this process, she vicariously seeks and experiments with different methods of self-injury. Eventually, she makes a highly effective effort to kill herself. She is rescued by accident.

As with life itself, the reader of *The Bell Jar* comes away with vivid images but no adequate explanation for any of the self-injury phenomena described. The novel's failure in this regard is no criticism of its literary merit, but does indicate the limited understanding of the author about self-injury and her own motives. To her credit she provides sufficient detail to permit the kind of conclusions possible in psychological autopsies.

Esther Greenwood suffers an array of problems that add to her burdens as an aspiring young author, but why should any one or more of these be a sufficient cause for self-injury behavior? For every woman who suffers frustration and disappointment sufficient to motivate suicide, there are literally hundreds of thousands who do not. Even in combination, why should social rejection, male contempt, and feelings of inadequacy be sufficient to trigger self-injury? Esther, like everyone else, carries an implicit standard for judging the meaningful life. She describes it in her fears that she cannot seem to write anymore. At this time in her life, becoming a successful writer is her most compelling goal. The prospect of marriage in which a wife's duties override every other value is offensive to her. These are described in the characters of Dodo Conway and her mother, Mrs. Greenwood. Of all her psychiatric symptoms—not eating, not sleeping, not realizing, apathy, depression—she is most bothered by her inability to write. The background of Esther further documents her total investment in wanting to develop this capacity further. It represents her only purpose in life at that stage of her evolution. Also implied was Sylvia Plath's inability to fully accept her own father's death.

Like so many other able and hard-working people, Esther discovers she is on some kind of a treadmill that isn't as wonderful as she had been led to expect. If she were like the other girls who won the *Mademoiselle* guest editorships she would not especially care about the discrepancies. Of the girls, Betsy is simply insensitive; Hilda is superficial; Doreen is cynical. They all seem to manage fine. So far these are all garden-variety problems of adolescence and growing up. Most kids eventually find some answer or muddle through this period. All seek help from parents, peers, ego-ideals, friends, teachers. Esther does so as well, but she is increasingly disappointed by what she finds.

Mrs. Greenwood is portrayed as an inadequate hard-working widow whose own ambitions were betrayed by marriage. She does not really manage or control her difficult situation—widowed, working as a stenographer, raising a son and a complicated daughter. These seem to overwhelm her limited understanding of the situation. The mother's efforts to help Esther seem pathetic. She uses the prevailing mores to manipulate her daughter, who reacts to the whole thing with negativism and withdrawal.

Jay Cee, the ugly female editor, is a potential ego ideal. "She had brains, was honest, and knew all the quality writers. Jay Cee wanted to teach me something, as did all the old ladies I ever knew. But suddenly I didn't think they had anything to teach me." Jay Cee triggers memories—of her mother, Philomena Guinea, a successful novelist patron, Mrs. Willard,

her boyfriend's mother. They are all perceived as sexual
failures. They carry traditional expectations toward female
options but all of these are disappointing to Esther.

Another potential help is her friend, Doreen, who is beautiful, smart, intuitive, and unfettered by stereotypes. "Everything she said was like a secret voice speaking straight out
of my own bones." Doreen externalizes what Esther's inhibitions prevent, but acting on these impulses causes her distress.
She resolves to become like Betsy, a proper Pollyanna. However, neither extreme worked. Esther vacillates on both horns
of several dilemmas. One conflict is sexual versus intellectual;
another is proper versus improper; others are marriage versus
a career, and eventually, the wish to die versus the wish to live.

At any point in the time covered by the novel and certainly during the summer of her acute distress, Esther Greenwood could have answered frank questions about her wish to
die had they been asked. Even conventional Dr. Gordon could
have obtained relevant information, and certainly Dr. Nolan
with her better rapport. Mental health professionals don't
usually ask questions about death; they may inquire about
suicidal thoughts, but tend to penalize frankness by extra
observation or medication. Often they don't scrutinize superficial answers deeply enough. If they did, patients like Esther
would react by reexamining all their thoughts concerning
death. For example: "Under what circumstances would you
prefer to stop living?" Esther has already indicated several
conditions which interfered with pursuit of writing—marriage
to anybody, but especially Buddy Willard, and having children.
An opposite, but less acceptable answer to Esther is the not
quite explicit notion of being too ugly to enjoy sex; like Jay
Cee, and implicitly Mrs. Willard or her mother. These unconscious conflicts contribute to her distress and help induce
"writer's cramps." She perceives this last as a total failure of
her reason for living. She suffers increasing distress and
depression. Attention to conflicts that threaten her reason for
living would be prophylactic. Routine inquiry could have elicited this concern. Any discussion might have introduced an
alternative formulation or started her perceptions moving in

a different direction. A similar comment is appropriate with respect to her thinking about self-injury methods.

Esther's search for a plausible way to kill herself is certainly authentic. She may have been a fictitious character, but her trial-and-error experiments, abortive and superficial gestures, all eventually prepared her for the one "right" method. All of these have meaning as rehearsals. Consider the range of choices and especially her reasoning about each of them.

In order of appearance:

1. *Jumping from a seven-story ledge*
   Need to pick the right number of stories or else still be alive. She sees the description in the local scandal sheet—murders, suicides, beatings, and robbings—every page featured a half-naked woman with her breasts surging over the edge of her dress.

2. *Disemboweling with an extremely sharp knife, hara-kiri*
   Takes a lot of courage to die like that, and this is discrepant with her current self-evaluation.

3. *Starlet succumbs after sixty-eight hours in coma*
   Esther makes no comment except to note her identification with the victim.

4. *Gillette razor-blades in a tub of warm water*
   Rejects cutting wrists; "they are too defenseless." What she is trying to get at is placed somewhere else, deeper, more secret, a lot harder to get at.

5. *Drops razor on right calf—leg crossed, ankle on knee of opposite foot*
   No time for cut on calf to bleed long enough.

6. *Drowning*
   Cold ocean, her flesh winced in cowardice from such a death.

7. *Gun wound*
   She thinks that it's just like a man to do it with a gun; she couldn't get one; wouldn't know how to shoot; danger of missing; too many risks.

8. *Drowning—two additional references*
   First compares drowning with burning; second, says "water spat me out."

9. *Hanging by the silk cord of her mother's bathrobe*
   Couldn't find suitable place in the house. Pulling the
   cord while lying in bed didn't work. Part of her body
   blocks further effort. She would need to ambush her
   own body.
10. *Overdose of sleeping pills*
    She takes fifty pills and leaves her mother a note,
    "I am going for a long walk." She hides in the cellar,
    elated, certain, and efficient at last. "She knows just
    how to do it."

The evolution is not random, but a unique expression of
Esther and Sylvia Plath. Each argument is predetermined by
previous experiences, her expectations, and the human compulsion to externalize the kind of person she thinks she is.
There is nothing whimsical about her thinking, the final method
chosen, and how she attempts to prevent possible rescue.

Another example of this psychological over-determination
is illustrated in the novel by the death of Joan Gilling, who is
described as "horsey." Joan is engaged to Buddy Willard, the
medical student whom Esther rejects. Joan is also hospitalized for a psychiatric problem. She propositions Esther for a
homosexual affair. Esther rejects Joan, but later seeks out her
help when she hemorrhages following her first sexual intercourse.

Toward the end of the novel, Joan is found hanged; an
unusual choice for most women, but consistent with the character depicted. She is active, dominant, aggressive, even
masculine. Compare Esther's efforts to arrange her own
hanging with her mother's silk bathrobe cord. Hanging simply
is not appropriate to Esther's character, rather than reflecting
her inadequate intention to die.

Real people also think in these ways and, if invited, will
describe their reasoning. The whole process documents how
historically predetermined any self-injury can be—impaired
freedom to choose, narrowed alternatives, and mixed emotions.

Knowing about suicidal thoughts permits efforts by others
to block any immediate impulse by developing a prevention
plan. Mrs. Greenwood was quite right in trying to hide the
pills. But she was unable to sense her daughter's contempt

for her. If Mrs. Greenwood had been able to ask direct questions, the dialogue might have gone something like this:

Mrs. Greenwood: Esther, if you felt like killing yourself, how would you do it?

Esther: Take a lot of sleeping pills.

Mrs. Greenwood: How would you get them?

Esther: Find out where you hide them.

Mrs. Greenwood: How would you make sure that would work?

Esther: I'd take the whole bottle and I'd hide myself where no one could find me.

This dialogue is, of course, totally unrealistic. Mrs. Greenwood and Esther had never had the ability to talk frankly to each other under any circumstances. There was understated, although observable, hostility between them. During that summer neither one would have been capable of anything but the most superficial conversation. The point, however, is intended to demonstrate the kind of questioning that is possible, other things being equal. There is no harm in attempting these questions, only in not trying at all.

During Esther's acute episodes of despair, Mrs. Greenwood could not, but perhaps somebody else could have kept in touch by weekly or even daily conversations with Esther. Clearly, Mrs. Greenwood wasn't the only one who committed the sin of omission. The professional staff of the private mental hospital failed to ask similar questions, knowing full well that once mental patients start getting better, the greater is the risk of self-injurious behavior.

Why did Esther Greenwood attempt suicide in the summer of 1954? She perceived reality as preventing her *raison d'être*, the desire to be a creative writer. She was less aware of her fears about being undesirable. She felt unable to remain honest about her own feelings. She was not able to reconcile her reactions with what was expected at home, in the career world, and in her social encounters. The convergence of her perceptions of reality and her own standards for preferring death increased her wish to die.

Her choice of self-injury method reflected a unique style—to go quietly, without mayhem or bloodshed, peacefully, by going to sleep passively. She obtained the pills and arranged prevention of rescue with intelligence, resourcefulness, and efficient effort. These were consistent with her character and personality.

Because there is a rationale for, and method of, self-injury peculiar to Esther, there is also a method for preventing her suicide attempts, but nobody tried.

The outcome of Esther's overdose of sleeping pills was not death, but this was due to chance. Following Esther's release from the hospital, she became a high-risk person with odds of one in one hundred each year thereafter. These odds are cumulative among potential suicide victims. Statistically, the odds for the individual to commit suicide are actually higher in the first year than in the twentieth year thereafter. In between suicide attempts, a high-risk victim such as Esther could aspire to a normal life, and like ordinary people suffer the kinds of disappointments that elicit wishes for relief through death. Unlike the majority, the high-risk person is more likely to act because of previous familiarity and surrender to despair.

A. Alvarez in *The Savage God* provides details that permit an extension of these remarks about Sylvia Plath's actual death. In November, 1962, she had rented a house in Ireland in which the poet William Butler Yeats had once lived. Her identification as a writer continued to dominate her purpose for living. She moved into the small house with her two children, Ted Hughes, her husband and also a poet, and she had become separated in September. On Christmas Eve, Alvarez dropped in for a drink with Sylvia and they discussed her most recent poetry. He noticed her different appearance as one "curiously desolate," and that she had "a sharp, strong smell from her hair like an animal's." In all their previous meetings, Alvarez had never seen her quite like this.

He noticed that her recent poems, especially "Death and Co." suggested a surrender rather than continued resistance as suggested in "Lady Lazarus" and "Daddy." Alvarez was unable to react appropriately. He ended up feeling disappointed in himself and was sure that Sylvia saw his failure as well. That was his last encounter.

In late January, 1963, a fellow editor described Sylvia

Plath's recent poetry as being "too strong for him" and added that "she sounds in a bad state." Friends agreed that she needed help. Her physician agreed, too, and prescribed sedatives. He also referred her to a therapist. These are the usual last resorts.

But Sylvia Plath didn't show much enthusiasm for any of this help. She had gone that route before and had no reason to think anything different would happen this time. Symptomatically, her visible behavior reflected changes associated with her clinical depression. She was unable to act on her own behalf, set up appointments, eat, or even wash properly. The apathy was circumscribed. She still continued to care for her children and wrote prodigiously. She was not psychotic, nor hospitalizable as a mental patient. To have attempted this would have been ineffectual or temporary at best. It is only hindsight that justifies the dramatic interventions available.

Alvarez goes on to describe the breakdown of communications between Sylvia and her friends. She visited friends for the weekend, planning to return on Monday. She appeared cheerful, but decided to return Sunday evening over the protests of her friends. At 11:00 p.m. she knocked on the door of an elderly, deaf artist who lived two floors below. She asked to borrow a stamp, but lingered to talk. He finally asked her to leave because he was tired.

About 6:00 a.m. she went up to the children's room in a different part of the house with two glasses of milk and a plate of bread and butter. She was expecting a girl from an agency to take care of the children about 9:00 a.m. Sylvia then prepared to kill herself by turning on the gas, sealing the cracks, and putting her head in the oven. At 9:00 a.m. the girl knocked at the street door. Receiving no answer, and seeing no names on the door, she checked a phone directory, and eventually called her agency. They advised her to try again. She did, but her knocking produced no response. The deaf artist didn't hear either. The girl finally got into the apartment by 11:00 a.m. through the aid of some workmen. They smelled gas and broke in the door. They found Sylvia on the floor, her body still warm, and a note to her doctor asking for help along with his phone number. She had apparently changed her mind and clearly wanted to go on living.

Technically, Sylvia Plath died accidentally while attempting suicide. Her actual death does not fit the dramatic or the heroic image of the artist making the supreme sacrifice for the sake of creativity. Instead she approached her own self-termination with all the doubts, confusions, and inadequacies that characterize all suicidal behavior. Her death was due to chance factors just as her previous survival was an accident. This does not mean that her wish to die was not genuine, but rather that her acts of self-injury reflected her unique ways of solving problems and achieving her goals. If her three suicide attempts are regarded as an evolving sequence that ended eventually in sudden death, Sylvia Plath's chronological behavior looks like this:

Summer 1953: Sylvia Plath crawled into a hole in her basement (grave?), diverted rescuers with a false note, and took an overdose of sleeping pills. She was rescued by accident.

Summer 1962: She drove her car off the road mysteriously, dangerously, impulsively. She escaped injury. The violence of this method is not typical for Sylvia Plath and suggests tension and conflict in her relations with intimates.

February 1963: She placed her head in a gas oven, apparently changed her mind, and wrote a note for help, but succumbed to fumes in room.

These different self-injuries reflect her situation, age, sex, and mental states at the time. Self-injury methods are predetermined by the kind of person one is. If her last attempt seemed poorly planned, impulsive, irrational, these acts also described her behavior during those last hours. Placing her head in a gas oven expressed how she felt about herself and immediately recalls the image of Hitler's final solution of the Jews. She used the same image in the poem "Daddy" where she imagined a Nazi father and a Jewish mother. Whatever the connection between the poem and the act of self-injury they most certainly reflect the actions of the same person.

Alvarez believes that Sylvia Plath was attempting to write her way out of a preoccupation with death. He suggests two reasons—the first was the recent separation from her husband which triggered a grief reaction based on the severe bereavement she suffered as a child over the death of her own father; the second was the more recent car accident/suicide attempt. Survival from the latter permitted Sylvia to examine death without the usual conventional restraints. She could write about dying as an observer rather than as a victim. In short her writing was a self-help approach to her own wish to die.

Alvarez, like other observers of suicide in the gifted, is judging her motives in hindsight; he is seduced by her death into giving more credence to her writings as evidence of suicidal motives. The death outcome for Sylvia Plath enlarges the context of her writing from literary and aesthetic to clinically morbid. Her poems stand on their own as works of art. Their implications of her mental status, her wish to die, or as data to account for her motivation are ambiguous. Sylvia's poetry provides a record of some of the sensitizing experiences she had had, her habits of examining and accepting taboo topics, and her contact with unconscious fantasies. This would be true of most artists. To seek from these evidence of clinical motivation is to pervert the context of her writing. Her poetry may provide clues about her fantasies, but offer nothing usable as a foreshadowing of future self-injury. Her poetry conveys the same meanings regardless of the author's fate. The poems of her last days would have received an entirely different connotation if she had survived, remarried, watched her children grow up, and received the public recognition her works justified.

Unfortunately, Sylvia Plath's role as Joan of Arc for the suicide generation—people in their twenties—still continues, aided by the heroic emphasis given her death. There are two fundamental arguments the young tend to use in identifying with Sylvia Plath's suicide. The first is the one previously challenged. Namely, the idea that artistic themes involving death are inevitably seductive to the artist who will eventually die prematurely. A series of studies of artists who painted suicidal themes, and those artists who eventually committed suicide was conducted by this writer. The evidence supported the con-

clusion that the two acts were unrelated and probably mutually exclusive. Those who painted the theme did not commit
suicide and those artists that died from self-injury did not deal
with the theme in their work.

The second argument is the heroic nature of suicide. The
details provided about Sylvia Plath's self-injury behavior
should make it clear that there was nothing courageous about
her three attempts. In this matter, she was more typical of clinical subjects than of the professional artist she most certainly
was. The confusion comes from popular notions based on the
example of Socrates, certain soldiers, and the self-chosen
deaths of Christian martyrs. What these premature forms of
death have in common is the willingness to die for a cause
greater than a personal need; in a way that advances this
purpose. Unfortunately, the heroic aspirations of the young
suicide victim are typically manifested in stereotyped symptoms of clinically-motivated, self-injury behavior.

These stereotypes seduce the young and intellectually
prone into risk-taking and eventually choosing self-injury
behavior under duress. The mass media aid in this seduction
by the pornographic-like usage they make of all violent deaths.

5

Installment Dying

Somewhere in-between fatal disease and sudden death lie a variety of life-shortening habits which effectively reduce life expectancies, but are never formally recognized as such. Occasionally someone will over-dramatize these examples and call them suicidal, but the very exaggerations often diminish their impact as warnings. Illustrations occur with alcoholism, obesity, smoking, drug abuse, and a variety of behaviors associated with poor cooperation by the patient in chronic illnesses. These include diseases such as diabetes, kidney failure treated by dialysis, circulatory disorders, frequent pregnancies, and so forth. The direction of these lifelong and dangerous habits tends clearly towards the reduction of length and quality of the individual's remaining health. This process has been called dying-on-the-installment plan. No matter what the name, the patient is hastening his or her end by an insidious process of self-injury.

A slow death is defined here as a predictable event, coming sooner rather than later, because of some systematic habit which threatens or injures health. This habit continues compulsively despite knowledge of the consequences, and whether or not a person tries to use his will power. The definition is clear, and the choices self-evident, yet individuals continue to accept the prospect of reduced life expectancies rather than to alter a bad habit. The most common example occurs with smoking. At this writing, everyone seems to acknowledge the conclusion that systematic inhalation of tobacco smoke reduces life expectancy by vulnerability to various terminal diseases. While the percentage of men smoking has declined recently, large numbers continue the practice in what is clearly an addictive pattern. These people are shaping the kind of death they will most likely encounter by permitting a compulsive habit to continue that is dangerous to their health. Exhortations to use will power, threats, or rational arguments are largely wasted on most of them. The choice is not theirs to make, at least not in the direct fashion implied by the advice-givers.

First of all, the addictive quality of tobacco has been vastly underestimated, mainly because of its familiarity and near universality. In a previous time, smoking was a symbol and image of masculinity. Adolescent boys traditionally lit up in the presence of girls and each other for a variety of motives familiar to any parent, but not directly connected with addiction or smoking itself. In time, however, these gestures become habits, and physical addiction follows. Regular inhalation of tobacco induces a physical adaptation to chemical ingredients such as nicotine. Medically, this condition is called tolerance, and yields a physical craving when deprivation occurs. The mechanism is similar to the process in heroin or alcohol addiction.

There is next the social habituation in which daily repetitions have reinforced the pleasure, or reduced distress, by the process of lighting up, inhaling, and manipulating the materials, when in the presence of others. Even after physical withdrawal is completed successfully, the social craving is stimulated again by cues such as dinner, social drinking, or company. The ex-smoker suffers awkwardness and a sense of being in limbo when stimulated by the familiar signals, but is unable to light up in the old way. These perennial reminders of the lost habit stimulate the act of smoking and during times of special vulnerability relapses will occur. Once resumed, a snowball effect occurs and the victim loses his minimal option to give up smoking.

There is thirdly the additional obstacle of society's failure to take the problem of cigarette smoking seriously. Modern advertising essentially exhorts every American to partake of the good life through smoking. Even today, few people are condemned for smoking. Given the known hazards to health, the tolerant acceptance of cigarette smoking is comparable to encouraging reckless driving in adolescents or by intoxicated adults. The failure to criticize, especially in the context of prior approval, represents a group-sanctioned license for the addiction and diminishes the individual's resources in attempting to assert his or her will power.

The very universality of smoking and the deceptive ease with which many appear to give it up is seductive. Everybody expects will power alone to be sufficient. As the individual finds his or her resolve insufficient to break the habit, he or she becomes defeated and gives up. Or worse, a person tries to make a virtue out of necessity, and proclaims the freedom to choose what he cannot reject. If the pernicious hold that tobacco has over normal users were known, the individual would recognize the need for assistance and would be less vulnerable to defensive rationalizations.

Tobacco is certainly more addictive than marijuana, which is considered merely habituating. While marijuana is more intoxicating, it is different from tobacco and there is less chance of developing even the habitual pattern that frequent repetitions create. Successful members of Alcoholics Anonymous testify that giving up tobacco is far more difficult than doing without alcohol. Even heroin addicts note that it is easier to "kick" than stop smoking. Addicts will often quit "cold turkey" in order to reduce their tolerance so they can get high later on smaller doses. This phenomenon is unknown with nicotine addiction.

The smoker and other victims of slow dying lack the freedom to choose. In effect, their will power is impaired as a significant force in altering their self-injurious habits. While there are many examples known to everyone of people who can give up by strength of character, what is not so immediately apparent is that they were able to alter the conditions under which they smoked. Successful escape from the cigarette addiction requires the victim to recover some ability to choose, or never to have lost that choice completely in the first place.

Most of the familiar social problems involving a compulsive behavior hinge upon an effective loss of control because a habit has become rigid through regular usage. There are, in addition, often predisposing, unconsciously motivated, and irrational forces at work. However, even when these are resolved, there still remains a compulsive habit that continues to exert force.

The dismal record of treating and controlling alcoholics, drug addicts, or sexual deviants reflects a tactical failure to deal with relevant daily patterns which continue the compulsive habits and predispose to problem behavior. An illustration of this can be found in the heroin addict who decides to reform. Whether under the auspices of a correctional program or on his own, many former addicts have decided to stop their life of drug abuse. Firm in this new resolve, they often return to their old neighborhood. Meeting old friends, they renew associations, go to a bar, or to a party. When the drugs emerge, it's too late for an effective choice. Regardless of the intention, under those circumstances, the former addict cannot maintain his resolve, or has stacked the odds against success. Failing once, he is more vulnerable to giving up and going along with the bad habits that block his freedom to choose. Pride leads these victims to assert that their failures represent a free choice.

Most treatment programs emphasize psychological hang-ups, and give lip service to relationships, but fail to provide alternatives for the addicts where they can begin to exert choices. An illustration of this last point occurs with heroin addicts. As members of the criminal world, their addictions were part of their way of life. To really give up drugs, they also need to give up life in the underworld with its crime, prostitution, "scoring," "fixing," and "coasting." Yet the square world is clearly not ready to accept them and especially with their impairments, lack of skills, and low-status income. Efforts to rehabilitate have failed to create a reference group appropriate to the ex-addicts that satisfies their need to belong. The

most obvious answer should have been the ex-addict soci-
ties, such as Synanon or other self-help groups. Yet the official correctional position was to penalize ex-addicts who
sought to form non-using reference groups. Their parole status
was violated for associating with "known" criminals.

Poor nutrition is another illustration of slow death. Because
under- or overeating are lifetime patterns, the threat they
pose to life is typically minimized by the victims. Some cultures
regard overweight as a sign of love, good health, and prosper-
ity. Others regard being thin as a positive or aesthetic achievement. There are, of course, complicated and obscure connections between body chemistry and eating habits. These in turn
are connected with physical activities. The tendency of fat
people to be sedentary has been noted before, but some sedentary people are also thin. There are physical limits to what
an individual can do without going against his tastes and
body rhythms. The choice lies in eating habits, not quantities
of food. The kinds of eating habits that produce excess pound-
age are obviously self-injurious.

Any diet can help some people lose weight, but which ones
will keep weight down over the long haul? To extend life, eating habits must be acceptable and effective over a lifetime.
Every person has some optimal balance between intake and
activity at which his weight is stable. A stable weight of ten
percent above the ideal in one person has a different meaning
from a recent ten percent gain in another. Both need to look
at the probability tables for heart disease and overweight.
While the life-shortening effects of both are the same statistically, the first person may decide the increased probability
of death is easier to accept than a significant change in eating
habits. The recent weight-gainer may be scared into a successful weight loss. However, that success can be attributed to the
recency of the habit and the comparative freedom to alter it.

Arbitrary exhortations to use will power are neither realistic nor effective in the long run. They may yield a weight loss,
but will they hold up over a two- to five-year period? There are
no easy answers or effective gimmicks in developing a lifetime solution. There are many recommended books on good

nutrition and weight loss for different kinds of problem eaters. The important consideration is for the victim of slow death to change his eating habits with a lifetime goal in mind. Better fewer, and longer-lasting changes, than frequent crash and rebound cycles. Chemical assists in losing weight by repressing the appetite carry the danger of chronic dependence. Diet pills pose the same problems of drug abuse as with heroin. It takes more and more to achieve less and less effect. If the weight control method does not offer the promise of a permanent change, forget it. There are fewer risks in being fat than in taking unnecessary chances with fad diets, pills, or sudden and irregular exercise.

Excessive pregnancies, in relation to health and intentions, are obviously bad for the life-expectancies of the mothers. The controversy about birth control has had a religious emphasis, out of all proportion to the real issue of choice. Aside from the "sinfulness" of natural versus unnatural methods of contraception, the tendency of some mothers to have many more pregnancies than they wish is attributable to a default in application of preferred methods of birth control. The largest identifiable group of reluctant mothers are those in the lower-income groups. The major obstacle to effective contraception for them is apparently a lack of motivation. Even the ubiquitous condom and diaphragm require the trouble of putting them on. While none of these is 100 percent reliable, they are certainly not as fallible as the recurrence of unwanted pregnancies would suggest. There is, in addition, the tendency for lightning to strike twice or thrice in the same place when it comes to unwanted pregnancies. The real failure here is that of a sustained effort in practicing any chosen contraceptive. There is instead a surrender to the path of least resistance, either during the heat of passion, or during the more exploitative situation when women are overwhelmed by the demands of an impoverished life. Often the element of choice is effectively absent and the social pressures are on the side of continued exposure to monthly risks of pregnancy. The women in this situation are less able to alter or escape the dangers.

In the context of chronic disease, it would again seem obvious that taking the right amount of protein (as in kidney failure treated by chronic hemodialysis) would be obvious and easy. While most patients do watch their diets successfully, every treatment unit seems to have one or more eating delinquents. The artificial kidney machine manages to keep patients alive indefinitely by replacing the functions of their own damaged kidneys. However, it is never as efficient as the natural organ and the patient can never go back to prior eating habits. In time a sense of deprivation comes over the patients.

Given the life and death situation of patients on chronic hemodialysis, most manage to conform to medical requirements, even though their existence is difficult. Eating binges are always tempting. Periodically, they do occur. Many observers have construed this behavior as suicidal but this reflects some confusion. Eating delinquency is a slow-acting behavior expressing a wish to die, but not a direct act of self-injury, nor even one whose lethal effects are certain. While some dialysis patients have literally pulled out the surgically implanted shunt between artery and vein, these are different kinds of self-injury behavior. Here death is certain from rapid ex-sanguination and reflects different motivations than dietary excess. The former is an example of suicidal intent, while the latter is a compulsive but slow self-injury.

The phenomena of slow death are known to everyone although often poorly formulated. The perniciousness of this mode is the inability of the victim to alter his habits and preferences so as to facilitate his or her continuation rather than death. The undramatic nature of these life-diminishing behaviors allows them to escape attention, let alone intervention. The outlook for prevention is typically grim. The most positive suggestion is to identify this problem more clearly so that all parties can be on their guard, and alert to optimal alternatives.

Other chronic diseases provide similar examples. The specific disease is not the critical factor, but rather the observation that some victims react to the chronic treatment and its limitations with less rational actions. In time, these victims seem to get locked into a high risk or self-injurious pattern of behavior. Casual discussion always documents the fact that they understand the implications of their behavior, but feel unable to prevent it. Like reformed alcoholics, they will often promise never to do it again, but most are vulnerable to repetitions.

Sometimes this behavior is especially obscure even in psychiatric settings, let alone in the usual surgical or medical units that are for the chronic patients, such as in kidney disease. The major problem appears to be one of motivation, the wish to continue a meaningful or worthwhile life. Since dialysis patients are selected for the limited number of dialysis beds on the basis of prior evidence of social worth, their dietary indiscretions represent impaired motivation or morale, rather than lack of ability or original intent. Existence in a chronic dialysis way of life is extremely arduous, debilitating, and exhausting. Eating binges provide instant kicks and are inherently seductive to any deprived person. The individual patient, while knowing better, has not found an effective choice, or an appropriate alternative for satisfaction.

Unfortunately, traditional medical care of individual patients tends to neglect such human needs as beyond their province. Yet an effective resource in dealing with this problem is always present, but typically neglected. Patients with similar problems are a potential help in providing instant support, and approval when most needed. Patient-to-patient-effort as a standard resource is rarely encouraged. Group encounters or task-force approaches to relevant common tasks provide substitute kicks which reduce the need for eating delinquency, and give the individuals a greater choice in enhancing their own life expectancy.

In the context of diabetes, it would again seem obvious that taking the right amount of insulin, at the right time, is the most important consideration in the daily life of a victim. While most of them do, and also manage to extend their life expectancies, there are always a few who don't. Every diabetic victim is vulnerable to periods of instability in which they end up with too high or too low blood sugar levels. Aside from the technical problems of arriving at an adequate dosage, the patient himself has to accept the self-evident limit that he will need to spend the rest of his life replacing the insulin his body no longer can manufacture. While any one patient may have disappointments that affect his ability to live within this limit, some victims fight this necessity the remainder of their lives. The principal symptom in living with diabetes is the tightrope act of taking the right amount of insulin daily, which metabolizes the sugar into the form usable in blood circulation. Failure to replace sugar supply will lead to a lack of blood sugar and blackouts. The early signs of such deprivations are often mistaken for alcoholism and are psychologically similar. As the judgment of the victim begins to fail and he or she surrenders to unrealistic desires, the symptoms are equivalent to alcoholic intoxication. Essentially, the diabetic victim in this situation need only take candy to alleviate symptoms. The specific motivations of a diabetic victim who is unable to eat or take candy at the right time become dramatically curious; especially with repeated episodes of blackout and near death. The simplest explanation is to say that there is a reluctance to accept the fact of diabetes, with its resulting necessity for insulin and carbohydrate ingestion. Regardless of why, a chronic pattern of risk-taking and self-injury occurs with a continuously increasing probability of early death.

Thus far, death on the installment plan describes victims who partake of self-injurious behavior in an insidious fashion. The mode is acceptable to their reference groups, and the freedom to alter is effectively impaired. Some of these victims of slow death also manifest conflict behavior with respect to living and dying. In terms of premature death, these victims tend to act episodically and impulsively as if in conflict with themselves. The conflict suggested is between the more usual wish to live and the recurring wish to die. The latter, unlike the overt suicide, is not admitted into full awareness of the victim. Instead, it is repressed much like the sexual desires of the Victorian Age. The banished wishes tend to re-emerge when controls are diminished such as in sleep, intoxication, or in rationalized and displaced behavior. In general, the wish to die breaks through in uncontrolled and unpredictable impulses.

However, sufficient control remains to block any deliberately suicidal act. The resulting compromise of conflicting wishes gives rise to the self-injurious behavior described as slow death. However this latter motivation is sufficiently different to warrant a special name, and especially since the phenomenon has already been described under the term, "indirect death."

The conflict between the wish to die and the desire to live is more familiar to suicidologists as ambivalence, usually observed in the attempts of victims to end their own lives. Both before and after such self-injurious behavior, the victims often express a wish to live and a wish to die, simultaneously.

Fortunately, this ambivalence often prevents some victims from killing themselves outright. What is less well-known is that this same conflict usually is resolved in favor of life immediately after some self-injury effort. This dynamic is what permits rescue from suicide and also allows many victims to have years of normal life in between suicide attempts. In the context of indirect death, the same conflict blocks overt suicide but at the price of some compromise to health in the various insidious and slow-acting, self-injury processes described here.

When death does come to these victims, the modes and methods are typically multiple. Accident-homicide or accident-suicides are frequent. Methods of self-injury usually involve alcohol or chemical aggravations of some pre-existing disorder. Chance- or risk-taking behavior is also a prominent cause of death.

The essential difference between slow death and indirect death is the presence of conflict behavior. A further difference seems to be present, but is mainly one of degree. While the slow-death victim can see the implications of his or her current behavior in terms of eventual self-injury and death, the indirect-death victim cannot. This is consistent with the unconscious nature of the conflict.

Where the cigarette smoker can see the life-shortening consequences, the alcohol or drug-abuser cannot, or does not, really feel the threat. Where the overeater is unable to alter eating habits for the long haul, the risk-taker can. However the consequences come faster. The victims of slow death are acting under compulsions even with the knowledge of their consequences. The candidates for indirect death have minimal knowledge, and tend to act on impulse.

Intervention with either type of death-seeking is made difficult by the perennial taboos. However, the slow-death victim needs assistance in gaining control of his choices. Since he is knowledgeable about the implications of his behavior, the problem is one of developing effective alternatives; ones that not only work but are applicable to the individual. For the victim of indirect death, intervention is more complicated because the conflict generally involves an unknown quantity. The wish to die is either denied, temporary, or motivated by unconscious wishes such as guilt and expiation needs. When these victims are able to make the death wish explicit, this is a first prerequisite to achieving control of impulses. Usually controls are impaired by denial of awareness. Making the choice clear and conscious introduces a rational element in responding to the danger.

Where most people are aware of circumstances in which they would prefer to die, very few have arrived at a deliberate desire for immediate death. Death wishes are aroused, or break through into awareness, on sporadic occasions, typically following some personal loss. A preventive effort with victims of this conflict is possible through the usual psychotherapeutic efforts used to resolve any conflict. The difference, of course, is that death is not any old type of conflict and most therapists avoid the subject. However, the problem is soluble by direct efforts. Simply making the victim aware of his wish to die can give him a little more direct control over the wish, and later over the behavior that is self-injurious. The technique is simply to engage the potential victim in discussions about death. Later chapters will provide questions and points of view relevant to helping people think about the prospects and consequences of their own deaths. These notions are changeable by intellectual argument, and, in turn, the motivational result of such beliefs can be diminished.

In both kinds of death-seeking, victims make their own diagnosis and develop options in the light of their own preferences. The lacking ingredient is the simple intellectual opportunity to discover alternatives. Reading a book on survival is one step. A class on death is better. A discussion with fellow-victims offers the most optimism for mutual aid, self-control, and the reduction of unnecessary death. This will require the cooperation of many others and some form of professional leadership.

Alcohol and drug abuse represent the most common forms of slow death in America from the point of view of numbers and public concern. While the remarks in this chapter are intended for all forms of insidious self-injuries, there are specific problems unique to the diseases and the mode of life-shortening behavior. The remainder of this chapter is devoted to alcohol and drug addiction. Efforts to point up the prevailing culture of each, and some constructive suggestions appropriate to the individual seeking more control over his compulsive behavior are also offered.

There are, of course, all kinds of alcoholics and addicts. Clearly, not all drinkers are seeking death. Among those who drink compulsively and who suffer disruption of work, home, health and community rejection, there are also degrees of self-injury. In addition to the social damage, there are some who kill themselves slowly; there are others who kill themselves indirectly; and of course there are many who kill themselves deliberately in the act of suicide.

The difference is the degree of choice; first with respect to the compulsion of drinking even in the face of increasing degrees of self-injury. Second is the degree of awareness the victim has of his or her life-threatening behavior. Any compulsive habit exercised frequently enough can exert a compelling force on the individual. An ingestion process such as alcohol consumption provides physical satisfactions. The intoxication effect itself is inherently rewarding, regardless of rational arguments against continued drinking.

Most humans find an occasional degree of intoxication a pleasant release from the serious business of living. Whether the source is a chemical or a social occasion does not alter the need or the satisfaction. Every society has its approved rituals during the course of which the members achieve some degree of release through a social or chemical process of exhilaration, controlled release from inhibitions, and acceptance. In American society, alcohol serves that function. The degree of use and habituation varies, primarily with opportunity and age of the user. It takes a lot of drinking to achieve the status of an alcoholic, and that is why the average age is well beyond thirty. Heroin addiction and drug abuse are easier to accomplish, and require less effort. Typically, most addicts are below thirty.

The people who are killing themselves slowly with alcohol have lost the freedom to choose *when* they will drink. Will power is irrelevant. Calling alcoholism an illness should imply a need to receive assistance. Instead, most alcohol-treatment programs put the burden of control back on the patient. These victims usually accept the notion that they have a choice and pledge "never to drink again." What makes this process appear reasonable is that in a treatment program of any kind, alcoholics have less need to drink and derive more ability to control their desire by association with others like themselves. The majority, though, find themselves helpless to resist further drinking once they are released and are on their own.

Turning now to the alcoholics who are killing themselves indirectly, the basic difference is in the area of awareness. These victims are simply not conscious of their wish to die. If the subject is raised, they will often express a defeated "what's-the-use?" attitude, and say things like, "If I had the guts I would kill myself." However, these remarks do not represent a genuine awareness of their own impulses to accelerate death. More indirect evidence for this conclusion comes in efforts to understand what alcoholic drink represents to them. Typically these drinkers think of their favorite beverage as some kind of poison; one that will kill them.

In contrast, there are the alcoholics who are frankly suicidal as evidenced by efforts to destroy themselves in the past. Their notion of alcoholic drink has the characteristics of mother's milk, nutrition, and other positive qualities. In effect, the difference boils down to the difference between suicidal alcoholics and alcoholic suicides. The former are excessive drinkers who kill themselves by drinking a poisonous amount of alcohol. The latter are alcoholics who kill themselves by a means other than alcohol, although they may use it to facilitate a self-injury, e.g., pill overdose, alcohol for courage to use a knife, gun, or jumping method.

Assistance for all three kinds of drinkers must start with some additional resource outside of themselves which provides more immediate control over the drinking. Alcoholics Anonymous and institutional programs are current resources that have their value precisely in the additional control they give the individual alcoholic, but only as long as he or she is physically present and participating. What these programs lack is an explicit plan to make the individual a lifetime member in a special group from which he or she can derive continuous approval, direction, and standards for personal behavior that are credible and relevant. Clearly, the alcoholic cannot go back to the drinking group from which he or she came. The explicitly non-drinking group would be offended by these people or the ex-alcoholic would find himself uncomfortable in their presence. The ex-alcoholic society represents the most appropriate, worthwhile group for the problem drinker to join. A similar suggestion is appropriate to any group that needs outside help with problems of self-control.

In recent times, the heroin user has received increased attention. The indirect modality of death with these victims incorporates elements of accident, suicide, and homicide. Each time a user takes a fix, he is engaging in excessive risk-taking by the lack of sterile injection procedures. These often cause infections, hepatitis, or other complications. The variable and unknown quantity of the illegally-obtained substances makes each fix a pass at Russian roulette. The need for secrecy adds another element of risk in the event of accidents. Subsequent rescue efforts are blocked or made less efficient. The knowledgeable pursuit of another fix, despite these hazards, has often suggested the element of suicide. To some degree, it is self-injurious, but the operations involved seem more consistent with the criteria of indirect death; the accidental result of impulsive but pleasurable goals, all of which are enhanced by conflict between the wish to live and die. The homicidal aspect is, of course, quite rare even in the context of heroin use. Still the possibility gives rise to fantasies of its occurrence, substantiated periodically by an actual event. Any fix can be manipulated by the pusher to contain an overdose. The victim not only cooperates by taking it, but very conveniently removes his body from the premises. Every fix has elements of being the last one. Is this an expression of the wish to die or the pleasure of living dangerously? Do all of these combine in a social and psychological force to produce the kind of death reported for Janis Joplin or Jimi Hendrix?

Efforts to prevent or rehabilitate either alcoholics or drug abusers have been dismally unsuccessful. Unfortunately, when these social problems surface, they usually do so only amid panic with consequent efforts cynically or superficially planned. The same is happening today. Even though all participants know better, there is a surrender to the least common denominator and the typical treatment program for drug abuse becomes a treadmill where bodies are processed—detoxification here, evaluation there, treatment in the community. The last is a euphemism for transfer to a flop house, return to the same environment, or once-a-week psychotherapy groups.

In between the drug-abusing, a person gets into a self-alienating processing that makes him feel like a misfit. The current total effort to rehabilitate is guaranteed to increase the desire for more drug abuse, simply in order to tolerate the denigrating efforts at reform. Add to this the symbiotic flocking of pushers to these detoxification environments and the real miracle is why any one addict is ever able to give up drugs at all. In part the problem is made worse by a failure to recognize that drug abuse is not a simple use versus non-use affair. There is a culture peculiar to each drug. Every statement made about drug use is true for at least one and untrue for others. Table Two provides an array of substance users with three general circumstances of abuse.

Situational use of drugs refers to an occasion and place where a drug is available and persons present are expected to use it. Examples are an off-duty area in Vietnam, a campus party, or a high-drug use neighborhood. The individuals present are generally using drugs because of curiosity, sociability, or in a group-pressured way.

Symptomatic use refers to the person who is suffering some continuing psychological disability which is not only distressing to him, but impairs ability to function on the job, in school, with close relations, or in other settings. Drug use allays pain, provides the chemical support to continue functioning, and much like psycho-active drugs used by psychiatry, represents self-medication. There are of course three differences—first, the patient is medicating himself with little training and second, with unknown chemicals. Thirdly, tolerance and changing habits make any continuing medication difficult with problem people. The result is a psychological catastrophe where sudden deaths are more likely to occur. Parenthetically, the mass media's description of drug-induced tragedies usually relates to symptomatic users rather than to the other varieties.

Syntonic users are individuals, otherwise normal, whose drug abuse is part of their regular life and who go about daily functioning unimpaired. Sometimes they are members of the criminal world or could also be participants in organized crime. They include people in favored circumstances whose money and affluence permit regular usage.

Successful tactics must start with a response to the whole personality of the drug abuser and his or her particular kind of drug use. This means grouping by predominant drug and usage pattern.

Situational users are individuals most capable of choice and will-power approaches. They can be managed in their conventional environments. A reprimand, a lecture, a rap group is sufficient.

Symptomatic users are individuals who need extensive mental health assistance. In earlier days, they would look like schizophrenics and would spend considerable time in a

Table II   Spectrum of Substance Abusers

Substance	Situational	Symptomatic	Syntonic
Alcohol	Executives, business lunches, and housewives	Withdrawal reactions, depressions and psychotic symptoms	"Skid Row" or drinking drivers
Marijuana	College students	Schizoid, dropouts	Jazz musicians
Morphine and heroin	Vietnam soldiers	Inadequate, anxious	Prostitutes, pimps, pushers
Amphetamines	Truck drivers, college students	Clinical depression, paranoid	Overweight persons
Barbiturates	Hypertensive individuals	"Nervousness," agitation	Chronic insomniacs
L.S.D., mescaline, psilocibin, peyote	Psychotherapeutic research, Indian rituals	Psychotic reactions in marginal personalities	Persons seeking "instant" Zen
Cigarettes	Cocktail parties, other social encounters	Smoking behavior as compulsive or hysterical defenses	Chain smokers with heart disease, circulatory, or respiratory diseases

mental hospital. The drug use with them is indeed a symptom of mental illness.

Syntonic users are most familiar as criminals. However, if marijuana is legalized or methadone substitutes provided, some of these users can take their place in society as respectable citizens. Parenthetically, methadone substitutes for the syntonic user are guaranteed to compound the problem unless psychological approaches are also available. Conversely, methadone with situational users will also convert curiosity seekers to addiction.

The symptomatic and syntonic users present the greatest problems in rehabilitation, mainly because of the failure of society to provide alternatives for these victims who have no effective control or choice. The symptomatic user has lost control because of his or her mental illness. The syntonic user can shape his or her use, but not give it up. Both need alternative lifestyles.

Other illustrations of the drug-abuse culture can be described in terms of the drug's source; whether it's the neighborhood pusher, or boy friend, or another friend can make a big difference. Most female-users are introduced to drugs by their boy friends. Most drug-users sell to their friends in order to support their own habit. The so-called drug rings that are always being "smashed" by the police often involve several friends with drug-using experiences who also have money, talent, or other angles that prompt them to attempt free-enterprise on a different scale. Implicit in their behavior and in that of many drug users is the universal availability of drugs and the high visibility of users. A new attitude is surfacing now in public awareness via the news media and its portrayal of the involvement of "nice kids." As long as ghetto kids and jazz musicians were abusing drugs, no one really cared.

With the advent of the drug-use era, many kids, especially on the college and university campuses, began trying drugs. In the early 1960s, college students experimented with LSD, then peyote, and other drugs. Heroin remained primarily the drug of the criminal world—users and peddlers tended to be felons. Marijuana users were traditionally apprentice-level criminals in that the source was frequently a pusher of heroin as well. On judicious occasions, a marijuana habitué was supplied with heroin, typically when marijuana was not available. This condition of drug supply accounts for the phenomenon and general notion that smoking marijuana leads to taking heroin.

Today most college students have tried and many continue to use marijuana. Most college and even high-school youth either use the weed or have been present when it was smoked.

It is not enough to say: "Give up drugs" or "Give up alcohol." Neither is it realistic to think in terms of a little drug use and a little alcohol. In habitual users, a substitute is needed. Alcoholics Anonymous talk about positive sobriety in which the thirst is quenched by a psychological intoxication—the exhilaration of helping others and feeling in control of one's own choices. The most essential element is a genuine reference group to which the ex-alcoholic can belong.

Drug abusers are motivated for the mystical, puristic, and "perfect" experience. In seeking these states, they bring handicaps, diminished capacity, and limited drive. To expect drug abusers to exert sustained effort, with no reward in the here and now, is like expecting a cripple to run without his crutches. Yet the greatest "kick" ever made available to humans is the satisfaction of sharing with a fellow victim one's own problem and its solution. Every drug-abuser is potentially an agent of help to every other one and can derive his greatest kicks by turning his or her efforts to this end. The obstacle is that one can't do it all by himself. He needs a license and a group mission to provide him with a proper role and sustaining forces to keep him going during his "off" days.

Any addict who decides to start a one-man campaign to save another addict will automatically get the worst of both worlds. The addict's attempts to help will turn on him, and the square world will never believe him. Even when groups of addicts such as in Synanon attempted to organize themselves for self-help, the official reactions were all negative. Police surveillance, parole revocations, and neighborhood objections were constant obstacles. Public institutions for the treatment of the alcoholic or the correction of the drug abusers are doomed to failure because they reflect the communities' prejudices, fears, and irrational needs. The naive public wants these people removed physically. It never wants to see them again. The compromises apparent today destroy any hope of rehabilitation and tie the hands of individuals trying to do the right thing. In the meantime, alcohol- and drug-abuse patterns provide indirect death to millions of victims, primarily young men and their survivors.

There is nothing new about drug use. Drugs have always been available. Morphine was legal up until 1913, at which time one-third of the adult population was estimated to be addicted. President Nixon's War on Drugs was an ineffective public response to the increased awareness of drug abuse. The change that has occurred is in community awareness. Nobody knows what the usage is, thanks largely to the hysteria of the last forty years with respect to drug and marijuana legislation. As long as drug use was regarded as a crime, the forbidden activities went underground, out of official sight, and out of community control. The major beneficiaries of this approach were criminals and law enforcement officials. Not that they were in collusion, but like a biological symbiosis, they tended to feed off each other. One example is police enforcement or "cracking down of a drug peddling ring." This type of bust occurs in every community at least once a year with appropriate publicity.

To set up any one arrest, the police vice squad needs a string of informers and undercover agents who are given drugs to peddle in order to entrap possessors. Aside from the immorality of that, the more arrests the police make and the more the supply is reduced, the higher is the subsequent price of drugs that are still peddled. In effect, law enforcement raises the price of drugs and increases the amount of crime to support existing habits. There is a curious poetry in the law of supply and demand still flourishing in the world of crime.

A redefinition of drug abuse is needed. Is it a crime or some kind of social problem? If it really is a behavior problem, then a law-enforcement approach will be ineffectual or aggravate an existing situation. The alternative is to allow the full extent of the issues to surface by removing penalties and threat of reprisal. In the treatment of venereal disease, the military achieved more success by educational and prophylactic approaches than by punishment. Soldiers were more willing to accept treatment and name contacts when the threat of punishment was removed. Today venereal diseases are recurring in groups that are most suspicious of authorities, homosexuals and teen-agers.

A moratorium on drug abusers is needed with opportunities to seek voluntary assistance from publicly-supported clinics, which try to control the chemical addictions with whatever effective substitutes are available. However, these need to be linked with rap sessions by peers and professionals for support, encouragement, and specific assistance with problems. Such clinics would need to be placed prominently in every community and supported by the majority of community leaders.

Drug abuse is a social problem reflecting discrepancies in the American ethos, rather than moral or legal misbehavior alone. While methadone is the currently popular substitute for heroin, it should be remembered that heroin was originally introduced in order to reduce morphine addiction.

There are increasing signs that drug abuse as a fashion in slow death is diminishing. In its stead, there is an increasing shift toward alcohol dependence by the younger generation. Alcohol abuse is the single largest form of mental illnesses, and substance addiction is prevalent today. As a form of installment dying, it is the single most lethal force in causing premature death. The discussion offered in this chapter has pointed to the larger than individual factors that prevent free choices among victims of drug abuse.

6

Future Shock
After Thirty

*T*here is no socially acceptable way to grow old gracefully in America. The stereotypes of "successful aging"
are people who retain the youthful qualities—physical activities,
enthusiasm, and continuous play. Admiration and acceptance
of older people is based primarily on the degree to which they
can act and look young. In many circles, changes associated
with aging are considered symptoms of a disease, a curable
one at that. This expectation dominates the American orientation toward aging, and has even greater meaning as a denial;
an attitude that death can never come in the here and now,
either to you or me.

If one can accept the obvious, that biological life requires
everyone to die, it becomes possible to build an attitude
about the aging process which recognizes that growing old
is simply a series of changes in the body's functioning. Aging
requires certain accommodations peculiar to maturity, but
these are also comparable to the adaptations of youth. Just as
young people must function within the limits of their size,
strength, and experience, so too must older persons accept
certain restrictions. Growing old, like growing up, represents
a series of adaptations to biological changes, first in adolescence and later in senescence. Psychologically, these adaptations represent new coping tactics. Such evolution also implies
a shifting of expectations from others. Certain behaviors are
deemed appropriate for children as compared to adults, and
for older people compared to younger people.

The problems of growing old in America are only partially those attributable to physical limitations, or even illness. Adjustment to old age is mainly one of reconciling the discrepant expectations of others with the ways in which the individual sees himself or herself. In turn, this leads to complications in finding a comfortable niche in contemporary society. An example is unemployability of those over forty, and the mandatory retirement of those over sixty-five, whether or not they are capable of continued contributions. American mores denigrate people who do not work, earn, or produce, effectively creating in the senior citizen a double dilemma. If a person stops working for whatever reason, mandatory or otherwise, he or she is immediately in a class that is less productive and therefore less admirable. That older people might well have earned the privilege of retirement does not reduce the problem, since most of them value the work ethic even more than younger people. The retired individuals tend to reject their own status and are in conflict with themselves. The problem is only partially psychological, since there is a reality in that the older and retired citizen has no accepted role to play on the stage of life.

The majority of the elderly population are alone, unwanted, not needed, and in desperate search for a real purpose. The tragedy is that Americans as a people do not recognize the need for the services of the elderly. They do need the wisdom and counsel of their accumulated experience. Who else has the time if not the old to advise the young? Who else can offer a credible interpretation of parent-child relations in this age of family breakdown?

Instead, older Americans are avoided and ignored. They in turn cluster in ghettos with their own kind. More often they fall as casualties to the calamities of being alone and having no purpose in continuing the old life. Many simply die of old age, while others require supervision in nursing homes or state hospitals. Yet there appears to be no alternative that seems appropriate. There is much about the problem of the older person that is reminiscent of American prejudice toward all minority groups. The rejection of the laborer over forty has received some publicity. However, the similarity between the self-rejection of blacks and the self-hatred of the elderly has not been noticed. "Black is beautiful" was a slogan that helped the Negro recognize his intrinsic value as a human. "Gray is gorgeous" would be a nice counterpart if it were acceptable. The solution is to identify the positive qualities in the elderly that are intrinsically admirable, but peculiar to that particular age. First however, one needs a point of view about the physical limitations associated with aging.

The distresses of adolescence are regarded with optimism and occasional patronizing indulgence. Still there is enough evidence to suggest that it is increasingly harder to grow up in American society and find a socially proper place as a young adult. Aside from that commentary, Americans still generally view adolescence as a positive experience. The desirable qualities in youth are the obvious good health, vitality, and lack of fear with which young people approach adult life. Are there good qualities in old age that correspond to those in youth? Of course.

Take the quality of good health. To be healthy in one's old age is clearly different than being healthy in youth. Young people hardly ever think of health because most of the time they are well, or recover quickly. After forty, even the healthy are aware of the temporary and fleeting quality of physical well-being. This greater awareness and concern is appropriate. It reflects not only reality, but a potential wisdom in avoiding additional or unnecessary illness. It is also a reminder to live each day well, because the next day may bring new limitations. The fleeting nature of robust health is one of the conditions of aging; however, it can be a basis for wiser living if accepted and used as an early warning symptom to prevent abuse. The tendency is to denigrate this awareness as hypochondria when sensitivity should be expected. Instead, caution is scorned as a surrender to old age.

Vitality also changes in that it diminishes the older one gets. This change is simply a condition of biological processes. While some people retain more of their vitality, and do so longer than others, they are usually the recipients of some kind of random largesse. Regardless of the exceptions, there is still an obvious difference in vitality between the old and the young. A young man will tend to smother a problem with wasted movements and much noise. Older people approach problems more analytically and make their efforts count. This is partially due to experience and sagacity. Also, older people have to be wiser in order to make their limited energy more effective. The implication here is that the body changes which reduce vitality facilitate greater discretion in its use. Wisdom is a perennial answer to youthful excesses.

Optimism is also universally characteristic of youth. It is only partially due to the reality of good health and opportunities; some comes from sheer ignorance. Problems always seem soluble to the naive. Anybody can be optimistic if he doesn't understand complications. To comprehend fully the complexities and dangers in life takes a lot more experience than even today's sophisticated youngsters can possibly accumulate. To be optimistic in maturity requires an act of faith about the inherent goodness of human nature, despite the ugly reality.

Indeed, unabashed optimism is often a natural by-product of senility and other kinds of brain damage. Euphoria is a frequent symptom of elderly patients assigned to the senile wards of state hospitals or nursing homes. This particular response has been considered as nature's way of making a human's last days bearable given excessive impairments. Genuine wisdom does not justify optimism and hardly euphoria in old age, especially in America with its rejection of the non-young. Optimism is possible at any age and place, no matter what the ugly realities are. First it should be recognized that in the absence of immediate deprivation or trauma, there is no barrier to feeling good or optimistic. By definition an optimistic outlook is one that anticipates good experiences in the future. A conviction about the future is always nourished by evaluations of the past. Previous experiences dominate, but note that optimism has to do with the perception of the events, and not necessarily the reality. How one has evaluated the past, as basically good or basically bad, is a preparation for one's orientation toward the future. The past is a rehearsal for, and prologue to, the future.

In youth, everyone is generally optimistic in spite of the

real hazards of achievement. In the process of growing up and older, everyone experiences disappointments. In maturity, as everybody's achievements fall somewhat short of aspirations, there will be further evaluations and a summing-up—"Life's been good to me" or "It isn't what you know or do that counts." Optimism that is still apparent in the forties and fifties is an expression of the individual's earlier evaluations. If a person has difficulty finding optimistic perspectives in his or her middle years, final years will tend to be even more pessimistic.

How can people of intelligence be optimistic when there is so much evidence to support pessimistic conclusions? Noting only the failures and faults, adding to zero rather than subtracting from one hundred, looking only at omissions, accumulate and document discouraging conclusions. On the other hand, the case for a positive perspective occurs very easily. One can count all the calamities that did not occur; and consider all the good things already achieved.

The underlying theme is that feeling good or bad about the future is influenced by the same feelings one has toward the past and both are terribly whimsical. A shift in either direction does seem to be a matter of will or of grace. Not that it is easy, but somehow being aware of a choice makes optimism more probable. There is no age which does not provide opportunitites for the achievement of real satisfaction, regardless of how much, feeling optimistic about any age has little direct relation to the actualities. There are appropriate options open to anyone at any age that generate feelings of satisfaction and support optimism. The difficulty is in recognizing what the specific choices may be for a given person in a given circumstance.

There are several contexts in which special problems occur for the senior citizen or for the people who make decisions for them. Appropriate expectations for the elderly in general and for those who need additional care will be illustrated with observations on nursing homes.

Meaningful Continuation or Psychological Cessation

Life begins at forty, Mae West said, and the years beyond sixty are called golden. But despite this type of optimism, we all know that in later years physical hazards increase. For those who live on, the usual expectations are reduced physical activity, restrictions in natural functions, and limitations of sensory capacities. Despite these changes, many senior citizens grow old gracefully, and find pleasures in life commensurate with their wisdom.

To those of us who are middle-aged or younger, the infirmities of old age are generally ignored, except when we visit a relative in some last extremity. We usually find the poor old soul a shadow of the person we once knew, and his last days seem to be a living death. No wonder, then, that our notions of old age and nursing homes are morbid!

Despite these public preconceptions and the real physical limitations of patients, nursing homes and hospitals attempt to sustain life for an increasing number of elderly, infirm, and withdrawn citizens. Is it possible for these institutions to offer a person more than mere existence? Can patients in nursing homes carry on a meaningful life?

It was with this question in mind that I visited several nursing homes in the Los Angeles area. As a psychologist, my object was to look for the human qualitites remaining which any particular nursing home might either facilitate or diminish in providing care for its patients.

I visited several homes and noticed a wide variety of patients in terms of physical impairment, socio-economic backgrounds, health, former occupations, education, and so forth. This commentary will be more concise if discussed in terms of several concepts implied in the definition of a meaningful life. These are 1) personal identity, 2) involvements, 3) leisure activities.

Personal identity refers to those perceptions we have about ourselves as human beings. It is the answer to the question, "What am I?" We build our ideas up through time in terms of past experiences with other human beings, such as parents, spouse, child, boss, friends, and so forth.

In observations of nursing home care, I noticed that there were usually some patients who were perceived as mere objects by the nursing staff. Certain patients projected no personal identity to the staff, who responded in turn by treating them as sexless, faceless, things to be fed, cleaned, and changed. The care I observed was ostensibly correct, well-intentioned, and adequate, but devoid of human quality. Since these particular patients were not seen often by other staff members, and infrequently by visitors, their total human contact was limited to that described above.

These individuals were feeble, brain-damaged, and unresponsive. Nevertheless, the kind of care they received would not improve them, and more likely would accelerate those very qualities that had reduced their humanity, leaving them to exist as little more than vegetables.

On the other extreme were male patients who provoked very unique staff responses; such as one eighty-nine-year-old man who kept inviting the nurse to crawl into bed with him. The girl responded in mock outrage, protesting the threats he posed to her virginity. Both of these people were at their most human in this little give-and-take. It didn't require more than five seconds for the nurse to give the man a sense of identity as a male and as a human being. She managed to accomplish this while carrying out the bed pan and gave the old gentleman a pleasant experience that may have lasted for several weeks.

Involvement with significant "others" always decreases as old friends and associates die, or when the patient is moved to a new environment. The degree of concern one patient can develop for others in his immediate environment provides a measure of his or her residual ability to carry on a meaningful human existence. Involvements also provide a life-line to the real world that sustains hope and enthusiasm.

Here too, there was a range among patients from the total unresponsive self-absorption of a former socialite to the bachelor and spinster who had developed a love affair in their seventies. Generally, most patients in the nursing homes visited tended to be isolated and responded only to the staff. In this manner, they acted as if none of their fellow patients were worthy of significant involvement. Consequently, these people deprived themselves of natural sources of human pleasure. Now there were a few old ladies who exchanged gossip, but these seemed to be in the minority.

The patients in the nursing homes studied were technically members of a leisure class. But the big issue was how to absorb them in satisfying, meaningful activities, that is, with life itself? The problem is aggravated by the diminished vitality which is overtaxed by the sheer struggle for nutrition, elimination, medication, and sanitation. However, for the minority of people in nursing homes who do have additional vitality, the nursing care offers minimal resources in the kind of leisure pursuits that make life significant at any age.

The best nursing homes provide activities, classes, arts and crafts, music, television, reading, and volunteer workers to help. But all of this is approached in a manner that connotes a greater dedication to feeding, toileting, and cleaning. There is an attitude that other activities are less important, not necessary, expendable, and frills with respect to operating costs. However, if life in a nursing home is to be significant, satisfying, and more than a mockery, leisure pursuits must be conceived and provided in the same spirit as work, religion, and the more elementary nursing procedures. Any nursing home can keep an old person physically alive, but only the best concern themselves with providing a milieu that encourages meaningful living, by unique individuals, in significant human associations.

How can this be accomplished? There are no gimmicks. There is no substitute for human relations—between staff and patients or between patients and patients, and with the survivors who care enough to visit.

For the ordinary survivor, his own common-sense observations provide a first guess of how much life exists in any one person. Having made this evaluation, the survivor is more ready to arrive at optimal decisions with respect to medical procedures, hospitalization, or nursing homes. Typically, these choices will be presented as options to save life or postpone death. Neither the patient nor his survivor can ever say no if the alternative is posed as life or immediate death. However, the medical context in which this decision is made rarely permits the survivor to develop an adequate understanding of the alternatives. Frequently the choice is between some terminal condition and some radical intervention. It turns out that "terminal" can mean anywhere from six months to ten years before death occurs. On the other side, radical procedures such as organ transplants reduce the quality of the life saved, so that in hindsight at least, the question of psychological cost-benefit can be raised for the victim as well as the survivor.

Since organ transplants are increasingly available, some of the specific problems associated with these procedures will be presented next as background for possible decisions faced by patients and their survivors. The emphasis is on the preconceptions that impair informed consent for adequate decision-making by all concerned parties.

Transplants and Psychological Survival

Recent medical progress in organ transplants has produced any number of ethical controversies about informed consent, the rights of donors, and the responsibilities of decision-makers. Psychological conflicts have also been reported for the survivors of these procedures—both the donors and the donees. Their problems are made worse by prevailing preconceptions on the part of those who must make decisions. Distress has been reported in relatives and in significant others in their efforts to choose an appropriate donor who in turn faces some personal danger in giving, or guilt in avoiding the donation of a kidney. Controversy has also erupted among the experts in terms of when to transplant, what, and for whom. Along with these are the psychological and ethical hazards of developing effective and appropriate selection procedures. In brief, the issues focus on who gets it, who gives it, and who shall decide? Because of the longer history of kidney transplants and the relatively successful efforts to graft and replace kidney function by dialysis, this discussion is restricted to the renal organs. However, the intent is to develop a perspective on all medical efforts to achieve surcease or survival by radical procedures.

Who Gets It?

The usual ethical problem with renal transplants occurs in the sense of who shall live and who shall die. Given a greater number of patients with end-stage kidney failure, about 50,000 per year, than people who are willing to donate usable organs, the problem narrows down to selecting a worthy recipient for this gift of additional life. Criteria for "social worth" are reported by every dialysis and transplant center. Yet on closer scrutiny, these observations are hopelessly ambiguous or embedded in middle-class value systems. More significant is the absence of relevance to rehabilitation. In the same context, additional criteria needed for selection are those of "emotional maturity and stability."

The usual goal of medical rehabilitation is the return of the patient to active participation in life. The operational criteria for such successful treatment, at least for men, turns out to be paid employment. During an economic recession, unemployed workers with a history of kidney disease are less desirable than unemployed men with no history of any disease. If in addition, twenty to thirty hours per week are devoted to dialysis, the patients become unemployable, and treatment has failed. The paid-work standard is simply too restrictive, and probably not essential to medical rehabilitation. Some psychiatrists in this field have suggested that "sociological rejection" should be rare and based only on extremely deprived environments which prevent proper hygiene for patient care.

A more fundamental premise that impairs selection is the implicit notion that a renal transplant represents a cure, however imperfect, while dialysis is always symptomatic treatment, no matter how successful. Kidney transplants are still fallible with attendant risks so great that one medical writer called the operation a research procedure. The art of renal

transplantation has improved considerably since that statement in 1968, especially with the development of the Belzer
machine to keep cadaver kidneys alive for up to thirty-six
hours after removal. Additionally, the development of a
national typing center at the National Institutes of Health has
made a greater range of choices available in pairing cadaver
donors with living donees. Even so, kidney transplanters, as
with other organs, have not been able to deal completely with
the problem of biological rejection. As a result, hemodialysis
remains an appropriate alternative procedure for some
patients.

As of mid-1973, there have been about 14,303 kidney transplants and some 5,500 patients are still alive. The current
experience suggests that only a small percentage of those
have continued functioning longer than a five-year period.
This does not count all those patients undergoing major surgery for a "second-hand kidney" which failed during the first
year. Recent reports with optimally selected donors suggest
that as many as 80 percent of prospective donees can expect
their kidney transplant to survive at least two years; a level
more successful than surgical intervention with cancerous
tissues. While the state of the art is improving continuously,
the caution to be considered is that surgical replacement of
kidneys is accompanied with enough hazards to warrant
limitation to certain kinds of patients, and even then to expect
symptomatic relief rather than total cure. The quality of life
even after a successful transplant is not the return to a prior
healthy existence, so often anticipated by the public and
sought by the patient. There are regular examinations, starting
with two or three times per week, and declining to every two
or three months in the absence of complications. Crises and
other disorders are frequent. Where the organ is not rejected
by natural body defenses, the patient becomes vulnerable to
garden-variety infections.

The resolution to the choice of dialysis or transplant in
response to kidney failure is to recognize that both have a
place and both are appropriate responses, even though each
carries different kinds of risks. For patients selected by the

criteria of age and sex, expected activities, and other relevant aspects, hemodialysis may be far more appropriate than transplant. By presenting dialysis as the treatment of choice, morale and cooperation can be significantly altered for the better. Many of the crises and reports of uncooperativeness can be attributed to the lowered morale of patients waiting to be "cured" by organ transplants. Food delinquency, in which patients eat foods considered inimical to successful dialysis, appears to be irrational but common while on dialysis. Many physicians call this behavior suicidal, but fail to note the predisposition to this behavior given by the definition of dialysis as a holding operation until a suitable kidney transplant can be found.

An illustration of the tendency to label this behavior suicidal comes in a recent clinical report, published in the *American Journal of Psychiatry* in 1971. Reported is a suicide rate 400 times higher than that for Americans at large. An examination of this report indicates that the researchers failed to compare their obtained rates in dialysis centers to the appropriate age, sex, and clinical status groups. Additionally, they used accumulated frequencies for a ten-year base period rather than annual rates in which all suicide indices are reported. Comparison of accidental death rates in dialysis victims and the national frequencies demonstrates no significant differences. Dialysis patients who withdraw from treatment, as often occurs, may be indirectly suicidal, but are more appropriately compared to death rates in psychiatric populations where suicide indices are highest.

The uncooperative or difficult patient in dialysis is a victim of a progressive disease who is vulnerable to self-injurious behavior as his or her morale declines, and expectations however false, are disappointed. Identifying the treatment outlook more realistically prevents these declines in wish to live as the dialysis process continues. Labelling dialysis as offering the same effective control for kidney failure as organ transplant, gives the patient a more optimistic basis for living with either choice.

For those who are kept alive by whatever method, the prospects for the next five years are quite good. Current developments with artificial kidney machines augur significant improvement in efficiency, cost, and ease. The rejection problem in transplants may become more soluble too. The ethical issues diminish considerably as soon as supply begins to equal demand, an event that occurs with the availability of alternative resources. The ethical issue then becomes not who shall live, but which patient shall live with transplant, which one with hemodialysis, and which one with combinations of diet? Who gets what becomes a question of medical competence, and relevant criteria for assigning the appropriate treatment. Medical decision-makers in the area of kidney failure are already at this point, and the ethical controversies first reported have begun to diminish. The choice for the patient and his survivors is not life or death, but which procedure to implement in order to sustain the existing level and quality of life.

Who Gives It?

The choice of donor is a poignant issue since certain relatives by virtue of genetic similarities are often more likely candidates than strangers because the donee is better able to tolerate this transplant with reduced dangers of rejection. The physicians are in the position of saying survival of the patient requires "this relative to give up one kidney." The moral alternatives presented the chosen relative are essentially that of "murderer" or "sacrificial lamb."

This perceived choice is an artifact of the medical premise that the transplanted organ is a gain to the donee and a loss to the donor. The failure to consider other values besides anatomical profit and loss, narrows the issues, and impairs participants from making an informed choice. An example of an aspect usually given insufficient attention is the significant increment in the self-esteem of the donor earned by the act of giving. This gain may produce a behavioral sequence that improves the value of the life for the donor, even though margin of safety is diminished by the sacrifice of the second kidney.

Another aspect is the implied necessity of assuring a potential donor that his gift will sustain life indefinitely or be appreciated forever. In the effort to justify the donation, the professionals find themselves attempting to offer arguments for accepting the sacrifice. The actuality is that the donor makes this gift with the same risks he might face in more conventional acts of charity. Traditionally, all religions have identified the human need to give, expiate, or sacrifice. With increasing secularization, many people may find organ donation more satisfying than gifts to impersonal organizations. There are psychological gains to the donor beyond the narrowly perceived organ-gain, organ-loss dichotomy usually seen.

Paul Blachly, a physician writing in the *Journal of Life-Threatening Behaviors,* has recently argued that organ donation be considered as a substitute for suicide. He perceives transplant centers and suicide prevention centers as symbiotically referring calls to each other for complementary services. The would-be suicide victim may achieve survival by donating an organ as a substitute for total death. Conversely, the study of donors and volunteers documents that informed consent achieved in kidney transplants today is a myth. The donors interviewed made decisions impulsively, and for irrational motives, not the least of which was expiation of guilt feelings.

Such a joint service as described above would be more likely to cope effectively with self-injurious motives in all kinds of clients, while at the same time eliciting more organ donations. Enlistment of a suicidal patient in the cause of saving someone else may appear unrealistic to knowledgeable suicidologists. However, most victims see their own suicide in heroic terms. Giving them a chance to sacrifice organs helps diminish the impetus towards self-injury, and the delaying of any suicidal act for specific intervals permits the death wish to subside and increases the chances for continued life. The deficiency of this proposal comes in the premise that suicidal people are merely exercising their inherent right to choice, and therefore they will partake of rational, or orderly, medical procedures such as the complicated process of donating organs. However limited the prospect may be, any effort to inspire individuals calling for help in the direction of organ donation would have a place in the range of legitimate responses.

The essential consideration in the selection of organ-transplant donors should be the opportunity to make a relatively free choice and with as much informed consent as possible. The detection of irrational and self-injurious motives in would-be donors is not necessarily grounds for exclusion. The saving grace comes from carefully considered clinical dialogue between the donor and donee, in which professionals once recognizing the irrational motives, use additional criteria for evaluating the decision. Donors have psychological needs that are often in conflict with their consciously verbalized statements. There is a social and ethical place for acts of self-sacrifice and these are not all self-injurious. There remains of course some inalienable right to choose an action, especially in relation to a significant person in what may be part of a last encounter.

In a similar fashion, perhaps even as an extension of the above issues, familial pressures are always present so that family members rarely have a totally free choice in relation to each other. The role of a professional is potentially that of a meddler unless considerable effort is expended in working with the entire immediate family. Two resources are suggested. First is the use of patients who have been successfully transplanted or dialysed, to act as explainers and orienters to candidates. This lateral communication supplements professional advice, even when it seems to be contrary to the formal position. Such "senior" patients can provide an in-depth and more effective explanation than professionals precisely because they are patients, experienced in the procedures. They can tell it like it is. Their explanation alone is insufficient, but does complement, repeat, and make vivid the details of the procedure. In a broader sense, this helps to develop more informed consent, while permitting more opportunities for doubt to manifest itself. The same advantages accrue to the second suggestion, which is to conduct professionally-led group discussions in which potential donors, donees, senior patients, and staff participate as social equals in examining motives, options, and procedures. A spin-off from these discussions is better comprehension by the applicants, and more informed decision-making by providing opportunities for patients to act out the variety of roles they can be expected to play. Typically, the only role observed is that of patient, as a needer of help. This group meeting permits them to act as givers of help, peers, even colleagues.

Given these kinds of efforts, family dynamics can be allowed to influence choice of donor. The professional team can and should provide technical information on suitability such as rank ordering of all family members. However, a line must be drawn between the role of the staff as information-givers and decision-makers. Assuming some minimal suitability for organ donation, any choice reflecting a consensus between the donor and donee is probably most acceptable, especially if others tolerate the decision. Professionals most prepared to participate in this process are discussed next in the question of "Who shall decide?"

Who Shall Decide?

This ethical issue is that old devil "the Jehovah complex." Clearly, the decision as to who shall live and who shall die is a godlike one. Everybody knows it's stupid and destructive to play God. Yet such is the seductiveness of this role that most people succumb when given the opportunity. The physician in his role as "healer" often falls into this trap. The medical rationale used is that doctors are more competent to evaluate suitability of patients for transplantation. However, in the zeal to be objective, there is a tendency to ignore nonmedical or subordinate philosophical issues. Starzl, a physician-writer, feels that the ethical problems are too important to be entrusted to biomedical scientists or members of the "health professions." The prevailing use of "social worth" as a criterion for selection is an illustration of limited competence in the social and ethical issues.

Early criteria reported by transplant and dialysis centers tended to emphasize such middle-class values as previous work habits, income, presence of minor children, absence of criminal history, or other social failings like mental illness, divorce, alcoholism. From these it would appear that only nice people were "socially worthy" of a renal transplant. It is entirely possible that undesirable victims are equally suitable if not entirely worthy.

In the early days of kidney transplantation, expediency determined choice, and many donees successfully transplanted would not have been chosen. Psychiatrists knowledgeable with transplant problems question the entire premise of unsuitability due to mental illness. The only exceptions that achieve consensus seem to be the presence of mental retardation or such grossly psychotic behavior that ability to cooperate with medical regime is clearly impaired. There seems to be no reliable data to document that the lesser varieties of mental illnesses impede effective treatment by whatever procedure used.

Considering the emphasis placed upon cooperation by all the centers, it may well be that the most suitable recipient of transplantation or dialysis may well be a passive, dependent, highly institutionalized person who would then be socially inadequate by prevailing middle-class values. Other investigators have noted that clinical symptoms of psychiatric depression and defenses of denial are apparently associated with successful dialysis.

To meet the onus of bias, one transplant center in America adopted the strategy of using a citizens' group of lay people to make anonymous decisions based on medical prescreening. This has the advantage of sharing the decision-making with representatives from the community. The rapid turnover of committee members was designed to protect the participants from the stress. However, this may also have served to keep them inexperienced and more vulnerable to covert influence. Another limitation was the lack of representation or omission of minority groups such as the aged, the delinquent, the mentally ill, as well as the more familiar subgroups. The lay-citizen approach was eventually abandoned and choice is now handled more typically by the professionals administering the center.

Even where social scientists have been used to meet the preceding objections to the selection process, the emphasis is still on life expectancies rather than on the quality of life saved. Other professionals also share the prevailing middle-class notions of social worth. A secondary issue often raised in the ethical controversies is the use of psychological screening procedures. The obvious presumption that any kind of mental illness is an impediment has already been questioned. A more urgent issue is the exploitation of privileged information against the patient's own best interests. Answers, or scores to tests, are used to arrive at a decision of suitability, and hence treatment may be denied on the basis of information revealed.

This last controversy about the use of screening and the danger of self-incrimination is an artifact of preconceptions or naiveté concerning testing. Subjects seeking dialysis or transplants know they have to make a good impression. They approach all screening procedures with the same orientation as those who wish to gain admission to Ivy League colleges, country clubs, fraternities, or bank loans. These are familiar and realistic maneuvers invited by the implicit values of the selection committee. There is a psychological symbiosis between the standards of selectors and the responses of the selectees. Changing membership of the committee and broadening expectations of suitability will at least avoid the wasted motion of the existing process.

The more significant ethical objection to psychological screening is the one of effectiveness. Does it really identify optimal subjects for the proper medical alternatives? As presently organized, the effectiveness of any screening process is untestable because criteria of success are obscure. Kolff, the man who pioneered in dialysis, argues that dialysis can help any patient with renal impairments. However, the physical demands of this procedure tend to penalize the older, the more infirm, and the very young. The older patients also have less capacity for the traumas of surgical transplants. Since both procedures are fallible and extreme in their disappointing effects on or demands from the patients, screening can offer help with the degree of fit between patient and procedure. Given the current obscurity of normality in psychiatry and cooperativeness in renal disease, any selection process is doomed to failure. However, the information elicited by the process can be incorporated into decision making just as all other medical facts are reviewed prior to patient selection.

A more effective use of screening is for its impact on the participants. The effort to perform all the tasks involved in psychological testing gives the subject a feeling of having worked hard and having been involved. Selection becomes a *rite de passage* in which a sense of achievement and belonging accrues to those chosen. Later when the going gets rough, this result helps sustain motivation, and facilitates group support in a common problem.

The ethical issues of who shall decide the kind of treatment are even more of an artifact than who gets it, or who gives it. Clearly, the choice belongs to the donor and his donee. With proper attention to informed consent by family process interviews, and the use of patient selection-orientation, committee decisions can be made effectively in tandem with professional consultation. The ethical controversies surrounding transplantation are due to the limitations of the professionals who are responsible for the decisions and their failure to incorporate the community and the patient as equals.

The emotional heat generated by organ transplants is fed in part by the prevailing preoccupation with eternal youth, and the avoidance of inevitable death. Medical intervention is the *sine qua non* of secular and scientific immortality. Growing old need not be the depressing prospect most Americans perceive. There are compensations possible at every age, as long as each senior citizen acknowledges the biological changes he or she experiences. Having accepted these, they can choose to pursue developing interests, or goals valued within the limits of their vigor. The ultimate measure of successful adaptation to old age is the continuing pursuit of things one deems important, the satisfaction one derives from these efforts, and the wisdom to know one is preparing for appropriate cessation.

7

Rap First, Pass Later

D eath is a forbidden subject for ordinary conversation. While there are no explicit penalties for violating conventional taboos, each person feels an awkward sense of nervous discomfort when such a topic is raised. Most people avoid the subject of death, most of the time. The resulting conspiracy of silence blocks thoughtful discussion of fatal diseases. The fear of death or the morbidity of the subject still does not adequately explain the avoidance.

The larger motive is the feeling of unseemliness in dealing with an improper topic; of having imposed possible distress on others by acknowledging the reality of death; and most of all, in the absence of standards for appropriate reactions. In order to cope with last things, all survivors need a license to discuss any aspect of dying just as they have belatedly achieved with venereal disease, sex, divorce, and drug abuse.

Prevailing social expectations permit only stereotyped gestures in the presence of death. Polite expressions, sympathy cards, or flowers signal only that the senders have noted the fact of termination. These gestures in themselves do not convey a message and in turn do not invite a genuine response. While it is entirely possible to argue that there is no adequate message for the bereaved, this obstacle does not prohibit a human effort to express sentiment. Indeed the survivors need such tokens in order to achieve a sense of participation, a sharing of grief, and a confirmation of the emotional loss called bereavement. However, these signals only provide opportunities for communication. If not followed by genuine efforts to talk, they impede subsequent communication. The survivor gets the non-verbal message that talking about a resent loss is distressing to others.

It may help to consider historical reactions to the necessity of coping with a dead body. The last remains require some response on the part of the survivors, even if it be one of abandonment. Despite the wide variety of disposals, resulting funeral rituals observable in every culture appear to serve only four goals.

The most prominent ritual is for relatives and intimates to express their grief. Among primitive societies, the most frequent expression of affection occurs as a simple exaggeration of the feelings conveyed in daily life with respect to separation. With death, the separation is longer and the farewells more intense. In the more complex societies, the outward gestures of mourning have become more stylized in that an expected ritual defines proper behavior. The correct mourning behavior has meaning as the expected way of signaling farewell. The euphemisms in America about funerals are frequently those of "travel" and "departure." The American way of expressing affection for the victim of dying is some variation of saying "goodbye."

Simultaneous to the expression of affection, is an obscure dread of the deceased in his present dead state. This fear of a dead body is seen most clearly in primitive people, whose rites are often intended to confuse the spirit and protect the living from unwelcome or sudden return. Some funeral customs include efforts to make the corpse confused by turning the body around many times. Australian Aborigines are reported to remove fingernails and tie hands of their dead in order to prevent their digging themselves out from graves. Other cultures literally tie or amputate feet. The fear of ghosts is well-known in all cultures and is apparently based on nightmares about the deceased returning.

A third need, again simultaneous with the previous two, is a concern for the welfare of the remains and the future of its former spirit. Most of the rituals for the deceased include some effort to prepare for the spirit's well-being, such as providing means for the journey into the next, but invisible, world. These efforts include the burial of necessities with the body such as food, drink, or tools. The latter has included money, jewelry, horses, wives, and servants. The living survivors were obviously put to death, willingly. The Greeks used to put a coin in the mouth of a dead person to pay the boatman Charon for ferrying the body across the River Styx. The Irish placed a coin in the hand of the dead for a similar reason.

In American funeral services, reference to the future well-being of the soul occurs universally. In the devoutly religious context, explicit prayers are offered for the future of the departed soul. In the secular service, references are the same but given in more acceptable terms. These include exhortations to achieve peace, contentment, or even immortality in the memory of the survivors. All of the circumlocutions express a concern for the non-physical well-being of someone who recently died.

The American way of death was described vividly by Jessica Mitford in 1963. The emphasis in the American mode of burial is on the physical accouterments—cemeteries, tombstones, graves with a view, or elaborate services. All of these efforts are only partly devoted to the dead; they reflect complicated needs of the mourners; one of which is a profound concern, however obscure, for reassurance that the recently dead spirit will be well.

The fourth need is for one or more occasions of affectionate recollections. These may take any form or content appropriate to the relation shared. Usually these affections are expressed incidentally to periods of mourning, wakes, or services. More informally, monuments, and mementoes stimulate personal recollections. If in company, conversations and poignant memories are stirred. Eventually residuals of grief are fully expressed. However, affection also is rekindled and simultaneously the survivors may recall humorous as well as serious incidents involving the deceased. It is not uncommon for mourners to tell stories and anecdotes either about the dead one or even his favorite jokes. The ensuing laughter is often mistaken for lack of respect but is far more than this. It is also a human expression of familiarity, shared experience and love.

These four needs still flourish even within the current stereotyped, secularized funerals of today. The obscure dread of the dead is publicly countered by removal of the body and avoidance of the dying process. The absence of the victim is assimilated as some sort of separation or extended traveling; and like all travelers, the survivors wish them *bon voyage*, safe arrival, and continue to hope for speedy return. Once departed, occasions of poignant recall and affectionate recollections recur. Often there is humor, both genuine and forced, as survivors attempt to recover from their last encounters.

Every survivor needs a chance to express his loss by modes that are unique to the relation shared with the deceased. To recover from a loss, it is necessary to start with an expression of regret that includes ideas or words which may appear unseemly, improper, or cruel to the memory of the victim. The essential criteria must be that these are authentic for the relation pertaining between the survivor and the deceased. Any act that reflects a quality of the lost relation has a place in the mourning process. The advantage comes from the opportunities such actions open for the survivor to discover that others experience similar sentiment. The need to find consensus is universal in the human effort to cope with distress. Agreement of others about the nature of an experience provides a validation of one's own perceptions and generates reassurance as well as opening up new perspectives in problem-solving. The need for consensus and gratification is even more poignant in the context of bereavement.

While individual differences are usually emphasized in American culture, the corresponding uniqueness of any relation gets ignored. If the two individuals are really different, this quality will be most apparent in the ways they behave towards each other. More specifically, they will develop mutual expectations based on their previous acts; confirmed and expanded by new events. In time, they will experience a special familiarity and quality in their relation which will be different, but expressive of the unique pair.

When one dies the family survivors are left alone. The deceased is now a memory and a painful one because familiar acts become reminders of pleasure shared; now lost. The distress occurs whenever a strong association is disrupted, be it by travel, divorce, or illness. Corresponding names for the pain of separation are called homesickness, loneliness, or separation distress. The label doesn't matter, the loss starts a cycle of emotions: irrationality and impaired decision-making are the consequence.

Following a death, often months or even years later, survivors are vulnerable to consequences of bereavement because of grief over the lost relation. Impulsive remarriage as a replacement is the obvious example. Selling former homes or buying expensive but unneeded gadgets is another. Taking up some of the newer hobbies that require manipulating complicated equipment is a variation. The tragedy is that these decisions are motivated by sorrow, unresolved and repressed out of awareness. Like the old sexual impulses that were also denied, only awareness is lost. Behavior is still influenced by forgotten emotions to everyone's ultimate detriment.

To counteract this process, survivors need to deal with distress at the time of loss. The usual rituals are not sufficient because they tend to be diluted by the avoidance phenomena and socially-approved grieving. The latter is proper and has a place but does not permit the survivor to deal with the memory of the unique relation.

A survivor must start with the recognition that all relations change—from strangers to intimates, from superficial to more insightful, from common to specific. The process works in two ways in that both can be reversed: Friends and relatives are known to outgrow each other and spouses tend to move away as well as toward each other. Similarly, a relation to one who has died can also change if the relation is continuously shared with living others. Since the memories hoarded in private moments tend to remain constant, in time they act as a ballast on the survivor's relations to others. They stabilize but also provide resistance to changes.

Talking about the lost relation helps the survivors begin to work out alternatives to loss. After a death, they will experience distress when they attempt to resume simple daily activities once shared. Eating, working, playing, walking, and other activities will remind the survivors of the lost relation. Any attempts to work or keep busy, while distracting and eventually helpful, always rub salt in the emotional wound at the most vulnerable time.

Sharing this distress with others is a start towards change and recovery from loss. Remarks about the specific acts which occurred in the past interactions are a natural and appropriate response to loss. These may provoke tears, laughter, often simultaneously. All are potentially helpful. The value comes from the increasing awareness and confirmation that the relation has changed and the last encounters were indeed the final ones. A shift in these awarenesses accelerates the recovery process in moving from existential relations towards recollections; from major towards minor portions of daily life; and from disrupted towards replacement relations. These changes and the sequences implied help the bereaved make room in their emotional life for new relations and the business of carrying on.

If survivors are made to feel ashamed of their spontaneous reactions to loss and the memory of the deceased, they suffer more distress than if they could acknowledge these in relation to others. In time, the failure to find opportunities for these grief efforts impairs the survivor's ability to cope with the recent as well as future bereavement. Every survivor needs opportunities to deal with his personal reactions to any death. The closer the relation, the greater the needs, and the greater the necessity of providing opportunities to talk about death, before, during, and long after a termination.

The ability to talk about death does not occur naturally. It requires effort, especially if the survivor's first learning comes during, or immediately after, a terminal disease. In coping with the initial awkwardness, it helps to recognize that conventional practices aggravate the problem. It is reassuring when suffering from doubt and uncertainty to realize that one is an innocent victim in whatever degree of universal ignorance is imposed by social default. However, any solution always requires personal effort, with tolerance of the learner's distress so observable in the struggle to improve skills.

A good starting place in learning to talk about death is to achieve some preparatory orientation. Degrees of dying occur to all living tissue throughout the entire life of the species rather than at the end only. There are really many organic processes that can be called dying. More correctly these are really cellular changes. Some are named growth, others, decay. In American culture, growth is regarded positively and decay is considered negative. Given the current taboos about death, the former gets labeled as living and the latter as dying.

The natural and universal changes implied in decay and dying are given a poignant and dramatic meaning only with the passing of a "death sentence." The concept refers to some sudden and extra knowledge that now life is coming to a sudden end. Usually this information is medical with the diagnosis of a terminal disease which in turn has a known prognosis. However, other sources are also possible. These include the probabilities of surviving another year given a specified age, specific genetic history, sex, nationality, geography, occupation, unique circumstance. The latter include soldiers in combat or prisoners facing execution. The model and certainly public stereotype come with the recognition of a terminal disease such as cancer. In practice, all terminal diseases require several years to induce a death. Most patients are ambulatory and potentially able to pursue their usual activities during this period. While various distressing symptoms recur, medical management of pain, vital functions, and activities permits normal existence to continue for much longer intervals than the public generally recognizes. The great dilemma is the victim's ability to assimilate the death sentence; to accept a finite life without disrupting continuing interest or responses to others. Survivors typically aggravate the quality of life remaining because of their corresponding ignorance and false expectations for this last period of life.

The most obvious focus for these misconceptions occurs around the diagnostic phases, when the victim and his survivors finally realize that the patient has a terminal disease. The devastating nature of this information is not in the reality of illness and eventual death, but rather in some ill-considered and ugly presumptions concerning the dying process. This is the expectation that the patient will die very soon, in an ugly manner, as compared to more typical ways of dying. However, they are wrong on both counts. Terminal disease takes many years to run its course and much like old age, the victims of terminal disease die a little bit every day over an extended interval of time, often years and sometimes decades.

The ugliness of dying is attributable more to the victim's default in preparing for an appropriate death than to the vicissitudes of the disease. Most people think terminal disease is rare when in fact it accounts for 90 percent of adult deaths every year. The natural mode of death is medically caused by failure of vital organs which in turn are overloaded or damaged by the common diseases called fatal. The eight most common causes of natural mode of death are indicated in Chapter Three. The table listing these gives death rate per 100,000 live people.

Currently, dying demands more informed decision-making and preplanning than actually occurs. The basic error of omission comes with the naive expectation that death will come fast. The effective result is a rather extended period of limbo in which the victim is regarded as neither dead nor alive by his or her associates. While medical care is usually adequate, the victim's social role becomes ambiguous since there are no proper expectations for a dying person. There is a role for a sick person and for a dead person, but not for one who lingers on. Typically, dying becomes far more grim and cruel precisely because nobody, neither the victim nor his survivors, has an adequate sense of what is appropriate for the victim. The survivors lack a corresponding sense of seemly behavior for themselves.

Treating such a person as a sick one, while accurate, has

the built-in limitation of a false optimism; to wit, very shortly the ill one will be well. This patently false notion cannot be entertained very long because the extended period of dying demonstrates the inaccuracy, and makes liars out of survivors who persist in this notion. It is even more false to react to the victim as if he or she were already dead. The tendency to do so is irresistible even though irrational. The compromise is to treat the dying person as if he were a non-person, one who is not quite there; this bizarre but common tendency avoids the prospect of death, and the real things which count to the victim. Their omission is purposeful since real concerns generate emotions. These easily lead to the most relevant concern of all, the prospect of death. The subsequent avoidance behavior results in a pretense of social life, which alters the relation of the survivor to the patient. The whole process rings false, and the victim becomes increasingly alienated from genuine feeling, real activities, and authentic values. In time he gets treated as an object to be fed, cleaned, even talked at, but never regarded as a human with whom one has real encounters.

The principal tools to counteract the current neglect are any and all efforts at direct communication. The most central concern in doing so must be a willingness to respond and attend to those issues that are the most important to the dying patient. These are immediately and inherently everything that has to do with the prospect of cessation, the dying process, and the efforts to continue those personal activities that gave his or her prior life its unique meaning. The principal obstacle to this goal is the fear of emotions—regret, tears, sorrow, shame. If people ever have a right to express emotion, it is precisely during the period of dying. Accepting any emotional response in this context is a gateway to liberation and authenticity. An emotion shared is a mutual distress resolved. Accepting the inevitable and struggling to maximize the positive brings sufferers together and makes any objective calamity that much easier to assimilate.

For the vast majority of victims, recognizing a diagnosis with its attendant life expectancies is automatically a trauma.

Fortunately, early symptoms, diagnostic procedures, and medical caution in conveying conclusions generate a protracted period of uncertainty which stimulates an intense period of soul-searching. While some will continue to deny implications, most patients come to the death-sentence portion of their illness with some readiness to hear dire predictions. Their survivors may have even better preparation since they are not as directly threatened as the patient is. Both will need to put the diagnosis in a context of general life-expectancy such as suggested in the table given in Chapter Three. The rest of the present discussion is centered around the knowledge and choice areas that can help the victim and his survivors avoid default and prepare for a seemly death. The choice between an ugly or a beautiful end can only be made *before* the death occurs. The earlier the preparation begins, the more likely survivors are to choose the kind of dying they prefer.

The death sentence nature of a diagnosis is only partially related to the terminal nature of the disease. Life itself can be considered as a terminal disease from which no one ever escapes. Remaining life-expectancy can be reduced to a matter of probabilities even for those without disease. For those with an ailment, and therefore under a death sentence, the difference is that of a boogie man under the bed versus a monster in plain sight. The advantage of the latter comes from the greater ability to deal with a real hazard as opposed to a phobia. The major terminal diseases carry an extended period of dying, requiring months and years for termination to occur. The practical difference between knowing and not knowing such a diagnosis comes from the word "terminal." The recognition of this dying state has often successfully converted a meaningless existence to a meaningful life for the victim. Knowledge that dying has begun often brings a compulsion to make the remaining time significant.

In this alienated and dishonest age, it is the rare individual who does not harbor some reservation or some distasteful habit induced by expediency, frustrated hopes, implicit errors or sheer fantasy wishes that will emerge during the first few days following a death sentence. Those who have lived the biggest lie will be the most tempted to act upon the remaining options. There are several risks to doing so, first is the exhilaration of achieving a long-wished for desire. The individual begins to act upon other delayed choices and starts a cycle of intoxication, poor judgment, and "damn-the-consequences." The result is a runaway situation in which the hazards of poor judgment begin to accumulate. The second risk takes longer but begins to emerge as a growing disillusionment—"It wasn't all it was cracked up to be." Still later comes a third risk; a poignant regret for that which was given up in order to indulge the first choice. At this point, true wisdom begins to emerge. The original existence as lived was an optimal compromise, or result of conflicting forces, such that the habits practiced were not random but determined by all the pressures operating. The victim can begin to realize that the whole package had some sufficient value so as to make the life a worthy one in the first place, regardless of the perceived deficiencies.

At this point, the application of the new-found wisdom permits the patient and his survivors to incorporate into the dying process all those habits of prior life that provided meaning and satisfaction. Whether living at home, nursing facility, or hospital, most of the prior habits can be continued. Where medical emergencies, vitality, or the hospital environment pose limitations, the simple expression of preferences is often sufficient to permit continuation. Where genuine conflicts exist as between diet and food tastes, an informed choice is often possible, so that nutritional equivalents are possible. Even when not possible, some calculated risks can enhance the quality of the terminal process without significantly altering life-expectancy.

The prospect of dying provoked by the death sentence usually releases many fears. Three of these deserve special attention since they tend to impede acceptance of the dying process. Many physicians wait for questions before offering information in these areas. The working assumption is that there is a danger of suggesting problems where none were anticipated. In an other age, this was more likely to be correct than it is now. Today, most people are so phobic about death that they experience every possible dire consequence because their fantasies fill the vacuum of ignorance created by the American denial of dying and the totally negative orientation given to death.

The first fear is of pain. Pain is always subjective in that there are great individual differences in recognition and toleration as well as in response to pain killers. There is no cut and dried position on intractable pain. Most people equate terminal disease with intolerable pain, but the two don't necessarily follow. Knowledge of pain thresholds suggests that an important factor in the ability to accept pain is the patient's relation to survivors in the immediate environment. Some relations strengthen tolerance, others weaken it. A key suggestion for survivors eager to help a patient accept whatever pain he or she must suffer, is to come to terms with the meaning of pain themselves. If the survivors' attitude towards pain is optimal, neither denying nor escaping, they can help the victim tolerate his or her own pain.

Impairment, another fear, is more distressing at any age than pain in that the victim often suffers a damage to his self-image as an adequate or worthy person. Despite this threat, many people are able to accept and grow from the experience of amputation, loss of sight, hearing, or even cruel disfigurement. Even the skin acne of adolescence represents a damage which the once beautiful child must accept. It's no big thing. Everybody runs into it, but this small triumph represents a rehearsal for a bigger loss. In older ages with less vitality, the capacity to cope with such losses is more restricted, but the ability to succeed is measured by previous achievements in coping with damage and loss.

The survivors who recall the victim at an earlier time are especially shocked at the obvious signs of deterioration. Like all changes in health, appearance and capacities decline with aging. The reaction of survivors comes from their reluctance to accept the aging process; and their consequent shock when the reality is finally perceived.

The loss of mental ability is a third fear. This loss is commonly observed in extended-care patients, especially the elderly. Typical residents of nursing homes show a loss in recent memory or disorientation with respect to person, place, or time. They lose track of current events and are otherwise grossly impaired in ability to concentrate. These mental deficits, when observed, are distressing to survivors and even to the victim himself, when aware of them. To both, the distress derives not from the loss of mental ability itself but from the meanings assigned to the loss.

These mental losses are often construed as symptoms of psychiatric illness. Technically they are signs of central nervous system changes often thought to be brain damage because of their undesirability. The error comes in the assumption that any mental illness, and certainly brain damage, is an all-or-none process. Familiarity with any mental illness quickly documents the limited and reversible nature of the symptoms. The total maladjustment may continue, but each identifiable symptom seems to be variable. In deficits associated with brain damage, the impairment is also isolated but relatively permanent. It is rarely reversed. As the damaging process continues, additional deficits can be observed, or old symptoms become greater in degree. However, the total person will maintain his sense of identity. His or her awareness of a continuing existence is not disrupted until coma and death.

The over-reactions of survivors and even the victim himself are not to the loss of mental abilities but to the fears that they will disrupt his awareness as a human being or his identity as a specific person. Once everyone becomes comfortable with the limited, nonetheless limiting extent of mental symptoms, the loss of ability is much less upsetting. Some evidence for this clinical assertion comes from observation of dying patients in state hospitals for the mentally ill. There, victims of mental deterioration or brain-damaging illnesses often develop a sense of euphoria. They become ecstatic and report feeling extremely well, all of which is totally unjustified by their physical and mental status. These feelings are construed as symptoms of their mental illness and correctly so. However, an alternative meaning is possible. This may be a natural adaptation to the dying process in which the patient's mental decline permits a self-generated sense of happiness. As with all mental illness, the symptoms are observable adaptations to the implicit expectations of others.

The three dire circumstances described previously are often cited as justifications for self-injury and the wish to die in the context of terminal disease. These apprehensions are born out of a phobic perception of the dying process. The previous ideas were offered as alternative notions to suggest that the actual dying experience might be less depressing than generally anticipated; and that the specific extreme examples are not the typical ones.

The basic suggestion has already been offered—all natural deaths are due to some form of terminal illness. All have in common a slow dying process. An appropriate expectation for survivors to entertain for the victims is the notion that terminal illnesses of one sort or another are universal and that dying is not a tragedy. It is as much a part of life as birth, marriage, work, success, failure, fatigue, illness. Given this orientation, one can begin to develop reasonable standards for appropriate behavior in participants of a terminal illness. To do so survivors must increase the candor with which they address the subject of death; for the victim and in turn for themselves.

The truth about dying is increasingly difficult to handle in American culture because everyone participates in various kinds of insincere communication: tact, diplomacy, white lies, and formal gestures are socially expected modes, but which effectively distort the experience as ordinarily perceived. Conversely, only the young, the naive, or the mentally ill "tell it like it is." They and anyone else who dare voice their actual perceptions get penalized in a variety of ways. The net effect of this general practice is a universal skepticism and credibility gaps. Conversely, every victim suffers some sense of being alone, misunderstood, and alienated from genuine sentiment.

The various euphemisms about a recently dead person

serve effectively to block survivors from recognizing their own feelings and wishes. "Loved one," "passed-away," "departed" are all softer expressions for the fact that someone is dead. However, the net consequence is to suggest that termination has not occurred; that the victim will be seen again. The danger of this process comes from the ambiguity imposed on the survivors. Are they supposed to grieve for someone who is not really dead? Should they be happy or sad? How can grief have a place if they will soon see the victim again? Should they continue as before even though the victim is no longer around? These contradictions make for an awkwardness in all social encounters but especially ones formerly shared with the victim. Until some redefinition can occur, every message and gesture irritate and block rather than facilitate sharing of experiences.

These obstacles are even more pronounced in the context of dying, since the victim himself is still present. There, his own social role becomes so ambiguous as to make every visit a threatening encounter. The answer suggested here is the hope of genuine communication which can offer all parties a foothold in the currently nightmarish context of dying. The starting point is quite simply the admonition to start with obvious reality. By definition a victim of a terminal disease has an illness from which he will not recover. This is never a secret. Everybody including the victim himself always knows that the illness is severe, progressive, and fatal. Public acknowledgement is what becomes blocked. In part this can be attributed to levels of awareness in the victim; he may simply be avoiding an unpleasant subject so as not to inflict distress on survivors. At a more repressed level he may have denied to himself that this is indeed a terminal process. Degrees of denial serve to accumulate and reinforce repressed content. These tend to return as conscious controls weaken; most typically in the form of nightmares. The same process is also apparent in twilight states such as heavy sedation, alcohol, or drug abuse, i.e., the so-called "bad trip." In the context of dying, repressed knowledge returns in the forms of excessive phobias about the illness, treatment, and concern for well-being of survivors—in short, the very symptoms that make dying grotesque for all.

A survivor who is willing to "tell it like it is" may verbalize a harsh piece of reality, but in doing so he opens a social process that permits an acceptance, and eventual easing of dying. Every message, gesture, gift, greeting card, visit should acknowledge some aspect of the real situation. The array of subjects is infinite and more detailed references are available elsewhere in this book, especially the chapters entitled "Last Letters About Last Things" and "Readiness to Die." These topics provide a relevant content which is appropriate and absolutely necessary in order to achieve an optimal dying experience.

The conversational openers are always difficult. However, like starting a discussion in any new situation, there are obvious points of departure. The criterion of an appropriate remark is always the person to whom addressed. Ideally, the subject should first be broached early in the dying process rather than late. When the survivor first appears, he must start fresh with the patient as he is. The most obvious question is to ask, "What's wrong?" Visitors always ask this and its corollary, "How do you feel?" whenever they visit any sick person, except one identified as terminal. The question is equally appropriate for the dying patient provided one is ready to hear some negative answers. Readiness to hear implies a willingness to accept reactions like "I'm dying." Most patients won't blurt that statement out, but that is what they are thinking, and it's also what the survivor thinks, too. The inability to verbalize what both are thinking is the problem. The answer suggested here is that the first time the subject is introduced, there will be no socially correct way of handling it. It will sound awful, and tears and distress will emerge. Seeing it through to some conclusions, without whitewashing or denying the reality, gives all parties some bedrock in their perceptions from which they can react and build further adaptations.

One of the optimal answers in the above context is to go on to acknowledge that the information is shocking, upsetting,

and regrettable. It does not matter who says it as long as someone does. It becomes an expression of how both people feel.
Again, this represents a foundation from which the participants can begin to build further responses. The worst that can
go wrong in this effort is the confrontation with emotion, the
distress of encountering the truth. However, the whole attempt
is an effort to handle painful knowledge constructively. All
participants will realize this, and have probably encountered
strong emotions in past relations. Once started, the whole
process can be mutually constructive in helping survivors and
the candidate to prepare for an appropriate dying.

This kind of distress and the suggestions given here for
coping with it would not be necessary were it not for the near
total default in the current culture of dying. A reversal is not
in sight, but the consequences are provoking complaints and
calls for alternatives. Regardless of what direction is taken,
there will be a universal need for death education; and the
earlier in life, the better. When the possibility becomes feasible, the locus of these efforts will probably take place in the
educational system. There will certainly be controversy and
resistance to first efforts much like those that occurred with
sex education in the public schools. Death is so inherently a
part of life that its natural incorporation into education about
sex, health, hygiene, and physiology seems self-evident. Any
first efforts to bring death into the classroom will require
thought about the preparation of the teachers to cope with the
recovery of traumatic prior experiences. Early bereavement
and incomplete grieving will predispose both the teacher and
the students to start remembering their losses, and the distress they encountered in any dying or funeral process. The
whole point of death education is to cope with this unnecessary
pain before, during, and immediately after it happens. First
efforts to teach the subject of dying can help the students by
permitting them an occasion when they can talk about their
earlier losses. The teacher need only orient the class to listen,
accept the emotion as natural, and offer comments about similar experiences. These memories need not be solicited, they
will occur spontaneously despite the teacher's best efforts to

avoid them. It may even be wise to warn students that this may occur.

None of this represents a license to practice group therapy in the classroom, or sensitivity training in the current usage. Neither does the teacher need to assume that these previous grief reactions are deep-seated symptoms of mental illness. However, when doubt emerges, consultation is always in the best professional tradition. Any competent teacher who is personally comfortable with death in his or her private life will be capable of conducting this type of class. He or she will need only the social license to attempt the goal proposed here.

In addition to the work suggested, there would also need to be arrangements for field trips to places and occasions of dying. As with any good instruction, visits to places that illustrate and make real the course content are always effective and practical enhancers of the classroom training. The same advantages can accrue to the students of dying. The difference of course comes in the taboo and distressing nature of the topic. For this reason, some further remarks may be helpful with respect to potential problems in developing appropriate resources for visitation.

The general object is to achieve an orientation to the actual places where dying, death, and final arrangements are conducted. The essence of these institutions is the staff and the procedures they employ. The hardware and buildings are secondary to their attitudes and purposes. In other fields, staff members are usually quite enthusiastic because of professional ideals, concern for clients, and goodwill with the public. The prevalence of taboos about death will raise resistance levels until death classes become an accepted routine. Even when staff members are otherwise cooperative, the overreactions of the public may well deter them from participation. The resourceful teacher will need to shop around and accept more disappointments than he or she usually finds with more conventional field trips. The teacher of a class on dying can start by inviting representatives of these institutions that deal with death to visit the classroom and start a dialogue with the students. This process should evolve over several academic years rather than within one particular course.

Illustrations of possible field trips are extended-care facilities, nursing homes, intensive care, or emergency units of general hospitals. These represent places where dying occurs in present practices. Examples of death prevention agencies are police departments, highway patrols, crisis intervention teams, hot lines, suicide prevention centers. Examples of services after death are morticians, coroners' offices, cemeteries, churches, florists, probate courts, assessors, claims adjustors, and so forth.

Another peculiar educational problem that will emerge and must be anticipated will be considerations of timely death. This may be especially poignant for those approaching the "golden age" of life. Asking older people to examine their expectations for continuing life and the meaning of death when life-expectancy is less than ten years is always a painful form of self-development. Yet the need is there and students presenting themselves for instruction will be interested in this aspect. Hopefully, the self-selection involved for adults will bring students with more courage and openness than usually occurs. Ideally, teachers will be individuals who have faced this problem of appropriate death in their private lives.

The preceding remarks have been oriented towards the emotional aspects that would necessarily emerge in any class on death, especially during the pioneer or early stages of instruction. Academic courses on death are beginning to emerge in college. Several textbooks have appeared and the classes themselves seem to enjoy a great deal of popularity with the younger students. The interest and knowledge are sufficient, and extension of the instruction available will occur to adult education and secondary schools. Course content will of necessity reflect interest and problem-solving information, best left to the discretion of the teachers and their students. There is, of course, a voluminous body of writing in the area of death, dying, and last things. The religious literature itself is overwhelming to contemplate. The more secular philosophers have also dealt extensively with human existence in a finite life, where termination stops consciousness as in existentialism, or where the after-life permits some form of continuation. Some of these viewpoints must be represented, and necessarily will conflict with religious and/or value systems of individual students. Some classroom controversy is constructive, other is distracting. This sort of material should be subordinated to the more recent literature on the psychology of death, dying, bereavement, and the denial phenomena created by the avoidance of personal cessation.

8

Comparative Shopping for Last Things

Everyone must die, and in this dying process, last things need attention. Hopefully, the victim himself will specify his preferences and spare the ones closest to him from agonizing over proper decisions during a time of crisis. Typically, Americans default. As death approaches, physicians, morticians, attorneys, social workers, and others preempt the options. The survivors are left with a dilemma—to agree with the experts and ignore their own feelings, or to attempt clairvoyance, the reading of the victim's intention. The risks can be catastrophic to the other survivors and to the peace of mind for the one held accountable. This dilemma faces every next of kin, and often more than once in a lifetime. Either the victim or his survivors must make choices and give consent to the professionals of death.

Effective coping with these choices is not possible unless considerable effort is expended prior to a dying process—before a patient is diagnosed as having a fatal disease. Ideally, the candidate for an appropriate death will have prepared himself or herself years before the anticipated end by developing prior knowledge, by desensitizing from the phobias and making informed choices. In addition a person will have made explicit efforts to document and communicate these preferences to the significant other people, especially those who will assume responsibility for their implementation.

To aid survivors, the actual decision points will now be

described. Most of these are obvious. They would insult the intelligence of any thoughtful reader, except for the near universal avoidance behavior in current practices. Comments will be made from the perspective of last things and the search for an appropriate death.

Life Insurance

Adequate life insurance is a pedestrian form of planning which is relatively universal in gesture if not in actuality. The original idea was to shelter a dependent spouse, parent, or child. Today the concern is to maintain an accustomed style of living in dependents, or to guarantee educational opportunities for children under twenty-five. Implicit is the intention to provide maximum freedom of choice to beneficiaries, which only an adequate income can assure. Most breadwinning males subscribe to this philosophy, but because they really expect to outlive the others they do not examine the specific financial goal or the unique beneficiary.

The starting point for anyone considering insurance is to recognize the different life expectancies for males and females. A wife is usually younger than a husband. Often she will be five years or more younger than her spouse. When these are added to the five or more years of greater life expectancy for women, it is clear that insurance must provide for ten or more years of widowhood. This estimate assumes the husband will die at age seventy. Regardless of what a surviving wife can earn, she will need at least $5,000 per year to continue her middle-class way of life. The total amount is a minimum sum of $30,000 to $75,000 to cover the remaining years of widowhood at 1973 prices.

The above assumes that the widow does not remarry. After the age of fifty the sheer lack of available men deters remarriage. Unless she is comfortable seeking the company of younger men, a widow is more likely to continue on alone rather than settle for any available man. Having the reassurance of some dependable subsidy can do a lot to give a sur-

viving widow the freedom to choose how she will carry on her
life.

Surviving widowers, while fewer, have financial needs
also, albeit of a different sort. Unless the former wife was
exceptionally successful, her financial loss comes from replacement costs. The reference here is to the costs of hiring a full-
time housekeeper, or baby-sitter. Even a mistress or girl
friend represents additional costs. The average minimum for
a housekeeper is approximately $450 per month by 1973
prices. Over a ten-year period of widowhood, a surviving husband would need $54,000. Very few men have that kind of
cash available. Nor can they afford the additional $300-$500
per month. While less obvious, wives should be insured also in
order to provide more freedom of choice for male survivors
through adequate insurance.

The kind of insurance recommended is term insurance,
which is the cheapest to purchase for the most protection.
After the age of seventy the couple can protect the survivor
better by other alternatives such as cash, savings bonds, or
other liquid assets.

For surviving children, the problem is complicated by
their extended financial immaturity until the age of twenty-
five or even older. Most jobs are geared to educational levels
achieved; high school or college graduation. While the various
skilled trades do not require academic degrees, the apprentice-
ships and experience requirements can be considerable. All
of this requires years before the individual is admitted to full-
journeyman earning capacity. It is a safe assumption that
whether children go on to college or not, until they reach their
mid-twenties, they will be in need of some financial assistance.
If single, this aid may be minimal; but once married, the
money crunch is considerable. A parent wishing his son to
achieve a profession and early fatherhood will be stuck with
an even larger bill. If the father dies before his dependent
son's education is completed, survivors' benefits from social
security or retirement plans will contribute a monthly stipend
in the vicinity of $100 or less per dependent child. This will

never be enough for the style of life most Americans would choose for themselves or their children. Insurance can supplement these meager sums. The amount needed tends to vary with the sex, age, education, and marital circumstances.

Sex-role differences in American culture present different financial needs. Typically, wives used not to work, nor earn more than their husbands if they did. Where the reverse happens, the male interpretation becomes more applicable. Daughters usually marry earlier than sons, and usually the girls marry men older than themselves. Their financial dependency continues but is transferred to their husbands. With today's rapidly increasing divorce rates, and the tendency of fathers to absent themselves, the money needs of abandoned wives and dependent grandchildren always add to the financial burdens of all survivors. The financial inability of young people to support more than one home or family should deter divorce or remarriage. It doesn't and the resulting poverty limits everyone's subsequent freedom to choose wisely, usually at the expense of children. A prudent grandparent will want to consider ways by which he can provide alternatives for immature survivors—trust funds, or insurance payable through installments.

The sums of money involved in providing for survivors are large, too large to be given outright. The simplest solutions are to specify the manner in which these monies can be distributed. Before death, the decisions on how to accomplish this can be based on firsthand knowledge of the beneficiaries rather than stereotypes. Decisions frozen into wills rely upon impersonal executors to exercise discretion. They in turn tend to make use of conventional expectations in which they accept prevailing notions rather than considering the unique individual. An example is the old notion that women do not know how to invest or manage lump sums, or that they will fall victim to opportunists who will "flatter" the money away. Today's women are better prepared to cope with estates and large sums of cash. While younger people are always more vulnerable to romantic values, a female survivor especially one born after the war years, has sufficient skills to manage large sums of money. The possibility should alert the executor to the unique abilities of any female survivor. Some of them don't need protection, merely the opportunities that money can create.

Each of the surviving children will need some lesser amount for a shorter period of time. The danger with them is that the father does not know them as well as his surviving spouse. Since they will be young at his death, the kind of character these children may develop will be largely unpredictable. The safest procedure is to provide smaller monthly sums for children below age eighteen than those above. Eighteen is a watershed year, both from the point of legal maturity and increasing financial need, but not necessarily increased earning power. Even today, the cost of college is far greater than high school. For those under twenty-five who get married, money is a much greater problem than sex. Aside from college, just to maintain the existing way of life requires more money each year.

The psychological value of insurance planning comes from the practical advantages of anticipating financial needs in survivors. The candidate for an appropriate death helps to prepare himself for his own unique cessation, in the course of planning for the welfare of his survivors. By dealing with this universal last thing in all its concrete details, the individual achieves a sense of completion about one aspect of life. In repeating the process with other final things, he or she adds and builds further toward the graceful death everyone prefers.

Health Insurance

Again this pedestrian planning is so universal as to be insulting. The major reason for including the topic is to emphasize the habit as well as the advantage of preparation. A lifetime of good health or long-lived parents is no assurance that the individual can ever avoid extended hospitalization in his own dying. The evidence documents that the vast majority of patients suffer a lingering illness before dying. In addition, medical competence permits any death to be postponed for weeks and months. Barring death from homicide, suicide, or accident, it is possible to predict one or more extended hospitalizations during the last few years of life. Some form of health insurance in the later years protects the estate of the candidate for a graceful death.

During working years, the majority of the employed are eligible for group health insurance through one of the existing plans. As jobs change, the individual can usually transfer to individual or other group plans. The coverages vary widely with the fees. In recent years group health insurance has become universally available to those employed. Two general exceptions occur. The first has to do with poverty levels and the marginally employed, usually unskilled workers. They tend to resist health plans because of the premiums and the availability of free medical resources through city or county facilities. In addition, they usually adopt a shorter perspective on life's hazards. The second exception occurs with respect to major medical benefits and is resisted for the same reason.

The better paid, middle-income employees tend to resist the additional premiums of major medical benefits for the usual avoidance reasons. They simply "don't plan on getting very sick." While this argument is patently false, younger workers in the full flush of youth, especially the unmarried, don't fully consider the risks. Once past thirty, married, and with dependents, most of these convert to health insurance and a lesser number to major medical insurance.

Another area of resistance occurs with retired workers. Health care is now available from medicare as part of social security benefits. This coverage is automatically included in our federal social security program. However, for a nominal fee, some very generous hospitalization protection is available. This option tends to be resisted. The elderly may simply not be aware of the choice as part of the aging process. However, it is more likely they are resisting the five or six dollars per month for the premium. They also tend to share the great American delusion that death will come suddenly since they have always enjoyed good health.

For those who subscribe to maximum health coverage, the

great concern is avoiding death. They flee to the hospitals and expect further continuations. This process is now accelerated by hospital staff commitment to avoidance of death. Hospitals are designed to postpone death and prolong the existence of every patient. At this writing very few have developed a systematic service which can help patients die gracefully.

Patients resist major medical health insurance because they literally expect good health to continue. Those who subscribe expect the hospitals to keep them alive indefinitely when they do suffer major illness. Because of these expectations, they are doomed to disappointment. Even worse, the collective history of these false expectations has created an atmosphere of hospital care that assures the patient *only* a prolongation of his dying.

This grim obstacle to a graceful death can only be avoided if the individual gives up the pursuit of his or her indefinite existence. In order to succeed in the acceptance of finite life with its associated deteriorations, the candidate for an appropriate end must do the things suggested in this book and make decisions about last things. The radical shifting of expectations implied by the reorientation towards death will manifest itself in a different expectation toward hospitalization in later years.

Ordinarily people go to a hospital because of an immediate condition; for this they receive some kind of treatment, pay high fees, and suffer a variety of social neglects from the staff. They are treated as objects rather than as unique individuals. No one complains usually, because the object is to cure an acute problem, resolve an emergency, or restore a temporary failure. The expectation is that treatment should hurt; medicine is supposed to taste bad, and attention is only for patients worse off. The net result is a public acceptance of less than adequate or aesthetic standards when it comes to hospitalization. No complaints are heard when it comes to acute illness. However, in the treatment of long-term, deteriorating illness known as fatal, the traditional hospital orientation impedes the patient from achieving a graceful end. The usual staff attitudes are neither optimistic nor affirmative. The net effect is one of interminable limbo in which the staff, visitors and patients eventually practice collusion in a make-believe optimism that permits everyone to avoid the essential distress. The resulting bad feelings are rationalized as grief and are inevitable in the face of an impossible situation.

Survivors also accept lower standards of service in the hospital than they would choose at home. They do so on the expectation that the illness is temporary. As the illness continues and cure is seen as less likely, the resulting disappointment is focused on the distressing aspect of the dying process. The delivery of medical care has impaired the survivors from an effective role in helping the patient to die, and has instead magnified the suffering of the family without ameliorating the patient's dying. By carrying over the usual hospital expectations to fatal or chronic disease, effective medical care becomes perverted to everyone's loss. By shifting to the expectation that the hospital should help the patient die gracefully, the starting point would be a clear affirmation that the site of dying should be a pleasant, attractive, and active place, where all of the patient's interests are facilitated within his physical capacities.

Unfortunately, the modern hospital is not likely to shift very quickly. In the hopes that it will change sooner rather than later the direction suggested here is to look for other institutions with respect to the delivery of services. An example is the luxury motel or resort that cares for chronic conditions.

The kind of medical and nursing attention needed by chronic patients can be distributed more selectively if the terminal ward or intensive-care units were replaced with alternative models, such as suggested here by the motel or luxury resort approach. It is only rigid professional custom that requires hospital settings for delivery of paramedical services to the chronic patient. The continuous care of a dying patient can be given at home in between acute episodes. In a crisis, emergency teams or hospital admissions can supplement home care. Whether at home or in a nursing care facility, services to the chronically ill are packaged in a rigid medical context. Some patients at least could receive these in other settings. The alternative suggested here is more like room service in a luxury hotel.

In today's economy, medical administrators would argue against this notion as prohibitive. The chronically ill will continue to be dissatisfied as long as their needs are ignored. The dignity of the patient always gets subordinated to physical care, convenience, and costs. In chronic illness, this is truly inappropriate. As an outraged public makes more demands for a change, any alternative type of care will become more feasible. In the context of fatal or long-term care, the patient should leave his or her home only for a similar or better way of life.

Considering the amount of time each person is likely to spend as a patient in the dying setting, it behooves every survivor to select the kind and delivery of services he or she would prefer when well, or at least when free from the duress of fatal illness. Choosing to die in a luxury hotel or motel makes more sense than accepting a hospital setting or nursing home. The effective choice is still currently not available. Costs could be lowered if a sufficient volume of patients were able to act on this option. The major financial obstacle is not high cost, but the restrictive nature of health-care delivery and insurance payments. Regardless of how it may be financed, a dignified death requires pleasant surroundings. Adequate planning must include some attention to personal tastes in achieving a pleasant environment. Typically, death comes slowly with most of the patient's faculties intact, sufficient to enjoy the company of survivors and settings.

Property Settlement

The disposal of property and assets is another last thing which immediately comes to mind as an appropriate area for preplanning. Even so, a rather large number of people die intestate, with no valid will known. Partly this occurs because of a reluctance to plan for death. However, the victim himself often discounts his real assets as being unworthy of formal planning implied in wills. This may even be effectively true in the sense of low equity in homes or rapid depreciation of equipment. Rapidly fluctuating values and inflation also effectively minimize one's assets. Even so, there is always some residual value that can be lost in the absence of a will. Unnecessary court costs can wipe out small estates. Preferred heirs are not necessarily the ones who get clear title to the property. If the estate is a home occupied by a surviving parent or aged sibling, the children would have the preemptive right to displace the occupants, no matter what the intent of the deceased.

A more relevant issue is the estate with sufficient value to qualify for federal taxes. Typically when a husband dies the internal revenue service assumes that the entire property belonged to him. The wife will need to demonstrate independent income in order to exempt her legal half from estate taxes. In addition, all life insurance will be lumped into the taxable body of assets. While there is a personal exemption of $60,000 and an additional marital deduction of $60,000, the face value of insurance is often sufficient to generate a significant tax bill to the survivors.

A simple decision to transfer ownership of life insurance is often sufficient to avoid a taxable estate. The husband need merely assign the "incidents" of ownership to another, typically his wife. Insurance companies supply the proper forms on request. This assignment is independent of beneficiary designations or payment of premiums. Effectively, the insurance coverage and source of payments to the company need not be changed.

In reviewing estates for disposal while still alive, several confusions occur. In attempting to give something of value to preferred survivors, there is also a danger of incurring unnecessary federal taxes or probate costs. Every dollar of property which passes through the courts of a given jurisdiction is subject to fees. There is a fee to attorney, appraisers, and the court itself, all assessed on some percentage basis. If homes or residences are maintained in two or more places, each of these jurisdictions can assert probate costs also.

The solution is to make use of the suggestions in the recent best-selling book, *How to Avoid Probate*. An alternative here is to use joint ownership with rights of survivorship for one home, one checking account, savings bonds, E and H Series, and credit union accounts. These will then avoid probate, but may run the risk of estate taxes, depending on spouses' independent income sources. The advantage of the preceding is a ready source of cash immediately after death.

Second homes, cars, stocks, savings accounts in banks and credit unions are safer in separate names of spouse or children. These arrangements will avoid estate taxes and probate costs, but may run a different risk. The danger here is the unreliability of a wife in this age of divorce or the unpredictability of children whose adult characters cannot be fully anticipated.

There is no final answer in any context, and certainly that's so with respect to finances. The suggestion here is to accept the inevitable. If the Internal Revenue Service doesn't take it, divorce settlements will!

Another alternative not considered thus far is the option of gifts while still alive. This has the advantage of donor satisfaction while still around to observe the results. Present federal gift tax laws permit each donor to give $3,000 per year per donee. If the spouse joins in giving, the amounts are doubled. This gift must be completed at least three years before the death of any one donor. Such gifts are non-taxable to all parties and represent a way of passing on one's lifetime savings to the survivors. Many patients who anticipate the prospect of an extended dying are reluctant to exercise these options because they lack familiarity with tax laws, or have some preconceptions about the evil effects of turning over their property while still alive. These preconceptions are part of the Puritan ethic and folklore of the culture from an era when death came suddenly, and property passed directly to the oldest son. The modern situation is different, but the victims have not become aware of the changes and proceed on the old basis. Potential survivors need to sensitize and orient the patients to these matters before it is too late.

The ultimate gift a parent can give his survivors is the old Biblical notion of a blessing. Aside from its religious connotations, the psychological fact consists of one person, a dying parent, expressing his best wishes about survivors whom he has known for decades. These occurrences have lifelong impact, most often for good deeds and positive influence.

Any person making plans for his or her estate should include a blessing for each named survivor. Where possible, he or she should prepare these in writing in the event of being too sick to give them orally. Money and property always pass, but a blessing is carried throughout life.

Site of Dying

Death used to strike Americans where they worked, lived, and played. So common was the occurrence of death that the standard elementary textbook, *McGuffey's Reader*, contained numerous references to death. These illustrations document an era when death was not only universal, but regarded as so natural a phenomenon as to provide worthy exercises for developing reading skills in children. It is not surprising then that the home was the typical place to die. With improvement in medical care, especially for the acute infections that struck young adults prematurely, the hospital became the place to care for the ill. In time, the hospital became the site of dying, too. As long as the victims were taken by acute conditions that caused a fast death, the hospital functioned adequately. With chronic disease and slower terminations, hospitals have tended to shift the site of dying to the intensive-care unit, or to the acute service dealing with medical emergencies. In these sites, medical staff continue the effort to postpone death. This traditional mission becomes inappropriate in the context of fatal disease. Current medical care in terminal illness has been called the prolongation of dying rather than the extension of living. Hospitals as they function today tend to block the pursuit of a graceful death. The usual medical orientation in the care of the dying patient makes the hospital the worst possible place to seek an appropriate death.

The candidate for a graceful death will need to choose a site that facilitates this goal. He or his survivors with informed consent will need to specify an optimal place. The recommendation here is to choose the home, or the environment that expresses prior lifestyle best. Such a choice retains respect for the unique identity of the victim while allowing survivors to serve both the patient's and their own needs. This suggestion is not as extreme as it may appear. The bulk of the dying process permits the victim to go about his or her daily activities as usual. He or she will need regular medical attention, some degree of nursing care, and assistance with whatever impairments there are. These can be managed on an ambulatory or out-patient basis, supplemented by help from survivors. Nursing or convalescent home options can be utilized with appropriate concern for the lifestyle of the patient. Discussion of this aspect occurs in Chapter Six. Medical procedures requiring hospitalization should be evaluated carefully. Some criteria for doing so are suggested next.

First, is the medical intervention the kind that produces shock such as in surgery? Even routine operations are a trauma in one whose physical resources are limited. Implicit in medical interventions are the probabilities of reduced quality of existence following these life-extending processes. The expected hospitalization period is a good index. The longer the period of convalescence, the more the intervention is to be resisted as a debilitating process in itself. The hospitalization interval should be numbered in days rather than weeks. If the latter, the medical intervention is generating a chronic situation, which diminishes the patient further.

Second, does the treatment create a permanent departure from the patient's prior lifestyle? The more deviations imposed by medical intervention, the more difficult a graceful death becomes. The criterion here is the quality of life remaining after the treatment. At some place in the value system of the individual, a point is reached where death is preferable. While there are many who can adapt to any loss or impairment, there are also some who cannot, with the majority falling somewhere in between. The individual patient should not be asked to accept either extreme in an arbitrary fashion. Flexibility is only possible in the context of informed consent where the candidate for a graceful death can choose according to his or her personal values. In such a choice, it is essential to recognize that some people are better off dying from the disease itself, rather than existing within the limitations of a specific illness and its treatment regime.

The third criterion suggested here has to do with when death occurs. The moment of death is ordinarily avoided under the mistaken apprehension that in a hospital it can be postponed indefinitely. As indicated earlier, the moment of death is increasingly obscure and can be delayed, but never avoided. There comes a time in the fatal illness when either the victim or his potential survivors must consider the idea that the delay of death is no longer worth the distress of hospitalization. Rather than allowing termination to occur in a hospital, it may be preferable to seek death in the home. This can only happen if hospitalization is rejected during the end stages of fatal disease.

It can be argued that such a choice may shorten the life which could otherwise be prolonged. The rebuttal comes in the enhancement of the life that is passing, and in the contribution to the ability of survivors to carry on. Dying at home gives the death dignity in that a person is surrounded by sensitive people who will respect that unique individual and provide the last comforts that only love can generate. In turn, these last encounters permit the survivors to give their specific relation a meaning consistent with their own value systems, and which can function in memory as a constructive force for future growth and carrying on. The choice between hospitalizing or dying at home can be distressing. The three criteria suggested here will help clear the air of misconceptions and give the participants a relatively free choice. In such a decision, the values of the patient must dominate, while conventional stereotypes or professional advice must be subordinated.

Disposition of Remains

After death, the body needs disposition. The modern situation permits an increasing variety of choices among burial, donation for medical research, storage, or abandonment. The body can be embalmed, burned, frozen, or left as is. Burial requires a casket, cemetery plot, services, shrouds, and tombstone. All of these are expensive. In total, death represents the largest family expense encountered outside of home and car. Typically, there is little opportunity to shop for any of these purchases. Decisions are usually made in an atmosphere of grief, guilt, or a combination of both. The victim, while still alive, may lean over backwards and choose too humbly, or inappropriately, with respect to his values or the needs of his survivors. There is a near total failure to consult with concerned others while still alive. Every candidate for a graceful death needs to explore and consult with others concerning the array of choices suggested in the table that follows.

Table III   **Choices for Survivors**

Disposition: Burial, donation, cold storage,
                        abandonment
Treatment: Embalmment, cremation, freezing,
                        leaving as is
Grave accessories: Shrouds, casket, grave marker
Cemeteries: Public, private, crypt, mausoleum

Further comments are added with respect to each of the options given in the table above.

Traditional burial is still the most popular mode of disposition. The body is simply buried in an available cemetery, after a mortuary has treated the remains, wrapped it in shrouds, and placed it in a casket. Later an appropriate marker or gravestone is placed on the grave. There is a growing discontent with this traditional service, as there is with all conventions. However, the disenchantment is also a response to rigid stereotypes of "proper burial," and the subsequent survival gaps induced by insufficient grieving. Underlying this motive is a more obscurely felt wish to avoid the whole experience of death in others. All of these converge to create a need for alternative modes of disposition.

Donation of the body to medical schools for research or training has become increasingly popular. This popularity can be gauged by the use of waiting lists, priorities, and sheer rejections of such donations by these institutions. It is increasingly difficult to literally will away one's body. Donations to organ banks can satisfy the need to give while still alive, and less so after death. The logistics of preserving organs, donated while alive, are increased significantly by death, since deterioration occurs within hours after death. All of these tend to impede gifts to transplant banks. It is still an option, but increasingly complicated for survivors to implement.

Cold storage refers to the cryonic approach where the body is frozen immediately after clinical death, and then given perpetual care in a freezer vault. At this writing, the mode is still prohibitively expensive. However, some two dozen bodies have been preserved in the United States. Prepayment plans are being explored, and the cryonics exponents are remarkably resourceful in overcoming obstacles. One does not have to subscribe to the revival aspect of this mode, since freezing does represent a better way to preserve the remains than embalming. One can choose freezing and cold storage over embalming and burial. Whether one expects resurrection or revival is a matter of personal belief.

Abandonment is no longer an effective choice for most people. Respect and health factors have generated local laws that require authorized dispositions, most typically burial. The only exceptions are accidents such as plane crashes, shipwrecks, or other disasters where the bodies cannot be recovered.

Treatment

Embalming is the most universally accepted practice of treating remains. The process consists generally of draining the blood from the body and replacing it with a preserving or disinfectant fluid such as formaldehyde. The procedure includes efforts to improve the appearance of the body for open-casket viewing. Embalming does not effectively prevent deterioration nor significantly prolong its integrity. Embalming is not usually required by local statute, nor does it do anything for the victim. The survivors achieve a sense of duty fulfilled by ordering this service. Morticians, in turn, derive a greater financial gain from sales of caskets and accessories. Embalming continues to be popular because of conventional expectations and the eternal need to do something when death strikes. One's considerations should recognize the fact that embalming offers nothing of substance to any party.

Leaving the body as is, or untreated, is still considered a deviant idea, but has gained in social acceptance in recent years. This choice has the advantage of not treating the remains with strange hands. This again is a matter of personal value, and expresses the not quite rational feeling of many people when contemplating the disposition of their remains. The deviancy comes from the American ethos of action, especially in a crisis. The notion of doing nothing is foreign. However, simply putting the body in a box is increasingly acceptable today.

Cremation

Cremation is becoming a more popular mode of disposition. However, most people who express a preference for this option are not aware of the complications in disposing of the ashes. The dramatic image of "scattering the ashes into the wind" is not accomplished easily in the city. Along the West Coast, charter boats offer a complete memorial service with ashes disposed in the ocean. Light aircraft can be chartered for disposition of ashes also. However, there are mechanical problems in scattering ashes. Ashes are usually returned in an urn and need not be scattered at all. Cremation gives the survivors the option of keeping the ashes. This can be done simply by leaving them in the urn, which has the added advantage of portability. A more permanent solution is to build a columbarium in the backyard or wherever the parties choose. In the state of California, it is legal to keep human ashes, or place them in sites outside of cemeteries.

Cremation does offer the advantage of flexibility and therefore a wider choice. A key concept in exercising this choice should be the recognition that survivors need a tangible focus to help them mourn and to derive comfort after death. This is most easily facilitated by a grave site. With ashes, the equivalent would be the repository of the urn. Scattering of ashes tends to deprive survivors of this resource. This need tends to get overlooked in the planning, most typically because of the wish to avoid the distress associated with conventional funerals. A candidate for graceful death is usually thinking of minimizing the burden at the funeral, rather than of his survivors' needs to mourn during the longer period of grieving following disposition.

Freezing

The complications associated with the freezing alternative have been discussed adequately in Chapter Two. At this writing, the freezing option is not commercially feasible. The exponents of this mode expect to solve the revival problem within five to ten years.

Grave Accessories

Into each burial go an array of accessories with corresponding decisions that typically get made by happenstance. The mortician quietly suggests the items needed and manipulates the price extracted by various sales tactics. An example is to present the recently bereaved with a selection of three caskets. The pauper's model is reasonable, but unattractive, and even offensive in some respects. The luxury model is priced higher than the one in between. However, the middle one is priced closer to the luxury than the pauper model. This presentation manipulates the buyer into paying more for a modest casket. Choosing this and other items immediately after a death places the survivor on the defensive. He is under duress to select from among the multiple choices provided. The best way of countering this difficulty is through comparative shopping in advance.

Caskets are needed where the remains are to be interred in a cemetery. Originally, bodies were interred without cover or protection. Only in recent and relatively affluent times have the dead been buried inside a box. Once the wherewithal gave mourners this choice, the functional casket began to evolve as a means of expressing other feelings than those of respect for the deceased. The tradition of using an elaborate or decorative casket is based on the very human need to signal the community that a very important person has died. In the use of this symbol, the mourners were helped to cope with their grief. The danger here is that a stereotyped, factory-made, overpriced box with phoney decorations can be a symbol of contempt to the memory of the victim. This occurrence contributes to the contemporary disappointment with modern funerals.

Another false premise in using caskets is the notion that somehow, the box will preserve the body. The stronger the box, the longer it will be saved from deterioration. Everyone recognizes that the remains deteriorate after death, no matter what is done to deter this. The box in which the remains are placed serves as a respectful way of carrying these remains in public ceremonies. The survivors can give it any symbolic meaning they choose, but its value in preserving remains exists only in the fantasies of the bereft.

Shrouds are untailored black or white clothes that are wrapped around the remains for open-casket viewing. They are a convenience to the mortician in lieu of actual clothing. Again this choice is really a matter of personal taste, best left to the discretion of the candidate in his or her advance selections. Here it should be affirmed that there is nothing fixed nor sacred about the choice. The recommendation is to use those articles of clothing that seem appropriate to the kind of person he or she was. In the absence of an explicit preference, it is more consistent to dress the remains as they appeared in the memory of the survivors.

The typical grave in any cemetery is marked. The marker has evolved in American society from a simple cross, to a carved wooden board, to the granite tombstone. The current marker is not just any stone, but one that will "last." This human vanity has increased with the recent denial of death. In addition a proper size, color, and inscription must be chosen. These are motivated more by pride than simple respect for the memory of the deceased. As with all human pride, the error of these motives is not immediately apparent to the participants.

Aside from the rather large costs of this symbol, there are some unanticipated disappointments. When chosen in a viewing room, the stone will appear differently than on a gravesite. A visit to any traditional cemetery will best demonstrate the effect. Public and many private cemeteries have limited space. Cost factors drive the prices up while squeezing the size of each lot down. A six- by four-foot grave looks smaller when a four- or five-foot stone is placed at one end. If all the graves use tall stones, the rows of markers look like tenements and the graves appear to be alleys. The net effect is to denigrate the individual grave and to depress the mourner.

Another disappointment is the durability of these markers. The choice of granite and cement foundation is usually motivated by a desire for perpetual identification, along with indefinite care of the grave site. The quality of the foundation, the weather, the soil, and the amount of human traffic can undermine the permanence of the chosen marker. Vandals or even inadvertent accidents by visitors can knock over the stones. No marker can last forever. It is only human vanity which seeks identification of graves beyond two or three generations.

The alternative suggested here is to consider other kinds of markers such as wood or the newer metals. These are unusual today, but again are not necessarily disrespectful. While all will deteriorate, they may provide an aesthetically pleasing and personally comforting type of memorial precisely because they are different. In this respect contemporary sculptors can be approached to solve the design problems.

There is no reason why a grave marker cannot also be a piece of sculpture, that is, a work of art to be enjoyed by any viewer. If this idea is accepted, it can be pushed a bit further. Why not commission and place the work while the subject is still alive? This gives the candidate for a graceful death the satisfaction of seeing the final piece and supervising the details of its placement. A further extension of this idea is to think in terms of a family marker in which the central sculpture serves to identify the graves of all members. The individual sites can then be marked by a simple name and date plaque. The additional advantage of doing this is the creation of an intimate park area where individuals can go for comfort and meditation throughout their lifetime.

Cemeteries

Every community has a range of burial places, the larger the city, the greater the choice. These include the public and private cemeteries, while the overall appearance goes from pioneer to conventional and contemporary. The choice is most effectively made during preparatory considerations. A cemetery must serve two basic purposes. It is first a place to dispose of human remains. It is also a memorial to the dead, which should provide some comfort to the living. Implicit to both should be some satisfaction to the person seeking an appropriate death.

The choice of an appropriate cemetery is usually dictated by availability and cost, when it should be made on the basis of taste or personal needs. An illustration of personal values is offered next by the author's own search for last things.

In order to make an informed choice, my family and I visited local graveyards. In the course of this cemetery shopping, we discovered the first two to be limited with respect to our tastes. The first was an older, but conventional one with a view of the Pacific Ocean. From the highway, it looked beautiful. For many years this one had been our implicit first choice. We drove in and walked around. It was in a hollow between a hill and the highway and there were no trees. It was hot and dusty with freeway noises in the background. It was tasteless and depressing to us as non-mourners. What comfort would any of us derive as survivors?

The next one was a contemporary cemetery without monuments, an all-grass sort of place. Each grave was marked by a flat plaque flush with the grass, and here and there were some plastic flowers. Each grave was indistinguishable from the others. The cemetery was about twenty years old, but could have been sixty. It was a timeless atmosphere in the sense of denying the passage of time—the sort of image that suggests immortality and validates personal notions of death as a long sleep. "Speak softly, walk lightly; else you awaken somebody!"

The third cemetery we visited was old with stones dating back well over one hundred years. As with all older cemeteries, the heterogeneity of markers from different eras emphasized the passage of time. This was heightened by the obvious signs of weathering, the use of wooden markers, and the epithets inscribed with sentiments and language of the last century. Their juxtaposition affirmed a human continuity that was more credible because it made no pretense to personal immortality. Instead, the assemblage of tombstones documented the eternal continuation between the human past and future with us providing the living connection between the two. Our preference for this third cemetery was based on a personal value. We are all part of some larger process, call it civilization, which is continuously changing. We are a very small and temporary part of this process. We ignore or deny this frequently. I preferred to incorporate this notion in my choice of last things.

My family purchased four lots in this last cemetery and will develop them as a family plot. There is no necessity that compels any one of us to be buried there, but clearly its existence will serve as a time-binder between parents and children. I will probably be buried there first, and my wife will derive the comfort of visiting my grave. It's quite possible the reverse sequence may happen, but not very probable. With one or both parents buried there, the children will be able to make the family burial plot a place of retreat and eventual comfort. To enhance this process, we have decided to plant shrubs and trees and otherwise develop this site as a living memorial to our family and its collective encounters. In time, we will erect a sculpture as a family marker. These processes will provide us with satisfactions as we evolve through our family history. When death us do part, the survivors will have some additional sources of comfort.

The essential caution is to choose a cemetery, and grave site, as carefully as a home, because the human needs are similar. Like homesites, graves vary in price depending on the neighborhood, the view, aesthetics, the social class of residents, demand, and upkeep. While human vanity is to be deplored in this choice, it can never be eliminated. In moments of sorrow, the survivors are entitled to whatever gives them comfort. Through advance selection, some of the irrational needs can' be resolved and others minimized. Overall the candidate for a graceful end must consider the welfare of all parties to his death.

Last Services and Memorials

Associated with human remains are some miscellaneous services that may be less than essential, but still difficult to avoid. In planning for these decisions, some of these can be eliminated or their costs minimized. At least a fuller understanding of their implications may help participants be less bothered by them. Increasingly, memorial societies help their members develop informed consent with the various options. A list of Service Organizations is given in the back of this book. Briefly, for a small membership fee they provide a simple one-page form that covers all significant decisions with respect to disposition of human remains. Copies are filed with the chosen mortuary, the society, and the member. This form documents preferences even as it induces informed decisions. Completing these forms when well and free of duress assures optimal decisions. These forms also include a vital statistics section which facilitates the financial-legal aspects. These include names and addresses of significant others, Social Security, veteran's identification number, clergyman, attorney, memberships, occupation, employer, family, and national origins.

Opening and closing a grave in this day of euphemism refers to digging a hole and filling it after the body is interred. Both of these operations are performed off stage, before the mourners arrive, and after they leave. This service can only be avoided if non-burial is elected. If cremated, the ashes can be buried in a shallow grave. The opening and closing charges are usually less costly in this event. Baby graves, for the same reason, are also associated with lesser charges.

Grave-liners are absolutely required in lawn or perpetual care cemeteries. This service prevents the grave-hole from collapsing when open and from sinking when closed. It consists of a cement wall around the periphery of the grave hole. This service is not required in the conventional or older cemeteries and is intended to avoid disturbing the lawn effect in the contemporary cemetery. The resulting depressions were countered by the traditional mound of dirt heaped up above ground level. Aside from the aesthetics of an even lawn, depressions or erect grave markers would impede efficient operation of the lawn-mowers and other equipment.

Perpetual care is one of those reassuring phrases like slumber room, loved one, opening-closing graves, and so forth. All of these seem designed to deny that termination really occurs to the nice people we knew. In recent years, perpetual care refers explicitly to a type of cemetery which is dominated by lawn with markers flush to the grass. It is a promise to assure the safety of the grave and its aesthetic setting. This service boils down to maintaining the lawn for the existence of the cemetery. While there are other services implied in maintaining any cemetery, these are efforts to run a successful business, and are not really a personal service to the individual grave. These efforts will be provided anyway in order to attract future customers. Aside from taste, perpetual care should not influence choice of cemetery.

Flowers have been abused in recent years as symbolizing the unnecessary in expensive funerals. The reaction against flowers in an age of denial and consumer outrage is comparable to taxpayers voting down school bonds. Both groups were only able to protest these items. There was little choice with the other costs. Hopefully future taxpayers and candidates for an appropriate death can exercise their right to choose and protest with respect to more costly items. The essential service that flowers or greenery provides comes from their inherent beauty. Flowers can never hurt and often generate pleasant moods. In an hour of acute distress, they can provide some comfort to the bereaved even as they cheer the sick or sentimental. A widow attending her husband's funeral will not be hurt by a modest spray of flowers. Later as she visits the grave, greenery will add to the surroundings and ease her grieving. Male survivors have similar needs, but in the chauvinistic American ethos are prevented from fully deriving this pleasure.

Between the excesses of the overdone funeral and the extreme of no flowers there exists some middle-ground appropriate to the needs of individuals seeking comfort for their survivors. During the course of an anticipated funeral, small bouquets of flowers and greenery suggest a cheerful note. Proper mourning does not preclude the kind of cheer implied in either flowers, or candles, or spirits.

During the longer period of mourning implied in visits to the grave, the same logic invites the use of flowers or greenery there. The optimal solution is to plant an appropriate bush or bulb. These will need some care and give a functional mission to the regular visits to the grave. A by-product of this approach is the opportunity to grieve through activity. The work of expiating one's grief is facilitated by doing something as simple and active as caring for shrubs. The regularity and frequency also help to resolve extensive sorrow through time.

An atypical item of service is the request for autopsy following certain kinds of death. Where the law requires this, there is of course, no choice. However, there are occasions when the hospital staff will request an autopsy in the interest of establishing a better diagnosis or monitoring the quality of care given earlier. The decision to conduct the autopsy falls upon the survivor. In making this choice, the optional nature of this service needs some emphasis. While the requests are always motivated by proper goals, the survivors are always on the defensive in coping with personal values that conflict and may appear irrational in the semi-public debates with medical authorities. The necessity of an autopsy occurs in establishing cause of death. In the traditional coroner's decision, the evaluation is difficult only where unpredicted modes are in question. The social circumstances will suggest the question in the first place and the consequent investigations are clearly justified. Autopsies in this context are required by law and establish the role of the victim in facilitating his own demise. In the hospital context, where the patient has died from a terminal process, the original diagnosis is usually known. The affected organs are also known from the symptomatology and laboratory findings. There is usually no essential question about the general cause of death. On the other hand, there are often legitimate reasons for requesting autopsies. One is the in-house monitoring of medical care. There are tissue committees who review all surgeries and deaths to assess the quality of service given and to reinforce higher standards for all hospital procedures.

Each person must weigh the autopsy choice by his or her own personal values. In seeking a point of view to establish a preference, it is helpful to recognize that the usual stereotyped reasons for requesting a *post mortem* do not always hold in the individual cases. In the absence of information or planning, the survivor is entitled to fall back on his own feelings about the subject. Most often the idea of a loved one being disfigured by the surgical procedures required is distressing. While it may be irrational, the idea does do damage to the memory of the loved one and distorts the lost relationship.

Funeral and memorial services do nothing for the dead. They aid the living insofar as they give comfort to the survivors, and provide a perspective on what will happen to them when their own time comes. Aside from the social necessity of disposing of the human remains, the survivors need the memorial service associated with human funerals. There is a folk wisdom embodied in the traditional funeral occasion in all Western cultures. The public opportunity provided survivors permits them the opportunity of putting their own emotional houses in some kind of order with respect to the relation disrupted by death. Typically, the survivors need replacement relations, but this requires some kind of acceptance that the old relationship is really gone. The superficial tendency is to find some human substitute and pop them into the old relation. The replacement usually fails to meet the old standard and everything changes even while attempting to keep the old relation the same. The consequence hurts everyone including the memory of the departed.

The funeral provides an opportunity to deter this kind of danger. It does so by the public acknowledgement that someone is really gone and that a death has occurred. This naive formulation reflects the equally naive and primitive need to deny that loss has occurred. The consensus of involved others, whether intimate or casual, helps to confirm at some deeper and emotional level of awareness that the dead one is effectively gone. Along with the preceding, the funeral rituals also provide some group effort to explain death and through this the cycle of life. From this public experience comes the matrix in which an individual survivor attempts to give his or her personal loss some unique significance and value. Contemporary funerals have moved in two apparently opposite directions. The first is the public-relations-type spectacle where everything is done for the sake of appearances. The second trend is the swing towards no services; cremation, or secular gestures. The second is a reaction to the first, while both are acknowledgments that the traditional funeral just didn't satisfy. All funerals tend to be deficient in opportunities for individuals to express and share their unique feelings about the dead one. Primarily this deficiency comes from the survival gap created between proper and improper feelings with respect to public behavior after loss. The absence of an opportunity to "let it all hang out" robs the survivors of a chance to participate, to discover their own meanings, and achieve corresponding values.

The failure of modern funerals to deal explicitly with this survival gap and the needs of grievers impedes a sense of completion, or wrapping-up of the disrupted relationship and the consequent making room for replacement. Survivors older and more contemporary survivor, the memorial service is a formal occasion for contemplating the end of a unique relationship; one that can never be fully replaced and therefore a loss that diminishes them in some respect. For all survivors, sions consistent with their unique relationships.

With some minimal orientation, survivors can begin to develop preferences in the event of a death. By sharing these with family and others *before* death is imminent, consensus and decision-making are facilitated. At least the survivors will know what they want. There will still continue to be obstacles to implementation, especially where preferences are unusual. Putting it in writing helps to assure that all survivors and the professionals will be more able to carry out the wishes of the deceased.

Even when communication is achieved, a larger problem is that what a survivor prefers for himself is not necessarily what his survivors need. Indeed it may well be the opposite. For example, consider a couple. She may want a simple disposition; cremation without a service. He may belong to a fraternal order that provides fairly elaborate social rituals at funerals. No matter who dies first, the other will get the opposite of what is preferred.

Shifting from funerals in particular to memorials in general, some further comments can be made about psychological needs and options in the longer period after a death occurs. Honoring the memory of the deceased in subsequent years contributes to the well-being of survivors in at least two general ways. The service, whether by funeral or subsequent memorials, is a reminder that a milestone in the psychological evolution of the survivor has been passed. For the younger survivor, further psychological growth is precipitated by the death of an elder. Coping with loss at a younger age is usually harder because of the absence of prior experience. The memorial becomes an opportunity to instruct and prepare them by the example and meanings assigned by their elders. For the older and more contemporary survivor, the memorial service is a formal occasion for contemplating the end of a unique relationship; one that can never be fully replaced and therefore a loss that diminishes them in some respect. For all survivors, there is in addition the reminder that death will one day come for the individual. This reminder is a provocation to start seeking or acting upon worthwhile and satisfying ways of life now rather than later. Time is always limited, but people tend to continue routines as if they will live forever. The shock of death and the occasion of a memorial service helps survivors to remember. Through this remembering, the individual gets an opportunity to reconsider his past ways and search for options more consistent with his values and self-development.

The range of memorial services usually covers all formal religious possibilities including the atheistic. The choice of which one is relatively simple if the deceased expresses himself beforehand. Otherwise the mourners contain subgroups who go away dissatisfied with the religious content of the services. For some there are too many and for others too few Bible words. These dissatisfactions are dispelled if it is known that the loved one "asked for it." Knowing the service was chosen and is an expression of preferences felt by the deceased helps all mourners to cope with their own distress.

Specifically, if a mourner is bothered by some aspect of the service such as guitar music or colorful dress, he or she will be more able to tolerate its inclusion, if it expresses the taste of the deceased. In either of the examples, the expectations of the mourners are discrepant with the rituals and therefore increase discomfort. When these funeral rites are seen to express the personality or lifestyle of the deceased, they become easier to bear. The survivors reconcile this discrepancy in the same ways they dealt with disappointments by the deceased when alive.

In the absence of stated preferences, the next of kin has the burden of decision-making without the advantage of good will with which the deceased's choices are usually honored. For the survivor who must belatedly arrange a sudden funeral service, the choices are hazardous. The preferences of the dead are unknown, while the tastes of the living are in conflict. It is appropriate to start with the preferences of the designated kin who arranges services. Two general limits circumscribe these tastes. First is the recognition that the best way to honor the dead is to provide a memorial that fulfills the needs of the living. Second is to recognize that the majority needs or expectations of the survivors will tend towards the conventional for that ethnic group. In the absence of documented last wishes, funeral rituals should stay within conventional tastes in order to please the majority of mourners. The essential goal is to mark the death of a person known well and whose passing creates a sense of loss. The service should provide a publicly shared acknowledgment that helps everyone accept fully the finality of this loss. The funeral should provide sensory details that enable participants to perceive death. This becomes essential when it is remembered that death now occurs off-stage in specialized settings which prohibit observation of actual dying. The service associated with the funeral or in subsequent anniversaries needs to provide substitute cues to help mark the reality of this passing. The failure to provide these experiences permits survivors to suffer from survival gaps derived from incomplete grieving or denial phenomena. These problems will be described more fully in subsequent chapters.

Along with the passing of a unique relation with a person is the opportunity to expiate regret—real or fantasied. It does not matter which is the source as long as the occasion permits the survivor to acknowledge to himself the regret he feels for having failed the deceased. Later in the memorial service, the mourners need reassurance of safe passage. The deceased will "rest in peace," "go to heaven." be remembered, and so forth. The phrasing will be different, but somehow the words uttered confirm that his or her image will continue untarnished in the memories of the survivors. In order to validate this safe passage, survivors need to be certain that adequate earthly efforts were expended to provide a proper disposition. The last idea is open-ended in that only the survivors can define what is "proper." However, they will need to convince themselves in order to achieve a sense of finality about the loss. This is best accomplished by developing some notion of what is an appropriate burial service. The actual ritual should have some consensus by the participating survivors.

The after-funeral reception fills many human needs not adequately covered by the formal memorial ritual. At these gatherings, subgroups cluster together and share their reactions. Inevitably, references to the deceased are made, recollections emerge, and in the absence of external restraints humorous stories are told with the dead man or woman as hero or heroine. The ensuing laughter is often misconstrued as disrespect when in fact it represents the profoundest tribute. The gamut of emotions elicited conveys the essential loss through the shared relation and the recalled pleasures of the previous encounters.

Music has always added to the mood generated by the memorial service. Traditionally, dirges have served in the past, but may appear too stereotyped by today's standards. Innovations such as guitar-accompanied masses or rock group musicians may be used in good taste if the deceased or survivors are decisive in their preferences. The very uniqueness of these options may contribute more eloquently to the memory of the unique person than conventional music. Similar comments can be made about dress, decorations, time of day, or whatever dimensions of the service emerge for consideration. The old stereotypes are no longer held so rigidly and it is seemly to examine any alternative that appears to meet the unique needs of the relationship disrupted by death.

Documenting Preferences

Each person seeking an appropriate death will need practice and derive growth from discussing his or her ideas

about last things with whoever is available. Such conversations will test and sharpen whatever thoughts the individual
may have as well as conveying his or her wishes more fully to
the people who care the most. They, in turn, will derive a
license to act upon these wishes when the need for decision-
making occurs. Ideally, these intentions should be communi-
cated to the professionals who provide the services. Relatives
and close friends provide the most effective assurance that
those who provide last services will get the message and
accommodate the unique preferences. Still some formal documents are always helpful. A formal will is the prototype. The
Living Will is illustrative. This simple form was developed by
the Euthanasia Foundation to convey a person's wish for a
dignified death in contrast to the prolonged dying that current medical practices permit. The individual signifies his
approval of the statement. In practice, The Living Will is not
legally binding on any party, but signifies only a preference
for the reduction or avoidance of excessive medical intervention that only extends the dying process without really
offering any meaningful continuation. Copies are available
from the Euthanasia Education Fund. See the Service Organizations section in the back of this book.

   There are other aspects of the dying process, preferences
which require some kind of documentation in order for survivors to act. A perusal of the list of last things shows the
array of choices possible beforehand and the large range of
options implied. There are few legally binding forms available
except for business contracts with professionals who provide
them. Simply discussing the items with potential survivors is
a step in the right direction since they will at least have an
inkling of what was preferred. Systematically consolidating
these last wishes in an informal list provides the most precise
and reliable means for communication. Most of the time, no
one will question a survivor making last arrangements and
especially if it is known that these did indeed express the
taste of the deceased.

   However, some choices, such as choosing to die at hime,
are more controversial and leave the next of kin vulnerable to

charges of neglect or facilitating an act of suicide. Since there would indeed be some element of shorter dying at home than in a hospital, survivors would be on the defensive. By specifying this preference in a legally valid document jointly prepared with the family physician, preferably before a fatal disease is diagnosed, the moral certitude of those who must implement this last thing is reinforced. Reconfirming this preference periodically helps strengthen the documentation.

In making deliberate decisions concerning death, the candidate expresses his prior habits and ways of living. The whole process becomes a rehearsal for an appropriate cessation; one in which his personal readiness is matched by an external timeliness.

9

Readiness to Die

*I*ncreasing technology has permitted contemporary medicine to postpone the moment of biological death for days
and weeks at a time. In some instances, medical skill can even
reverse apparent termination. The resulting options have
heightened long-standing ethical controversies by creating
frequent examples of people denied a dignified death. Instead,
the patient is given an automatic extension of life that has
been aptly called the prolongation of dying. Effort to resolve
the dilemma is called euthanasia if imposed by others, or suicide, if sought by the victim. Strangely absent from the debate
is the option in which everyone cooperates in helping the victim achieve an appropriate death. Avery Weissman, a research
psychiatrist at the Massachusetts General Hospital, Boston,
has described this as one which the person might choose for
himself, if he had that option. The solution suggested here is
to provide more adequately for a choice and to respect the
patient's preference when expressed.

The current controversies start with the default of individuals in preparing for their inevitable deaths. By failing to
consider last things or to contemplate the larger issues in
human existence, the patient approaches his or her cessation
with minimal preparation or preferences. It is only by making
advance decisions concerning the last things and long-range
preparations that a person can develop a sense of when he or
she is ready to die. Intervention in the care of the dying should
match the patient's readiness to cease.

Human awareness as experienced is continuous, despite certain kinds of interruption, of which the final one has been called death. The acceptance of continuation is considered proper, typical, and at least normal. Any interest in cessation is viewed with suspicion even if expressed by philosophers. When verbalized by patients, concern about death provokes alarm and is often construed as the wish to die. The latter occurs most frequently as preoccupations with and threats of suicide. Earlier, a distinction was made between the wish to die, the act of self-injury, and the mortal outcome. These three aspects of suicide permit greater precision in coping with the clinical problems associated with the prevention of unpredicted death. The wish is a necessary but insufficient condition in motivating self-injury actions and those actions do not always end in termination. The wish to die is contrasted with the readiness to cease, which is construed as neutral. Motivationally speaking, it lies between the more usual efforts to continue and the relatively infrequent wishes to die. While the wish to die can come to anyone, it rarely leads to self-injury. The readiness to cease also comes to everyone, but is manifested by an acceptance of final encounters.

The position here is that readiness to die is appropriate under specific conditions. The act of self-injury is never appropriate. Any effort to hasten death by the individual is an act of self-injury. The conditions under which readiness to cease is timely are difficult to specify for reliable observation.

Readiness describes a reduced motivation, recent in origin and long-lasting. Aside from verbalizations, or demeanor, this changed motivation manifests itself as a failure to seek additional continuation, or the converse, to avoid cessation in the face of imminent threat. The passing whim can be separated from a more enduring mood by taking systematic samples of the subject's orientation over periods of weeks and months. In addition, temporary circumstances and phases, such as illness, medication, or the start of involution, should qualify any conclusions. Beyond the necessity for adequate sampling is the need to ask for and elicit relevant data from patients.

The clinical task of recognizing the readiness to cease and

differentiating it from the wish to die is made unnecessarily difficult by the absence of clinical criteria and the current inaccessibility of data. A start has been made by investigators in suggesting behavior for recognizing readiness to cease, and more can be expected in the future. The wish to die is more difficult because of taboos that exist even among professionals. These block efforts to elicit relevant information, and to repeat these inquiries on a daily or hourly basis, if necessary.

There is no professional context in which a serious observer can ask the objectively neutral question, "Are you thinking about death?" One can now ask about the number and kinds of orgasms, bowel movements, size of genitalia, and even take color movies of copulating couples. However, inquiry concerning death, dying, and self-injury is still forbidden or at least subject to serious misinterpretation. This makes for difficulty in eliciting relevant answers upon which to base clinical judgment. Despite the formidable obstacles, effective inquiry and consequent preparation of the subject are not only possible but deeply appreciated after the license to explore is granted.

Reference to license is meant to convey, in addition to the usual rapport, a special permissiveness which in effect is a promise not to condemn the individual for acknowledging forbidden thoughts. Violations of the conventional taboos concerning death expose a patient to risks of enforced supervision, preventive hospitalization, unwanted medications, and more significantly, stigmatization in a psychiatric setting. Even in the professional context, confusions and impairments occur in differentiation of the readiness to cease from the wish for death. While the clinician is in a better position to plan for either state of mind, once he has elicited the appropriate information, controversy is usually provided by these ideas and typically in terms of euthanasia or suicide. Additional qualification may help reduce some of the confusion.

The phenomenon of clinical suicide, so familiar to mental health professionals, excludes heroic examples such as that of Socrates, martyrs, or war heroes. These are more accurately described as sacrifices for a cause which is rationally advanced by the self-injuries sustained. These subjects are typically superior in explicit ways. Victims of clinical suicide betray evidence of irrationality, ambivalence, compulsive narrowing of alternatives, "cries for help," and over-determination for self-injury methods used. The distinction between heroic and clinical eliminates much of the controversy around the "right-to-commit" argument, since the usual victim appears to lack informed consent in seeking premature death.

A possible prophylaxis occurs when a clinical motive gets converted to a heroic suicide. Indeed, it has been suggested that inviting a would-be clinical suicide to donate an organ for transplant represents a form of suicide prevention. The individual must delay action, and restrict self-injury to a specific organ. Through this process, he or she develops informed consent and thereby converts a clinical impulse to a sacrificial act. All of these considerations permit the re-emergence of efforts to continue, or at least elevate an irrational impulse to one of heroic proportions.

Another major controversy is euthanasia, which in civilized societies usually centers on their non-productive members. The most well-known illustration in recent times occurred in Nazi Germany with the "mercy" killing of many groups, such as the elderly, the crippled, the mentally retarded, or the mentally ill. This same rationale also "justified" the elimination of unpopular groups. Such abuse of "mercy" killings confirmed the apprehension of many people about the dangers of accepting the principle of euthanasia.

As long as society can afford to support its less fortunate members, there is really no necessity to make this cruel decision. Today, the more relevant situation is euthanasia of individuals who request surcease from terminal illness. In its strongest form, the patient begs to be allowed to die with some dignity, rather than to continue with prolonged dying. Posed in this way, arguments always ensue.

The resolution suggested here is that the controversy is not soluble, but that the victim is. There would be no arguments if there were no dying patients. The existence of a person implicitly asking others to kill him creates the moral conflict. The failure is that of the individual; not for being ill, or for dying, but for failing to consider the alternatives before he or she encounters a terminal illness. It is the patient's responsibility to arrive at a sense of when life is over in general, and when he or she in particular is ready for a timely death. An individual will require a great deal of help in doing this—time, emotional support, education, and consultation. However, no one can decide for him. If he defaults, the choice will be preempted by the professionals, who will decide on the basis of their own values. These are often whimsical, cynical, superficial, or irrelevant to the victim's tastes. Currently, the patient cannot legally ask for euthanasia, any more than those in attendance can officially grant this request. However, in practice, all physicians acknowledge that sooner or later they will permit a terminal patient to die. In this current mode, there are two aspects that aggravate a difficult situation. One is the general avoidance of and reluctance to face the frankly terminal patient. There is ample evidence that physicians quickly refer patients with fatal diseases to specialized settings that develop cultures described as "passing on." It is clear the staff spends less time with the terminally ill, sees them less often, and even responds more slowly to their calls for service. In short, hospital care is not geared to the needs of the dying patient but rather to the convenience of staff. At best, they are oriented towards delaying death, rather than to helping people die.

Because hospital culture is phobic about death, the moment of cessation is left to chance, convenience, and the values of attending staff, rather than to the wishes of the patient and his next of kin. While informal practice accommodates to the necessity of death, the net effects are to block options that might make dying more appropriate for the patient.

Today, if any victim expresses an overt readiness to cease, or rejects some medical intervention, the staff will immediately raise the question of the patient's competence and the physician's legal right to override. Prominent would be the assertion that the victim was expressing a wish to die and was therefore attempting to commit suicide. On the other side, any physician who accepted the patient's preference would immediately be liable to the counter charge that he is condoning clinical suicide or practicing euthanasia. In either conclusion, malpractice issues would be raised.

Clinical staff in fatal illness is not prepared to hear, nor respond to, patients who deviate from the conventional desire to continue. For the majority of patients today, this is probably a correct response. For an increasing number, however, this position is demeaning. While medical authorities must always opt for continued life where there exists the slightest hope, the present practice does not permit a graceful acceptance of dying. Because of this absence of choice, the modern hospital setting is a poor place to die. A candidate for appropriate death is better advised to stay at home.

The right to injure oneself and mercy killing represent effective limits to the concept of readiness to cease, which in itself implies acceptance of present continuation no matter how grim, even if it includes the prospect of cessation. Any act to facilitate death or postpone its arrival is a departure from the neutrality implied by the concept of readiness.

Avery Weissman and his colleagues at Massachusetts General Hospital have suggested that a timely death can be recognized by 1) reduction of conflicts between living on, or ceasing; 2) compatibility with ideals held; 3) continuity of significant relations; and, 4) consummation of prevailing wishes. Elizabeth Kubler-Ross, a physician who has written *Death and Dying*, describes the plight of the terminally ill and the readiness to cease, as the patient's *acceptance* of the readiness to cease. Lao Tzu, the Chinese founder of Taoism, has described true old age as the absence of regret with the foreknowledge that death is approaching. Here, readiness to cease means an acceptance of the next encounter, even when this includes a very high likelihood that it may well be the last.

Until a shift in current practices occurs with respect to hospital management of the dying, the burden will continue to fall on the victim. To assist the candidate for an appropriate death, the remainder of this chapter will focus on some of the specific activities that represent an optimal preparation for the prospect of termination. The last things suggested in the previous chapter represent preliminary choices of the specifics. Informed consent and decisions on these matters will facilitate sensitivity and provide the capacity to move on to the relatively more threatening areas.

Preparation for One's Own Death

1. Participation in the dying of others
2. Examination of the cost-benefit ratio in life-extension efforts
3. Contemplation of the preferred terminal illness
4. Use of intoxicants or substances to facilitate dying
5. Orientation toward death and an after-life
6. Conditions under which death is preferable
7. Readiness to cease
8. Continuity of last encounters

All fatal diseases typically carry a slow onset, with extended periods of deterioration, when compared to violent modes of death. Even heart disease tends to progress over months and years. During this period, the victim and his potential survivors must exist with an awareness that death is imminent. Preparation for this highly probable aspect of dying can best be facilitated by the recognition of cessation within some limited time perspective. For example, a forty-year-old male has a statistical life expectancy of another thirty-one years according to 1968 data. While this may seem long enough to carry on as usual, half of those males alive at age forty will be dead by age seventy-one. Anything beyond that age is fortunate; anything before is unfortunate. Knowing that 50 percent of all men alive today will die before age seventy-one should make one plan the remaining years differently. Most people carry on as usual. They do not act as if life were finite. Acceptance of a limited time frame requires planning of future activities as though life indeed would cease. Take that trip sooner, make amends now, visit your old friends before it's too late. Start acting on those New Year's resolutions or have the honesty to stop making them. Once the inevitability of death is fully recognized, the consequent sense of urgency helps to separate sincere goals from super-ficial or stereotyped expectations. For the readers who would like a quick estimate of years remaining, the enclosed table may be helpful.

Table IV   Remaining Years of Life by Sex

Age	Males	Females
50 years	23 years	28 years
60	16	20
70	10	13
80	6	7
85+	5	5

It should be stressed that the "years remaining" are merely averages, and half of the people in each age group die before the indicated number of years have elapsed. For planning pur-poses, a man of fifty should schedule his activities to occur *before* the next twenty years. Factors such as health and money may force action even earlier. Even if no change is elected, the decision to continue as is becomes more valid after an exam-ination provoked by limited time.

The candidate for a graceful death will need to consider his own preferences in the light of past and continuing encoun-ters with others in the areas to be considered next.

Participation in the Dying of Others

For the individual who is searching, visits to places where death is happening are the best starting experiences. Funerals occur in every city, and visitors would probably be welcome even if they were noticed. Most people are reluctant to attend any funerals let alone those of strangers. The absence of an excuse blocks the uninvolved from gaining experience before the loss of their own intimates. Older people usually get more opportunities by simply surviving relatives and friends, but also from growing up in an era when funerals were viewed

as a more positive human effort. Americans below fifty tend
to avoid or not use the funeral experience in any planned
effort to prepare for their own cessation. Any survivor can
start by attending three funerals selected randomly or by their
availability. Notice the different funeral procedures. Do these
seem to make the participants feel better? Do they permit
honest grief or do the mourners need to pretend respect for
the dead? If any detail appears offensive consider what the
alternative choices might be. Try to imagine some unique
procedures such as a guitar mass, colorful decorations, or
flowers displayed for aromas and aesthetic patterns.

Funeral directors welcome interest and take professional
pride in the services they render. A frank conversation with
any one available in the community might be sufficient to
open up whole new perspectives. There is nothing fixed about
modern funerals. It is within every person's competence to
name the details he or she thinks are optimal, including the
rituals and eulogies. The failure to specify assures that the professionals of death will fill the vacuum with the most stereotyped options.

These funeral visits are by no means an expression of
morbid curiosity. They appear strange only because of current avoidance and taboos about death. A visitor relationship
to the participants has the advantage of emotional distance
that can facilitate better observation of the whole funeral
process. A visitor who is not under duress due to grief is soon
capable of identifying the needs and deficiencies of the modern
funeral.

Next, spend some time with the bereaved. The worst that
can happen is that one or both of you will cry. If ever anybody
has the right to weep, it is people who have suffered a loss
and those who come to sympathize. Even casual visitors can
weep sincerely, even though the loss is not so personal. The
recently bereaved tend to be isolated by the avoidance of death
and the uncertainty provoked by grief or visible emotion. The
mourners lack opportunities to share a common feeling of
loss or pain and the associated emotional behavior. A visitor

willing to listen or talk about death and the recent loss would be welcome once the social inhibitions were overcome.

The simplest and most direct approaches are to be recommended. Any time is better than no visitation at all. Given the current taboos, it is better to wait until after the funeral or the reception that follows it. Start with an acquaintance whom you can call or visit within the first month of a death. The topic of loss is natural and should be allowed to come up in any way that seems reasonable to the participants. Most of the distress in this period comes from the effort to avoid the subject, rather than the relatively straightforward acceptance of loss.

Once the conversation is started, the subject of the deceased is inherently cathartic and offers a form of comfort to the recently bereaved, precisely because it's so rare. Discuss any aspect that occurs, even if it would not ordinarily be a polite topic. Politeness is the scourge of frank emotions in the context of grief. Continue these visits as often as they serve their purpose in comforting. These visits can have no harm by themselves. Nor do these conversations encourage unnecessary or prolonged grieving, but rather they shorten the period of grief by permitting the bereaved the self-expression needed in order to carry on.

Next, attempt a similar approach to situations where patients are known to be dying. A nursing home or extended-care facility is a good starting place because the moment of death is several weeks or months away. The staff welcomes visits, especially by volunteers seeking to provide a service for the patients. There is always a shortage of company for those hospitalized in a chronic service. Human interest is the shortest commodity and the one with most beneficial impact.

Several visits will orient the concerned student with the peculiar distress experienced by the dying. It is not that life is over. or that pain hurts, but rather the literal damage to their self-respect as worthwhile humans. Suddenly, they are alone, familiar activities prevented, old social roles no longer possible. A respected citizen is now fed, washed, toileted by an aide who barely knows his name, was not his social equal, and patronizes him even while ignoring his identity. Add to this the disorienting effect of a new environment at an age when adaptation is more difficult and the plight of the victim is clearer. After a few weeks of this regime, secondary effects appear in the form of mental symptoms such as confusion, wandering, suspicion, marked loss of memory, childish babbling including early recollections, and other symptoms of mental illness. All of these are made worse by the tendency to isolate the patient, which induces a lack of stimulation and creates a sensory deprivation.

A visit to patients in this state is automatically a constructive force, no matter how short a time or how little one can do. The staff recognizes this and welcomes visitations. However, human encounters always create more work so that some resistance does manifest itself even though it is irrational. Such visits will contribute to the comfort of the dying person, even as it helps him to regain some dignity. The quality of such last encounters with less intimate relations will reward, even as it sensitizes the visitor to the hazards of dying and the survival gaps created by current practices.

Other kinds of visitation are also appropriate. Conversations with staff of emergency hospitals, ambulance services, or police rescue units may also be helpful. Questions about their perceptions of sudden death and the last moments of victims are informative. The bravado of the young with respect to risk-taking is not sustained once an injury or threat of death occurs. The last moments of those facing death are not the heroic incidents portrayed in the mass media. While the technical care is typically excellent, the attitudes are often callous. The last moments of victims are not eased by concern for dignity even when conscious, or when the medical emergency permits it.

Jacques Choron, the philosopher-writer on the subject of death, told the story of his first heart attack. While waiting for the ambulance at 2:00 a.m., he dressed himself with suit, shirt, tie, and flower in his lapel, as was his custom. The ambulance men rushed by him when he opened the door, searching for the "victim." They were unable to accept his manner and appearance since he didn't fit their stereotype of a dying man. Someone other than Jacques Choron would have been made to feel worse by this self-fulfilling prophecy of how a heart-attack victim should look.

Frank conversations with the hospital staff about visitation may be harder to arrange. It helps to have a pre-existing relation with someone who works there. However engineered, the visitor should look for the attitudes about death, and accounts of how victims reacted to the sudden realization that they might be dying. Other possibilities are morticians, cemetery personnel, and coroners' offices. These people work daily in a context where death occurs regularly. What is their attitude to work? Probably like everyone else's. Unthinking! However, like all people who must cope with the facts of death, there will be a curious denial that their own services might ever be appropriate for themselves.

Questions of this sort may be too offensive. However, their personal preferences with respect to the kinds of services they offer may be revealing. How would they want to be treated? What kinds of procedures or equipment are optimal for the victim if it is themselves or their own families?

Visitations and participation in the dying of others will provide the survivor with new experiences that can desensitize the American phobia of death. At the same time, the orientation increases awareness of choices. The more impact each new visit has, the greater the necessity for a debriefing, to talk about the topic. Like any field visit in a class, the students need to discuss their observations and reactions with peers. In the context of dying, the visitor needs to arrange for associates who will either share with him or discuss his observations afterwards. Friends, relatives, or fellow students are the usual array of people to consider. The minister or other family-oriented professional may be another alternative.

Cost-Benefit Ratio of Life-Extension Efforts

Medical intervention can extend the length of life, but not its quality. Organ transplants, radical surgery, and the postponement of death usually reduce the quality of subsequent continuation. One of the cruelest decisions a survivor encounters is the request to give permission for this or that medical intervention. Ostensibly, the request assumes that the patient's life will be extended. The quality of this additional life is usually not discussed. In this context, the survivor has no effective choice. One must opt for life no matter what the odds. Later he may realize that his decision merely prolonged the dying process rather than extended the meaningful life of his loved one. In addition to grief, he is left with the guilt for useless and expensive suffering. It is only in hindsight that survivors begin to realize that the choices were less clear and alternative choices might have been more worthwhile.

Since no one can predict with certainty the actual end of a terminal illness, professionals tend to present the most optimistic picture they can. It falls upon the patient or his survivor to assert a value—this intervention is worth the effort or it is not. The major obstacle is informed consent. Knowledge about the medical consequences of any illness, or procedure to arrest it, is rather difficult to communicate. However, with enough effort by physicians, and attention by survivors, some comprehension is usually possible. At that point, the choice is between doing nothing or doing something ineffectual. Both extremes are laden with values. In American tradition, doing *anything* is better than nothing. Increasingly in the context of dying, doing nothing has value over doing something ineffectual with respect to prolonging the dying process.

There is a need to evaluate the human cost for any life-prolonging effort. The delay of termination is not a pure blessing. Some kinds of continuation are worse than death; even subjectively viewed by the victim. For an individual to prefer death in such extremities leaves him vulnerable to a charge of suicidal intent. As suggested earlier, there is a difference between the readiness to cease and the wish to die. The cost-benefit relation of intervention must be examined in the light of the patient's degree of readiness to cease and the quality of life expected after intervention.

Financial costs are usually mentioned but are rarely the

dominant issue in making these decisions. Insurance, medicare, and public generosity usually assist with the actual costs. The larger problem is the license to assert a preference for anything less than perpetual prolongation of biological life. The usual rebuttal by medical authorities is that they do indeed allow patients to die; however, this decision is seriously lacking in several respects. First, it is not public, nor subject to scrutiny by the consumer. Second, it is always belated, occurring far too late to give the victim surcease, let alone a dignified dying. Third, the current practice tends to increase the costs to survivors. Fourth, the decision to allow the terminal patient to die tends to occur whimsically with respect to medical practice or standards of care. In such arbitrary choices, there exists the opportunity for, and appearance of financial gain. Whether or not this is documented is less important than the suspicion it feeds.

An effective alternative is to create the choice of non-intervention where the patient is kept comfortable and treatment is restricted to an optimal cost-benefit ratio. In proposing this option, survivors need to be aware of relevant standards for readiness to cease and daily acts expressing a clinical readiness to die. These areas will be discussed later. Knowledgeability in these areas permits a survivor to recognize the personal preferences of the patient with respect to additional medical interventions after a prolonged downhill course with a fatal disease. Currently, the patient's wishes tend to be ignored because of the apparent absence of choice. Simply conceiving of the alternative invites the survivors to pay attention to the patient's degree of readiness for cessation. Knowing and recognizing these helps the survivor in developing his informed consent with respect to the value of any medical procedure.

If communication is blocked by inhibition, or mental impairments, the patient's preferences are difficult to elicit. In addition, even under the best circumstances, residual doubts always remain in the minds of survivors. Given the current dire consequences of a default, it is better to guess at what the patient wishes than to let the decision be made by professionals. Surgery is usually presented as an extension of existence on the basis of probabilities for additional survival. Most patients with a given ailment live longer with surgery than without. However, the quality of this longer life is never discussed in sufficient depth for either the patient or his survivor. This aspect should be weighed before electing radical procedures.

In addition to a medical briefing, patients should meet others who have survived that specific procedure. For example, candidates for colostomies should meet with those who have adapted to the radical changes imposed by this procedure. The sheer lack of orientation facilitates ignorance, regret, and predisposes to more negativism in adapting to changes in qualities of the altered existence. The same problems of choice exist in a variety of other surgical interventions for fatal disease. Mastectomies for women or castration for men are examples where over- or under-valuation of their respective sexual organs introduces irrational motivations impairing judgment and consequent choice. The loss of these organs by surgery will have unanticipated effects on the will to live. Given reduced vitality in the first place, these surgical losses may aggravate psychological states which in turn impair the quality of life yielded to the patient. In hindsight, survivors can question the net value of this intervention, even though their objection would be considered irrational.

Either the patient himself, or his potential survivor, must choose. This procedure is worth the quality of life to be extended or that one is not. The choice is between the disease process itself or the sequelae of a medical intervention, aggravated often by the victim's reaction to the treatment. The opportunity to reject radical treatment counteracts the more desperate efforts to prolong life at any cost when the patient himself is ready to cease. The survivors need to question treatment alternatives as presented. Is surgery an effective answer in the light of cost-benefit considerations? It is not always the life or death choice. It is more often death this way, or that way. Is a nursing home placement optimal? It may provide better physical care, but all new environments are disorienting in the feeble and intellectually damaged.

All choices in the context of dying are difficult because

the generalized expectation is that death simply must be post-poned. Wise choices require the participants to recognize that death is not the worst alternative, either for themselves or their loved ones. Coming to a full acceptance of this premise is not easy and is, in many ways, the burden of this book. An additional hazard to decision-making is the inevitable neces-sity to assert a value, a preference for this or that, and doing so on the basis of doubtful knowledge. The reference here is to the impossibility of ever fully knowing what a victim may prefer, and yet needing to make some sort of guess as to what is best. An alternative resource suggested here is to use con-structively the well-known psychological defense of pro-jection. Instead of ascribing to others certain unacceptable feelings in oneself, the survivor is urged to assert for the patient the wish he has himself. In a context of impossible choice, with uncertain knowledge of wishes, it is better to project know-ingly, than to default to others. The advantage of using pro-jection deliberately comes from the opportunities to build in safeguards. The first is informed consent. The second is con-sensus with other survivors. While agreement may not always be attainable, the process of trying can be informative and reassuring, especially in assessing the psychological cost-benefits.

Preferred Terminal Illness

Given a natural mode of death, each person needs to become familiar with the annual lists of death rates attributed to the various fatal diseases. Each individual has a multiple choice, complete with actuarial probabilities and symptom descriptions. Heart, cancer, and stroke account for approx-imately 67 percent of adult deaths annually, and in that order of frequency. While the prospect may appear morbid, any individual can relate such rates of occurrence to heredity and health history. One can guess what is most likely as a final illness. He or she can find common language descrip-tions in any library. Medical dictionaries are usually sufficient. Armed with this information, any survivor can select the fatal disease whose symptoms and progression he finds the least offensive, or the most acceptable. Within the range of alternatives, the person can choose one that expresses the sense of a seemly way to die. It is not necessary that the choice be the correct one. Nor is it necessary to prevent the occurrence of such an illness. The major reason for stating a preference of illness is the value of preparation. There is a wisdom of the body such that organs exert an influence and are themselves influenced by mental states. Body compliance with stated preferences may occur beyond chance levels of expectation. The individual is more likely to die the way he or she prefers, especially if he thinks about the disease process and its effects upon lifestyle.

The preferred terminal illness requires a process of choice that helps a survivor achieve an appropriate death. By naming, studying, and accepting symptoms of a certain disease, the individual works for a timely end. What is more important though, is that he is able to recognize and ready himself in a positive way. He can start by making a simple choice of illnesses. First he must familiarize himself with the range of fatal illnesses to which he is most vulnerable. Within the possibilities likely to occur he should identify an optimal process of dying; one that will be compatible with his preferences. Knowing what to expect, even if it's bad, helps to allay doubt. Uncertainty tends to feed the more morbid anticipations. Specifying the most probable disease is prophylactic in several ways. First, it facilitates early identification of symptoms, and permits the start of treatment earlier than might otherwise happen. In some cases, it is an effective antidote to the total denial of all symptoms until end stages are reached. Far too many cancer victims delay asking for medical evaluations in the early stages of their illness. Second, but more important in this context, the survivor receives the advantage of preparing for his or her own end by simply stating a preference. Having done so, a person will experience a compulsion to know more about this specific disease, its symptoms, treatment, and progression. In effect, that person will prepare himself to be a colleague of his own physician. While doctors tend to make bad patients, that can be attributed to their failure to shift roles from healer to needer-of-healing. The patient who is well-informed about any one illness is still in the role of one seeking help. However, he or she now has developed more informed consent. That person is more capable of acting as a partner in his own treatment. In short, every illness requires a division of labor in the treatment team. It is the patient's job to seek and accept help in the most knowledgeable manner possible.

The usual objections to this area of preparation are that the whole process is hypochondriacal, and how can anyone, especially a layman, predict his own fatal illness? While it is a clinical observation that anxious people protect themselves with somatic preoccupation, the opposite does not follow. It is very possible for anyone to study illnesses without becoming a hypochondriac. The various handbooks for home care and the newspaper columns giving medical advice to readers document the general safety of self-education in the medical sphere. The second objection ignores the suggestion in the first place. Trying to choose the fatal disease preferred by a survivor is not a prediction. It is merely the statement of a preference within the most probable range of illnesses. Ten years later, the probabilities may shift, or the individual could change his mind. There is always the chance he may die accidentally in an airplane crash, or be shot by his wife. Both are unlikely. More possible is the survivor's change of heart where the disease preferred at forty may be replaced by another at fifty. If another disease should strike, there is always some transfer of training so that the unexpected one is less strange, and the victim more able to retrain himself. One of the by-products of this extended preparation is the sense of destiny in coping with death. One can derive the feeling of being in some way a shaper rather than a victim of disease.

Use of Intoxicants, Analgesics, and Stimulants

Human existence almost always includes occasional intoxications. Religious ecstasy, sexual encounters, novelty, and public acclaim are non-chemical sources of a purely psychological euphoria. Alcohol and drugs are more familiar means and ones that require less effort to achieve intoxication. The dying process requires opportunities for the same sorts of release. Indeed, imminent death may create more deprivations that demand greater degrees or frequencies of release through intoxication. The dominant criterion is the prior source of relaxation *before* illness is diagnosed. The prospect of an extended dying process should not eliminate the accustomed kinds of pleasure. Permitting a dying patient to drink, or continue his previous ways of seeking release, is not a license for one long drunk or drug-abuse orgy, but rather human frailty towards the end of personal existence.

Currently, the use of pain-killers is not questioned even though they yield addictions of various degrees. Wine, beer, or hard liquors are used surreptitiously by the dying. More typically, benign authorities allow or ignore the presence of alcoholic beverages. Psychedelics, especially marijuana, are apparently unknown and would present legal problems if detected. However, medical prescription of Tetra-hydrocarbonal (THC) or Lysergic Acid Diethylamide (LSD) in sufficiently small doses would have some value in achieving a positive orientation to the dying process. These chemicals can also mellow reactive depressions if supervised carefully. THC, the active ingredient in marijuana, can be useful in reversing bad feelings about death because it does induce a pleasant physical state. LSD is far more powerful, but in smaller dosages also yields intoxicating and pleasurable experiences comparable to three or four ounces of alcohol. Minimal amounts of LSD avoid the more extreme reactions reported in the popular press. Neither LSD nor THC clouds awareness or memory afterwards, and both can contribute to a hedonistic sense of well-being despite the actual physical state of the patient with fatal disease.

In suggesting the use of chemicals to facilitate psychological acceptance of dying, the reader is invited to consider these as a resource in coping with what is an inevitable existential crisis for everybody. Modern pharmacology makes available new and powerful chemicals, uses for which have not been fully explored. LSD is the prime example of a chemical agent that may well rank as the psycho-pharmacological breakthrough of the twentieth century, but not until some human predicament is defined as appropriate for its use.

Orientation Toward Death and After-Life

The awareness of self—called identity, mind, soul, and personality—goes through some kind of change at the moment of termination. Does it cease totally? Continue in the form of immortality? Or does it return in some kind of reincarnation? Does continuation depend upon the preservation of the body such as mummification, embalming, or as implied in notions of resurrection on judgment day? Is it possible to revive a clinically dead person after freezing, storage, and defrosting? These ideas illustrate the kind of options people entertain about their own continuation after death. Currently, these represent assertions that are not testable in any scientific sense. However, each person can do and does his own testing up to the point of death. Every person asserts some belief about his own existence which can never be refuted by others. With continuing experiences, thought, and observation the individual can always change his or her ideas. Between these two extremes, a person asserts some notions about life after death, which are relatively permanent, and which dominate existence before death.

The belief in some form of continuation permits an individual to pursue his existence as if he will never die. This illusion appears to be universal and benign. However, the danger is that of default on daily choices. Recognizing that personal existence is finite and that at death a radical change occurs forces the individual to make each living day count. Whether termination is the end of self or merely a transition is secondary. Death marks a change in daily existence with everything beyond it unknown. It behooves prudent survivors to use that time wisely by their own standards, rather than assuming it will go on forever.

Once personal mortality is accepted, the sense of limited time forces the individual to examine present choices in the light of a predictable end, when he or she will be the judge. When death is imminent, candidates for an appropriate end will be comforted by the knowledge that they chose wisely, did the best they could with the limitations, and were satisfied with their achievements.

Sudden death is always easier, but occurs rarely in the context of natural modes of dying. No one can avoid some dying process, and typically everyone brings their own pre-conceptions to the situation. In these expectations, personal orientations to death and what follows will dominate their last preferences.

The prevailing orientation toward cessation, especially among those under thirty, and for those with scientific train-ing, is dominated by existentialist philosophy. People who feel that cessation is the end of personal experience often regard existence as absurd because death comes equally to the good and the bad. The only values that make sense are those which enhance the living process, and hence the popularity of hedon-ism. However, the self-limiting process in pleasure-seeking forces a search for a more self-transcendent meaning. The one suggested here is the achievement of an appropriate death, where daily life is construed as a rehearsal for the kind of dying most likely to occur. This equally untestable premise has the advantage of giving positive meaning to total life, while shaping daily existence according to the kind of values consistent with a good death.

Conditions When Death is Preferable

Aside from medical criteria or social circumstance, every individual can assert a theoretical condition under which the person would prefer to stop living. It is not a wish to die, nor in any way a suicidal impulse. It is merely a statement of pref-erence. Asking individuals to specify a situation when death is preferable to life is an explicit preparation for readiness to cease. Answers to this question provide criteria that are unique and which become descriptions of forces for readiness to stop living. Typically, these are imaginative statements which are future-oriented. They are data only in the sense that they express a feeling. By eliciting these before any such eventuality, and for a sufficient number of occasions, the observer can externalize an approximate standard. As perception of existence begins to converge on this pre-specified criterion, the individual will experience a reduced desire to continue existence. Whether this changed motivation is called the readiness to cease or a wish to die depends on the manifest behavior and its direction of alteration. A neutral acceptance of final events is readiness, while an affirmation of termination as a goal is the wish.

The usual answers offered to this question tend to include loss of relatives, most typically a spouse or lover. They and others like children, parents, friends, or partners are individuals whose sudden departure is felt most through the disruption of mutual daily acts. The losses attributable to money, failure, and even health are not as significant as most people assume or the press suggests. Time permits most people the chance to absorb many of these, everything else being equal.

The loss of physical capacity or appearance is distressing primarily when these qualities existed in a large measure within a person or were used extensively. An athlete will be more distressed by amputation while an intellectual will be equally upset by failing eyesight, memory deficit, or the inability to concentrate. Certain occupational groups are disturbed by reduction of roles or activities associated with their profession. Psychologists are disturbed most by the thought of brain damage, physicians by ill health, especially fatal disease. The activities pursued longest that required the most effort become sentimentalized, and are most upsetting when lost or disrupted.

Sooner or later, an individual will reach a condition in which he or she is ready to accept cessation. Death will not follow immediately nor automatically with this occurrence. However, termination is less likely to be resisted. Whether

death is due to accident, suicide, or somatic compliance is
not the issue. Simply put, when a person loses the ability
he held as a criterion for continued life, he will be more ready
to cease, and death will be more likely to occur shortly
thereafter.

Asking this question about conditions under which death
is preferable helps to develop informed consent with respect
to employing special interventions for the prolongation of
existence. In lesser degrees, it helps survivors plan for the
indefinite period of slow dying that occurs so frequently
today. Explicit answers help alert the patient and his significant other relations to the positive choices remaining in the
search for an appropriate end.

Behavior Changes and Readiness to Cease

If asked properly, with sufficient attention to rapport
and prior removal of taboos, any person can indicate a readiness to cease. More often than not, survivors are not able to
achieve this frank a communication, and the patient's motivations remain obscure. It then becomes necessary to observe
demeanor and activities to form an opinion about the existing
mental state. Items illustrative of readiness to cease would
be examples of giving up, waiting, passivity, disposing of
valued objects, especially in the absence of debilitating illness,
or acute trauma.

The presence of anger or other negative feelings is
incompatible with readiness, unless complaints and sarcasm
were a typical characteristic before the illness. Strong feelings, whether manifested as hostility or depression, bespeak
goal-seeking behavior and suggest the wish to die rather
than a neutral acceptance of the end.

The importance of this area has mostly to do with the
survivors' ability to recognize when another is ready to cease,
wishes to die, or is merely in between acute illnesses. It assumes
there has been an insufficient opportunity to establish open
communication about death. The survivor who must choose
some form of action will need to know what the patient pre-

fers, but will lack information. By observing current behavior, relating it to past, and allowing for effects of the illness, some opinion can be formed with respect to the remaining wish to live. The general directions of change and alternatives are suggested here.

Continuity of Last Encounters

The last encounters are the same as all the others in being moments of truth, in the here and now, and between two people as they do what they must in order to be what they are. Last encounters differ from others in that one or both parties recognize there may be no more after this. Knowing the imminence of death tends to disrupt the relationship, alters expectations, and makes the last encounters truly different.

In daily life, the usual mutual expectations are ordinarily felt, accepted and modified without deliberate thought. The most obvious examples are the shifting roles as a person moves from situation to situation. A parent includes different expectations than a spouse. Both in turn are different from friends or children. The shifts in demeanor are called roles. These imply a package of stereotyped expectations in which proper behavior is recognized for parent, spouse, child or peer in relationships and interaction. Potential survivors and victims have a unique variation of a conventional relationship with subsequent role stereotypes. These become strained and altered in the final events called dying.

In last encounters, every victim has concerns about the meaning of life and history that often prompt heroic aspirations, if not for the formal record, then at least for his personal self-image and its memory in the recollections of survivors. To fulfill this implicit wish, every person assigns meanings to his or her life, and to the kind of death anticipated. This tendency fuels the latent preference for conditions under which the patient would rather cease. In this context, the dying process will contain efforts by the patient to achieve the heroic meanings he has assigned to his prior life. One aspect of this psychological need in the person who is dying, is the explicit intention to give each survivor some significant token of self. Typically, this will be conveyed by an object of sentimental value passed on as an heirloom that ensures the continuing presence of the dying patient. Whatever form this desire may take, the survivors often overlook the need of the dying to serve others. Providing the patient with means and opportunities that help to achieve this personal goal are appropriate behaviors for survivors. By becoming willing recipients of such efforts, roles are often reversed whereby the victim helps the mourners to carry on after his or her death.

Accepting these or other needs facilitates the search for an appropriate death. Emphasizing the continuity of last encounters permits the participants to identify specific needs and pursue effective action. By going along with last wishes that are consistent with prior relations, the survivor helps the patient to die in the way he lived. Opposing these wishes makes dying that much harder.

The danger in last encounters lies in the current social phobia about dying and the absence of a proper role for the person seeking a graceful death. There is an expected role for those who are sick and their visitors. It consists mainly of one who needs care and those who will offer this help. The underlying premise of the usual sick-visitor roles is that complete recovery is expected shortly.

In the field of mental illness, this expectation has been observed to be detrimental to the recovery of patients with psychiatric disorders. Indeed, the major criticism of mental hospitals has been the impairing roles assigned inmates. Self-fulfilling prophesies have been observed when the staff expected the patient to act in a bizarre or schizophrenic manner and actually induced or prolonged the continuation of these unwanted behaviors. Ken Kesey's novel *One Flew Over the Cuckoo's Nest* illustrates vividly the injurious effects of the "proper" patient role in mental hospitals. Role conflicts come most dramatically when the patient role is resisted. The conflict manifests itself when new behaviors are resisted by the family who expect only the old patient role. These obstacles to mental health in the recovering patient are optimally treated in family interviews where role shifts can be facilitated and validated by trained observers.

In the context of dying, the vacuum created by current stereotypes for the dying person or survivor induces an unnecessary rigidity, where the patient is forced to function in the passive, indulged, sick role, whether it's necessary or not. Two fundamental errors make this tactic harmful. The finality of fatal illness prolongs the period of indulgence past a point of need. The prolonged nature of modern dying requires that an individual be allowed to return to some accustomed social functioning. This need gets blocked by the expected role of the patient rather than by the limits of illness or because of necessary medical management. The second error comes from overlooking the personal and unique wishes of the candidate for an appropriate death. He wants to die according to his own notions and in a role he deems consistent with his previous relationships. In order to act on this image, he needs a willing audience that will cooperate and accept different roles. It is only the last-encounter quality that blocks full cooperation of survivors. The preconceptions about it, rather than fatal illness itself, become the obstacle. Resolution requires a family willingness to permit the dying person some preferred role.

Examples of appropriate death in other cultures tend to start and stop with suicide. Hara-kiri by the Japanese was publicized during World War II. Suttee, the widow's death by cremation atop her husband's funeral pyre, is peculiar to India, though now outlawed. Human sacrifice of the entire royal court was customary when an Egyptian pharaoh was entombed. These forms of suicide were seen as transitional to another existence, and part of some larger, public ritual. A more relevant example was the killing or abandonment of the old in primitive cultures. Typically, this occurred where the survival of the tribe was threatened by lack of resources and the marginal economy. Usually the aged were not put to death directly, but in a ritualized fashion of dying, in some familiar context such as in the wilderness or the snow.

Contemporary examples of appropriate death are in the line of duty as with firemen, policemen, soldiers. "Dying with their boots on" is the American notion of an appropriate death. There is little in the contemporary scientific literature that describes, or makes credible, what an appropriate death might be. A search for examples must look elsewhere as in literature, philosophy, and history. The bareness of current ideology on dying documents the avoidance and taboos that block adequate contemplation of dying. Readiness to cease remains an elusive goal whose attainment must be sought in the examples set by the lonely struggles of friends and relatives.

10

Loss, Grief, and Carrying On

T he death of anyone disrupts the daily life of the survivors. In order to carry on, they must cope with the
facts of loss and the emotions of bereavement. The initial
shock sometimes requires emergency care. Later come the
more complicated impulses toward unique modes of grieving.
Typically, public mourning is inadequate for the actual sorrow
of the survivors while private action is often blocked by current taboos. The result is another survival gap in which effective carrying on is impeded by insufficient attention to the
work of grieving.

Carrying on demands acceptance of the fact that a termination has occurred. The first and apparently universal reaction
to the finality of death is disbelief, followed by an inability to
recognize or accept the consequence of a change in the prior
relation itself. After a death, everyone knows that the dead
person is gone, but the experience of human relations is a
process in which the mere absence of the other party does not
change the expectation, at least right away. There is a
momentum in human awareness of others, which continues
past the point of death. Images are recalled, especially in
activities shared frequently. Such memories generate daydreams in which the survivor enjoys the presence of the dead
one in his imagination. Effectively, the relationship continues
even as it gradually fades from real to remembered; from
daily to occasional; from specific act to general attitude. This

process takes time and is not pathological. Such thoughts are to be expected and occur universally. Unfortunately, when verbalized the general response is to label these as morbid.

While some survivors are more able to turn these images off than others, they do so at their own risk. The danger is analogous to the Victorian tendency of forgetting sexual fantasies and the later return of repressed impulses in the form of irrational behavior. On the other hand, the unchecked continuation of fantasy relations with the dead person feeds the illusion that he or she is still present, still available, and will return sooner or later. There is in short an equal danger in denying the death of the victim.

Denial of death takes many forms in America. The most frequent is that of eternal sleep, with the implicit possibility of waking up some day. Another common denial is death as a separation. The dead are addressed as the "departed" while the absence of a lover is compared to bereavement. Actually all separations are experienced emotionally as equivalent. The survivor cannot tell the difference between absence due to death, travel, or estrangement, because they all feel like separation. People know the dead cannot return, that travelers can meet again, and that the circumstances of estrangement can be remedied. But these are all intellectual knowledge, and are highly vulnerable to feelings or needs.

Because of this more psychological equivalence, survivors require sensory experiences to *confirm* that death has occurred. The most direct source is an encounter with the dying process—death, funeral, and mourning rituals. These serve to validate the more intellectual ideas about termination instead of permitting denial notions to continue unchallenged.

The persistence of denial is far more common than recognized. It is most easily observed in children. Their only preparation for death of a parent is prior absence or the more conventional explanations, such as illness, business, and more recently divorce. Children faced with the sudden absence of a parent due to death interpret the loss as a personal rejection—"Daddy doesn't love me." In less extreme form, the same danger occurs to adults. They tend to experience the loss of a

significant person as some kind of personal failure in themselves. The symptoms of this error show up as excessive guilt
for inadvertent or trivial errors; and more dramatically as
prolonged grief or thoughts of suicide.

The danger of denial comes from the seductive glossing
over of the facts of loss while offering only the most superficial level of support during the immediate crisis. Complications begin to emerge as soon as the survivor can begin to ask
thoughtful questions. If the loss is really a separation, it may
only be temporary. The survivor may expect to meet the victim again. Since the evidence of this perception supports
denial of death, he or she enters the bereavement period
predisposed to believe in reunion with the dead one. What
must the survivor do to facilitate another meeting? One
answer is the death of the survivor himself. Accidents and
suicides occur frequently and coincidentally during the first
year of mourning. Even terminal diseases appear to come on
suddenly and more frequently following dramatic changes
or separations in close relationships. Where the survivor is
elderly sudden death may appear appropriate. However,
younger people suffer from the same hazards, and often by
violent death.

Denial as a proper means of coping with loss is traditional
in Western, Christian, and especially in American culture. In
a strictly religious context, denial takes the form of survival
of the soul in heaven or hell. On some millennial day of judgment, body and soul will be reunited. Before that time these
souls contemplate the beauty of God, and possibly each other.
If part of a religious system, the denial aspects are adequately
countered by the congregation so as to enforce a dealing with
daily problems of living and later replacement of the loss,
including remarriage.

Actually, the contemporary context looks to alternative
systems, both for explanation and support of the newer denials
of death. Examples are reincarnation, poltergeists, magic,
astrology, extra-sensory perception, the prevention of aging,
the cure of all terminal diseases, and cryonics—freezing,
storage, and reanimation. All of these beliefs function to sup-

port a belief in extended continuation, and permit a default in coping with the facts of loss.

The curious mixture of comfort and repression present in contemporary mourning is difficult to question because it does offer some solace. However, it just isn't enough. In this day of future shock, to allow an inadequate practice is to face the prospect of a devastating consequence.

To really help the bereaved, all the traditional gestures to the survivors must be used as opportunities to open discussion about the areas of conflict, guilt, distress, and feelings of loss. Not by just anyone, but by those whose closeness, personal comfort with the subject, and willingness to devote time, combine to make them suitable friends in need. Some of the groups listed in the resource section provide aid and visitation during the mourning period.

Sympathy cards, flowers, condolence visits, and even public memorials, while well-intentioned, merely confirm that the loved one has left. All of these provide opportunities to open communication and share feelings, but they also serve to seal over distress. Typically, this consists of stereotypes: "gone to his maker," "the hereafter," "rest in peace," or "indefinite sleep," "speak no evil of the dead," and so on. The survivors are exhorted to forget the real person with his faults and virtues, and remember only the heroic.

The present social climate permits the risk of default in order to avoid dealing with excessive emotions in the recently bereaved. Anguish, however expressed, is disturbing to well-wishers who seek its immediate removal by any means. For the same reason, less extreme expressions of grief are even denied by the survivor himself. The consequence of such default is a failure to relate feelings of grief to changes in daily living arrangements. The alternatives proposed here are options for the survivors, whose freedom to choose is impaired by lack of informed consent and by the unnecessary dilemma of whether to give proper or genuine expressions of grief.

In general four suggestions are offered. The first is adequate preparation before death, and especially during last encounters. Specific details were given earlier. Second is the emphasis on the shock effect of loss which requires emergency care in the first few days following a death. Thirdly, is the attention to the prolonged period of "grief work" in which the survivor must examine, give meaning, and validate his or her perceptions of the disrupted relation. Fourth is the eventual attempt to seek replacement of lost relations in terms of specific functions or needs.

Immediate Shock Following Death

Conventional wisdom recognizes that death produces a shock in the survivors. Most people respond with sympathy, indulgence, assistance, and try to be helpful in every way. However, this is only the first response. Quite often, it is given exclusively in public. Like most unconsidered social practices, there is often a failure to follow through. When a survivor is overcome or prostrate, attending physicians initiate firstaid as they would for physical shock. But most survivors don't show obvious physical symptoms and they don't otherwise identify themselves as in a state of need. The majority suffer some degree of physical shock following a death, but many do not recognize it as such. As a result, there is insufficient attention paid to their physical needs let alone to the more complicated psychological ones.

Following a death, the initial shock requires psychological first aid given by total and immediate indulgence, support, and acceptance. This usually occurs the day or two following a death, if everyone recognizes the shock. Whether identified or not, the most prudent response is to continue this attention or diminish it slowly over the next few days. Simultaneously, the survivor should be freed of his daily obligations for a more extended period. Beyond the first few days of indulgence, the second and third week following a death should also be free of responsibility and decision-making. The analogy can be made to medical care following exposure, broken bones, or post-surgical nursing. Initial as well as continuing first aid is necessary.

In attempting to cope with the immediate shock, several

concepts may be useful to the survivor and his helpers. The first is to start where the survivor is; this concept refers to a subjective understanding of what has happened. No matter how exaggerated or discrepant the survivor's assertions may be, helpfulness requires a suspension of judgment and an acceptance of the personal point of view. The helper must attempt to see that loss through the eyes of the survivor, at least as a starting point.

The next concept is that of a time perspective, either chronological or psychological. They both aid the survivor by providing hope that the present grief will pass. Calendar time also helps to dissipate distress by a natural healing process or by a psychological mellowing and forgetting.

Psychological time refers to the stages of grieving and recovery. The initial shock is followed by efforts to absorb or recover from the disruption. The survivor moves from raw distress to private and extended grief. Later, some resolution occurs in which replacement of the lost relation is noticeable. These shifts in the survivor represent some growth or adaptation. The sequence is unique for every individual. If grief is a response to changes in a former relation, the resulting differences also mark a difference that represents a change to the survivor. The sequence of these significant differences represents psychological time. Knowing that even grief will pass helps all parties to accept the distress more patiently.

Another concept is that of the "right to grieve." During the immediate days following a death, survivors are entitled to any emotional response which occurs. None of these will be random or necessarily destructive. However, all will have the quality of extreme emotion. Responses such as screaming, weeping, tearing of hair, beating of breasts, and even continuous tears are resisted by many. Part of the reluctance to talk of death is the fear of the survivor's tears. It may help comforters if they can be reminded that loss does hurt, extreme emotion is appropriate, and its recurrence, or continuation, is to be expected as part of the grief work.

The distress of mourning is not restricted to the first two or twenty days following loss. It is always appropriate relative to the needs of the survivors. Extreme emotions in a bereaved person should never be labelled morbid or criticized, but rather accepted as a part of death, which will also pass. Traditional mourning rituals such as the wake, sitting-in shiva, neighbors providing food, embody the concept of psychological time by providing emergency, but temporary services, on the very practical assumption that the survivors will recover their self-sufficiency later. In addition, such care explicitly permits catharsis, while publicly sharing the grief. By relieving survivors of mundane chores, this helps to shield them from small reminders of the loss present in simple activities such as eating, cleaning the house, doing chores, or even hobbies.

For those who fear overindulgence or encouraging a lifetime of mourning, reassurance comes from the temporary nature of acute shock. This apprehension is also an underestimation of the prior strength of the survivors. Where there is a history of mental illness, or excessive dependence, the shock of loss may precipitate more complications. However, the most constructive approach to all mental illness is to start with an expectation that is appropriate to the mentally well. People suffering from mental illness often respond rationally to something as real as death. It's in the later mourning period that loss facilitates irrational complications in the mentally healthy as well as the ill.

In the initial reaction to the news, the phenomenon of shock is generally recognized by indulgence for the survivors. Would-be helpers are advised to accept the survivors' reactions as they find them. The concept of psychological time permits the helper to wait, assist, and work for changes that he knows will come as the survivor moves away from initial shock into later grief work.

Grief Work

The effort to examine the loss, give it some meaning, and validate perceptions of the changing relation to the dead is called grief work. The serious and prolonged business of grief work begins to emerge following the initial shock. The next recognizable response to loss is a pseudo-recovery in which the survivor will appear to have pulled himself together and go about the business of handling the complex details created by death. Some spouses may have no apparent reaction, in public at least. They may appear cold and unemotional. Regardless of what the initial response has been, some form of return to prior functioning will be observed. However, it won't be quite the same as before. Both kinds of survivors will resume the business of living, but with apparent changes.

A careful inquiry will elicit their feelings of sorrow, sense of loss, and searching for new adaptations. Since most people are uncomfortable coping with such feelings, they are reluctant to ask. The survivors soon realize that their distress is distressing others, and learn to dissemble. Eventually they turn off their bereavement. It is during this stage that much harm ensues to the grievers.

If the history of mental illness and its modern treatment have anything to teach it is the error of banishing unacceptable ideas and feelings into a limbo of unconsciousness, from which they eventually return to generate irrational symptoms. From the observations about conflicts and repression have come the justified value of catharsis as an elementary psychological first aid to any emotional distress. It's never enough, but it's always a prerequisite.

The survivor needs a sympathetic listener willing to accept him as he is, including the immediate emotions, no matter how extreme. After that, he needs a friend who can suspend judgment, listen to the gradually emerging doubts, mixed feelings, apologies, shame, and guilt about deeds of omission or commission. These are the unfinished business of any relationship disagreements, failures to comply with past wishes, shame about a dead one's real faults. In objective terms, these may be trivial but to a survivor, these items reverberate and need finishing rather than forgetting. Well-wishers can be constructive by taking the time to hear these out, reacting with their own opinions when asked, and permitting an opportunity to complete the details of a disrupted relationship.

Complicating the straightforward needs are conflicts and confusions on the part of survivors. Only good may be spoken of the dead, but in close relations, intimates always experience mixed feelings. These include the more critical, negative, or hostile kind. Hating the dead or speaking unkindly of them carries a burden of guilt or shame. The compromise behavior resulting from these conflicts often yields unpredictable, irrational, or inappropriate emotions which never make much sense to the comforter. All of these behaviors have meaning as expressions of the unique relation shared by the dead one and his survivors. However, understanding some of the more extreme reactions aids the person trying to comfort the particular survivor.

The first to surface will be items of "unfinished business" which are always present and implicit in close relations. Did the pair settle their last argument? Have they forgiven each other mutual errors? With any warning of impending death, the answers should easily be yes, but given all the denials, the survivor often finds himself alone with a guilty conscience. The reality is never that terrible, but the distress from even a minor sense of guilt can be excessive in the context of death. Tragically, these bad feelings about self in relation to a dead one are the most easily overcome, if confided to another concerned human being.

Following the period of shock, the survivor usually returns to typical behavior. The loss is rationalized, the dead one is buried, and memorialized. Yet two kinds of damage are apparent.

There are first the gross errors in judgment that survivors express in significant decisions following a death. Sudden breakups in relations occur between couples after the death of a parent figure or a child, and conversely, disruption of parent-child relations follows the death of a spouse. In the workaday world, significant job changes and business reverses occur. Accidents are also more likely in the year or two following loss. Younger men who are in transition, either in terms of work or intimate relations, including the loss of a lover or parent, are more vulnerable to automobile fatalities. For the older, accidents take other forms such as falling, burns, or even elective surgery with untoward outcomes.

There are secondly the internal kinds of damage that are called mental illness, melancholia, drug-use, risk-taking. Psychologically these are symptoms of distress experienced by people whose earlier adaptations have been disrupted by death. Even when these symptoms were present before a loss, their degree will now be accentuated. Moving into the majority who will not show mental symptoms, there will continue to be moments and areas of distress associated with continued memories of the deceased. Such feelings as guilt, pity, hatred, and sentimentality will fluctuate in an unpredictable sequence, and cause further distress because they seem improper and persistent. These feelings, while natural, will continue unnecessarily, precisely because they have not been given a place in the psychological awareness of the survivor. This help can be provided by anyone concerned enough to pay attention, and adopt the tactics suggested here.

The helpful person can be constructive by providing an opportunity to express these feelings. Having first accepted the survivor and his particular form of bereavement, the next step is to assume a share of the burden by acknowledging the loss, the validity of the particular feelings as a measure of closeness, and the difficulty of continuing within the victim. This sharing should be more than a verbal statement or gesture such as practiced in condolence visits. There is no substitute for time spent, and the literal acts of being there, listening, accepting as natural, and responding with feelings appropriate to the survivor's acts.

Such sympathetic responses will in time induce enough acceptance where the survivor can begin to identify his more negative feelings about the dead one. The kinds of events and acts which motivate resentment, guilt, hostility in people will begin to emerge. These may appear trivial, but to the survivor they are important. His efforts to dispel them are what cause his distress. Providing an opportunity, and the role of alter, but sympathetic ego, allows the survivor to reexamine and evolve his own perceptions. In this role, the helper can offer an assist to further evolution of the relation to the deceased. This permits the survivor to complete his grieving, validate some personal notion of what that relationship meant, and go on to make room for a replacement.

This process is sometimes called "working-through" in psychotherapy. That label should not intimidate the reader, since everyone practices some of this with their friends all the time. The danger of the non-professional approach is that of unreliability of effort and lack of completeness. However, there is a corresponding difference of expectations from friends than from the professional. Thus the mourner is fore-warned in not expecting too much from his friends. But the danger of meddling is exaggerated and certainly minimal in relation to the present default of needs in the bereaved.

During the period of grief, many survivors resort to work in order to escape the pain of loss. This solution is effective for some people, only because the current alternatives are so poor. Return to a job or continuation of housework does offer some superficial relief because it is distracting; especially when the activity is a return to old duties rather than learning new ones. The major drawback to distractions of any kind is the danger of ignoring or avoiding the kind of self-examination suggested earlier. If work is used only to avoid distress rather than to provide temporary relief, the survivor becomes another victim of the total denial from which everyone seems to suffer. Insufficient grief work predisposes to delayed reactions or depressions later as repressed mourning returns unpredictably.

Continuing or resuming work schedules following a loss is compatible with adequate grieving, but only if specific lim-itations are recognized, and compensations allowed. For example, routine duties will be familiar and comforting. When alternated with quiet moments of thought concerning the bereavement, regular work can be useful as well. However, critical decisions and new problems should not be attempted until other criteria document readiness to carry on fully.

Time alone is not a reliable standard for judging readi-ness to resume full decision-making after a loss. Immediate shock passes in hours or days, but the period of mourning may last for months or years. While not visible, nor apparent even to the survivor himself, emotions will impair judgment. The amount of bereavement is a function of closeness, which in turn implies frequent, long-lasting, and intense sharing of mutual need satisfaction. Closeness is ordinarily judged by blood relations rather than functional human interaction. The former are more limited in today's mobility and diluted by diminished contact. The brother seen once a year is functionally more remote than the friend seen weekly. Grief work will be greater when the friend dies, yet the social expectation is that death of a brother requires more public mourning. Grieving for the intimate friend is often not proper in public. These are further examples of survival gaps encountered today.

The survivor himself is the best judge of how intimate the relationship was and how much grief work needs to be done. If in doubt, one should consider the loss personal where weekly meetings once occurred. The more intense these meetings were, the longer is the period needed for grief work. In addition to the frequency and duration of contact criteria, there is the one-shot encounter that yielded a lifetime impact. This is more likely to occur in relation to outstanding personalities. The death of President Kennedy, or Martin Luther King, Jr., induced grief in many who had minimal contact or contact through mass media. The survivor is always the best judge of what he feels. He may not call it bereavement, shock, or depression, but he will recognize that something is not right within himself.

Unrelated people are not expected to mourn or suffer from loss. If they are observed to be so moved, there is a tendency to label them as morbid. Nursing staff in services where patients receive extended or continuous care are also vulnerable to grief reactions. An illustration is a hemodialysis patient who is kept alive by two or three visits per week for several years. The nurses who care for him often develop more involvement The nurses who care for him often develop more involvement with this patient than they do with each other. Sudden death leaves them bereft. Are they mourners or professionals? Do they grieve or do they ignore the loss? Displays of emotion are considered unprofessional, and publicly sanctioned opportunities to mourn are not provided officially. Unofficially, the bereavement is acknowledged by whispered condolences, tears, and sick leave. The fellow patients are even more in conflict. They are not supposed to be involved in each other's affairs, even though they have suffered the same affliction together for several years, much like combat buddies; they offer each other mutual aid, become friendly with their respective families, and support each other through the various medical crises so common to kidney failure. Suddenly they are bereft. There is no official acknowledgment that they have a right to mourn the loss of a fellow human sufferer.

These survival gaps occur to anyone who is acquainted with people who die. The problem is one of recognizing an occasion of grief and degrees of personal loss, no matter what the relation may appear to be.

In trying to judge such contacts, it is easy to overlook the closeness that long passionate enmity can generate. Without impugning judgment, the sudden death of one, even with good riddance, should not be overlooked as a source of bereavement. Anyone hated passionately will be missed; the longer the period of dislike, the greater the degree of grief work needed.

The death of an enemy needs further explanation. The initial reaction although "improper" will be a sense of joy or success. This first reaction is countered by the more stereotyped kinds of regret. After death, hatred is no longer permitted. In public and later in private fantasies, this immediate relief or feeling of joy gets denied. The degree and kind of denial generate a special survival gap between actual feelings and the expected kinds of mourning. In addition to the usual danger of inadequate grief work, there are several double binds when an enemy dies.

First, is the danger that an excessive guilt response will occur after the primary emotion was relief or joy. Even if this is not the emotion, the objective fact of hatred will stir some regret. The survivor caught in this contradiction is probably more vulnerable to prolonged distress than the ordinary survivor. The difficulty stems from the schizophrenogenic quality of the mutually exclusive choice for the survivor. His gut-level impulse is to rejoice as in primitive times, but his civilized conscience tells him that grief is the only proper feeling. In his efforts to maintain his own self-respect, this survivor may deny his feelings and try to talk himself into feelings of regret. As residuals of initial joy rear their now ugly heads, he or she will struggle harder to assert the grief deemed proper. Help for this survivor is more difficult since the problem will never be identified by observers, and is not accepted by the individual.

One approach a helper can take to survivors with this conflict is to stress the universality of mixed feelings following the death of anyone. Regardless of the prior relationship, there is always some basis for suggesting deaths stir guilt feelings in the survivors; sometimes just for still being alive, often for actual deeds against the deceased. Whatever the emotion or its cause, the unique feelings of the survivors include both relief and regret when a relationship is disrupted by death.

Unusual, bizarre, even socially improper forms of behavior such as laughing at the news can occur. Just as women are known to cry when happy, survivors may laugh when sad. This sort of inappropriate emotion is usually an expression of very strong and mixed feelings as well. Knowing these reactions can occur to anyone permits a helper to start unravelling the kinds of bereavement a survivor is suffering from, without the burden of seeing a psychotherapist.

The inability to know what one is feeling occurs to everyone in other occurrences beside death. The usual sources are conflicts in motives, loving and hating the same thing, wanting and not wanting a specific relationship. These are the stuff of mental illness and the focus of most psychotherapeutic efforts to resolve anxiety. A fuller treatment of the subject occurs in psychology books on mental health. One aspect does tend to get overlooked and seems to occur in normal families. Unacceptable emotions in children are often controlled by the psychological trick of re-labelling. Telling Junior that he is tired, and should be in bed, may get rid of him, but is also liable to confuse his notions about being tired. If repeated often enough he may equate, emotionally, being tired with being unwanted. Since children look to adults for definitions of their world, a great many mixed and confusing notions about feelings persist into adulthood because children's reactions are mislabelled or ignored.

In the context of death, confusion is currently the greatest because adults try to get rid of the subject by using euphemisms. The confusion is seen more clearly in children, who can go on playing, eating, or whatever following the death of a parent. Their ability to understand loss is so limited that death will not be perceived until some daily process is disrupted by the absence. Even when a mother is replaced by a housekeeper or relative, grief or emotional responses will not occur until some change is introduced. Older children may have a sufficient range of experience to perceive immediately that death means loss of the parent, but age is no assurance. A paternal death is even more remote since the usual contacts and practices are often less direct. The father's death will upset the mother, who will be less able to provide for the daily needs of her children. Only then will they "perceive" the loss of their father and demonstrate grieving.

Children can express emotions in many ways and especially when it comes to coping with loss of a parent. If at this time, well-intentioned adults try to shield the child from the fact of death, the tendency to incorrectly label their feelings obscures the problem and aggravates the grief work needed. In the period immediately following a loss, children's reactions can be identified by the range of unusual or new behaviors that emerge. Examples are nightmares, bedwetting, nail-biting, or school failures, which suggest an internalization of conflict and distress. The opposite might be delinquent acts, taking objects that belong to others, impulsive, action-oriented behavior where accidents or self-injury can occur. These last represent an externalization of emotion expressive of some kind of distress. In the context of loss, both internal and external kinds of changes suggest the child's own way of expressing his grief. When these same behaviors occur months or even years later, the connection with loss is not always made. These sequelae are more likely to ensue where the child was noticeably unemotional at the time of death.

The prophylactic suggested for children is the opportunity to secure some definition from responsible adults as to the nature of the events. Ideally, the adult figure should be prepared. Typically they are not. The next best thing is for them to offer their own perceptions. Hopefully, the child will ask after the adults have arrived at some personally reassuring position. Usually, the children need the definition when survivors are least able to give it. Regardless, when parent figures become aware of children with loss problems, it is better to attempt any definition than to avoid the subject. The major advantage to acting is that it gives the children a license to signal their own emotional states and understandings. These provide cues as to what comes next.

The antidote for all survivors is the permission to accept any emotion as legitimate in grieving for a death. This gives them a license to think and talk about negative qualities in the deceased. Such inimical expressions merely reflect the very human quality of the disrupted relation and the less than perfect actions of both parties. Grief work draws upon the recollections of participants in a mourning group and will recall examples of behavior that contain both complimentary as well as critical examples. Mourners will need to accept all statements as expressions of bereavement rather than speaking evil of the dead. Survivors need each other as willing listeners who accept all that is said about the dead one. In doing so, they give each other license to tell it like it was, and in the telling, to pull the pieces together. A disrupted relationship can be given some meaning which includes the idea that it is now completed. In doing so, psychological space is created for a new relation.

Replacement of Loss

Success with the preceding problems will permit the start of replacement activities oriented toward the lost or disrupted functions carried out by the one who died. The most central of these, if not entirely self-evident, is the lost relation itself. More precisely the reference here is to the human needs filled by the deceased. The problem shows up most poignantly when the survivor finds another person to replace the dead one. Typically this is a spouse relation. In an earlier time, before romantic love was a universal expectation, the solution was matter-of-fact and grieving, while genuine, was more simple. In those days, a widow and a widower in the same area would simply arrange to remarry as soon as they could join forces. The basic consideration was the right sex, a compatible religion, social class, and other factors in decreasing order of importance. Current resources permit more complicated criteria including the necessity of romantic love. Still, the first rational impulses following a loss are the possibilities for replacement. The booby trap in premature action lies in the danger of error and disappointment. Any person chosen merely on the basis of replacement is thereby doomed to a substitute role. An early remarriage implies an insufficient period of grieving, and with it a tendency to look for a fast, easy way back to the former relation. The danger is that of choosing any available partner, or one who is only superficially similar. When differences begin to emerge in the crunch of the marital relation, the need to accommodate to change is added to the burden of insufficient mourning.

Allowing an adequate period of time, say one or two years, allows the survivor to deal with the press of needs and put the disrupted relationship to some kind of order. The period of bereavement allows changes to occur in the survivor so that the person will both need and accept different kinds of partners. Shorter intervals will do, if adequate attention to grief work and need gratification is accomplished. When in doubt, delay is always preferable. The sad conclusion that must be recognized is that no equivalent is ever really possible that fully replaces a lost spouse. Nor is there a quick way to restore the equanimity disrupted by death. The survivor cannot escape a period of shock and painful working through of specific details of loss. Only when the survivor has assured an independent continuation, can he or she hope to find another mate without creating more problems than remaining alone.

An obvious area of need that can never be adequately satisfied alone is that of sex. Even more obvious is the difference between male and female survivors. More women survive men at every age and clearly females past forty will encounter more real obstacles in replacing a lost husband than vice versa. The hazards to both sexes are probably equal, but the imbalance puts women at a distinct disadvantage. A widow is more likely to accept the first available man because he may well be her only chance for remarriage. Conversely, there will be more pressure on her to expect less and live with disappointment. Compensating for this hazard will be a greater capacity for adaptation than in male partners of the same age. Whether this is due to biological differences or not is academic. The limited choice will induce a greater willingness to accept the distresses of a new relationship.

A man past forty would seem to have no need for remarriage at all given the surplus of eager women pursuing him. Sexual needs alone are probably the poorest reason for marriage in general, let alone remarriage. There is ample evidence the marital context is not the optimum arrangement for satisfactory sexual pleasure at any age, since the business of the husband-wife partnership tends to slop over to the connubial bed. The very real problem-solving tasks and competition apparent in modern domestic life affect sexual interactions, too. Each couple reacts differently, but all of them carry daily burdens to bed that frequently spoil sexual pleasures. Perhaps not enough to justify divorce, but certainly often enough to justify caution in choosing marriage as a means of satisfying sexual needs only.

The only continuing reason for a marriage today is the desire for a lifetime partner who can prevent loneliness while enhancing human pleasures and achievements. Yet in this respect too, modern marriage is also disappointing. Contemporary options permit other arrangements that gratify sexual needs for men more efficiently than through remarriage. Following the loss of a wife, it is more prudent for a bereaved husband to allow for an extended mourning period before attempting the battlefields of a new marriage.

In a similar way, the bereft should attempt to fill other needs as conveniently as possible in order to create the possibility of an optimal choice. While it may very well occur that success with these alternatives may eliminate the necessity for ever getting married again, they also prevent a lot of unnecessary distress.

Attending to all identifiable needs gives the survivor time to make a more reliable choice about replacement of partners lost through death. In this an individual fulfills the duty to himself and a future partner by becoming whole again, which includes a relative self-sufficiency for all those needs frustrated by the death of a former partner.

11

Common Conflicts After Death

*T*he sex, age, and relation of survivors to the person who died shape the kind of conflicts likely to occur. This chapter describes some of these and offers suggestions or approaches to the hazards of adequate carrying on. The basic answer is developed in other portions of this book, but can be summarized here as accepting the normalcy and inevitability of death in daily life. The notion of readiness to cease is both humanistic and positive in offering everybody a sense of seemliness about dying. From this perspective come the possibilities of developing more specific suggestions for a realistic and humanitarian approach to the grief of survivors.

Death *in Utero,* **Miscarriage, and Abortions**

Dying for the fetus is not an experience. Some people tend to over-empathize with the unborn child, by assigning perceptions appropriate to living adults. The awareness of the human fetus even into the last trimester of pregnancy is probably less than in unborn mammals, such as kittens and puppies. The individual of any species repeats in its own development the history of the entire species. Confirmation comes from the observations that during the early months of pregnancy embryos resemble various unborn animals such as pigs or dogs.

Dying *in utero* lacks several of the characteristics known

to occur with live people. First is the general absence of a
dying process. The embryo continues to exist and grow even
if damaged, until the right combination of factors produces a
spontaneous termination of the pregnancy. Second, the fetus
lacks sufficient awareness and foreknowledge to anticipate
its own death. Third, the awareness of pain is also minimal,
possibly even lacking, although embryos do react to stimulation. Fourth, an unborn infant develops little involvement with
its parents except in terms of their anticipatory images like
the guest who never arrived. The preparations are reminders
of a disappointment.

These differences permit parents to experience less grief
over an unborn infant than over living people. However, well-
wishers often overlook these differences in their effort to offer
consolation. While everyone is generally aware that grief is
less intense for an interrupted pregnancy, there is an even
greater tendency to deny the very real distress that does occur
in both mother and father. Both shock and grief work will be
less, but still occur, and require attention.

Dying for the fetus has no meaning simply because it
lacks the neurological ability to be that aware. The parents
and other adults assign a meaning to this event. Beyond the
obvious fact that pregnancy has been terminated each adult
places quite different meanings on any one death in *utero*.
These implications and their value will be influenced by the
conditions surrounding the interrupted pregnancy.

Rubella or measles represents one kind of calamity during
pregnancy. Typically the mother is exposed to the illness and
her fetus is damaged without her knowledge. Unless diagnosed
at the time, she may not discover the injury or death of the
fetus until a miscarriage occurs. The meaning of this event is
usually some random occurrence for which the mother is not
prepared. Possibly all women should be exposed to measles
before child-bearing ages, but the individual mother usually
explains the loss as bad luck. Most people assign the value of
no error, no fault.

If the fetus dies because of the mother's ingestion of
thalidomide drugs, there is a tendency to assign the meaning

of human error either to the physician or the mother. Eventually the values of guilt and blame are also given. The parents experience more distress about that loss than in the Rubella circumstances. In the same way, damaging conditions such as falls, drug abuse, venereal disease, or illegitimacy shape the meanings assigned to miscarriage and the consequent evaluation of the deeds. When the mother and father see themselves as guilty of some error, or are blamed for some otherwise innocent act, the resulting-conflicts will only add to the grief work they must do.

Additional sources of bereavement come from frustrated expectations. Parents who hope for certain changes in their relationship by having a child will be more upset than those who have no preconceptions. While children always change the family situation, the kinds of differences they generate are unpredictable, often negative, and currently, tend to exaggerate marital conflict.

A father looking for a son to carry on the family name will mourn more than one who is neutral about the value of sons. The mother's sorrow will depend on the meaning she assigns to sons and daughters. If she shares the husband's, she will also share his distress. In addition she will carry the burden of discrepant feelings, evaluated from a male point of view. The simple difference between her own and the husband's meaning will be exaggerated by a male expectation that she should feel the loss as much or more than the prospective father. In effect she may experience distress, but because she didn't show the same distress as her husband, who is reacting strongly to the loss of a son, she is somehow thought lacking. Female chauvinists impose the reverse burden on their husbands. The basic principle here is that each parent will have had some expectation for the child peculiar to their background, age, and sex, that miscarriage frustrates.

The kind of disappointment will introduce conflicts in what is simply the termination of an unborn object. A fetus is typically regarded as something less than an infant, who in turn is handled more like a non-person than are live boys or girls. The expectations imposed on this ambiguous idea, the

unborn child, introduce the possibility of personal frustrations and conflicts in motives.

If a mother did not intend to get pregnant, the miscarriage may be taken as a blessing. She has been rescued from
an unwanted child. Others will always expect her to be bereft,
and will question her pleasure as unnatural. The opposite is
also true. If the mother wanted the child, the regret or distress
will be countered by the expectation of others to forget and to
deny the loss of this fetus. No matter what the mother feels,
she will encounter conflicting expectations which provide more
examples of survival gaps.

In both reactions, the mother will suffer conflicts, mixed
feelings and unnecessary bereavement because her actual
emotions are not accepted by others. The mother will begin to
regret the miscarriage while not wanting the pregnancy; or
trying to forget the unborn infant while her fantasies about its
development continue. These mixed feelings are symptomatic
of conflicts internalized by the survivor and especially where
one feeling is deemed improper.

Among women who are not able to achieve pregnancy,
there will be a greater extreme of feelings about the miscarriage, because of prior efforts and failures. Mothers who
lose a fetus do suffer unusual but unrecognized distress. They
need more acceptance and grief work precisely because of the
conflicting expectations imposed on them. Fortunately, miscarriage is a pure example of conflicting notions about death,
and permits most mothers to work out their bereavement
alone, in spite of well-intentioned exhortations.

Abortion is probably a greater source of distress for the
parents than miscarriage. The obvious difference would be
the element of choice. The former interruption always appears
to be inadvertent while the latter always requires some intervention. The element of choice introduces a special meaning
and with it a value. In a miscarriage, the embryo goes away,
magically and without apparent interventions. The mother is
rarely blamed. Abortion requires an act and with it a decision.
From this act comes the evaluation. Is it murder or is it merely
a woman's right to choose what happens to her body? The case

for women always gets understated because the male frame of reference dominates the thinking. Traditionally men have made contraception a woman's problem. Illegitimacy and prostitution are female sins even though created by male needs. The restrictions on abortions merely create another form of crime much like bootlegging, gambling, and marijuana usage, while imposing unnecessary distress on the innocent. These cultural expectations complicate what would otherwise be a minimal grief response to the loss of an embryo as in miscarriage. The issues are the same for the mother, but the intensity of feeling needed to choose abortion, exaggerates her total response, including the frequent mixture of feelings following interrupted pregnancies.

While a mother who elects an abortion may react at first with relief or pleasure, in the weeks following, a mild depression can occur. The same is true when the fetus is lost because of miscarriage. Given this predictable emotional response, it may be comforting to the mother that she would run into these feelings regardless of what caused the termination of pregnancy. Unfortunately, many women are vulnerable to self-doubts and the guilt feelings that something they did caused the miscarriage. In abortion, the mother may have temporary guilt feelings which she will attribute to her choice. The important consideration is that these feelings of doubt, depression, and guilt are a response to the biological loss of the fetus. They are prototypes of the guilt and depression a mother may have following the death of a live child. The difference lies in the lesser degree of response to an unborn child. The danger is the failure to recognize that a loss has occurred and some kind of grief reaction is to be expected.

Generally, a father is more removed from the event and tends to feel this loss less directly. He may experience it by proxy through his wife, but usually he gets ignored. More typically he will regard the interrupted pregnancy as a woman's problem. If he does anything, it will be the well-intentioned advice to forget it. Telling his wife not to worry or grieve is useless and obscures a potential problem. Repressed feelings will tend to come back and haunt the victim in the form of nightmares, phobias, or hypochondriacal symptoms. Providing an opportunity for catharsis of her bad feelings is simple first aid that any husband can give his wife. He need merely listen to her guilt feelings, while remembering that she'll probably change her mind about them later, often as soon as she stops talking.

The listening process may also help him if his wife can reciprocate. However, the bigger value beyond this immediate first aid is the rehearsal aspect. The opportunity to discuss the death of a fetus is preparation for coping with the death of a live person later. In the same way, a husband may experience this distress instead of his wife. This does not mean he is weak or hysterical. In close relations there is often an emotional division of labor in which one mate experiences a process while the other suffers the emotions of good, bad, or indifferent feeling. Following the miscarriage the husband may suffer the depression. The same first aid is appropriate for him even though the wife lost the baby. In that particular pair, their way of coping with distress is reversed from the general stereotype.

Carrying on is facilitated in a mother by the cathartic value of discussing her bad feelings with her husband. While they may see the need for this in the first day or week following the ending of pregnancy, these distressing reactions may occur six months to a year later. The longer the interval, the less likely these will be due to a body or hormone response. However, whether purely psychological or not, they feel real, and are real in the sense of creating a problem.

Communication about the termination of a pregnancy is appropriate any time the couple are ready to share their thoughts—before, during, or after. In a miscarriage they will be dealing with an accomplished irreversible fact. They will also need to deal with friends and relatives who often know about the pregnancy but not the miscarriage. Matter-of-fact answers to direct or implied questions clear the air quickly. Youth describe this phenomenon as "letting it all hang out." The death of a fetus is not as overwhelming or as taboo as with the death of living people. Still, some awkward moments can develop and especially because the mother and father are not prepared, wish to avoid a fuss, or are disappointed.

Ideally it is far better to anticipate these possibilities before pregnancy by a simple discussion between husband and wife of "what would we do if you lose the baby?" It is unimportant how the conversation ends as long as they have it. Then both have some preparation for the event, an idea of what they should do about it, and most important, a basis for further discussion about this trauma should it occur to them.

The same suggestion can hold for parents who choose to abort. First they should discuss this option before she becomes pregnant. In addition to the three advantages noted in relation to miscarriage, abortion is still so questionable a practice in some circles as to require examination free from the duress of unwanted pregnancy.

Having elected abortion and now feeling badly about the termination of pregnancy, what should a woman do? Same problem, same advice. Her body doesn't know the difference between miscarriage and abortion. A post partum depression of some degree is probable and should be handled as if it were a miscarriage. Much later, when the mother is feeling better, she can reexamine the meaning and value of abortion, but only when she can be objective. That is why it is better to discuss it fully before pregnancy.

Dying and First Year of Life

Dying, death, and bereavement are telescoped together when a newborn baby dies. Infants are so fragile and helpless that parents customarily walk on eggs in their presence. For those who have just gone through the stress of a delivery, the additional distress of a premature death is double-jeopardy.

When the child is still-born, the parents suffer somewhat less, since the baby never assumed a real presence, except in the anticipation of the parents. Therein lies a clue. The loss is sensed most acutely by the acts parents ordinarily do with, for, to, or by another. The more they have done, suffered, enjoyed, the more poignant the loss. The yardstick is how frequently and how much activity is shared with the person who dies.

With an infant who dies at birth or while still in the hospital, the opportunity to share life is minimal, especially for the father. To a woman it is of course different. Death of a newborn or an infant poses dramatically different problems for the mother. These differences become more exaggerated by the biology of birth during the early life of the infant. Later, the role differences become more prominent. During the first four or five months, the anatomical events of birth, nursing, and post partum, keep the mother more involved in a twenty-four-hour cycle of activity. In the later months, this trend continues if the traditional roles of mother and father are maintained, i.e., the father works and the mother cares for young. However, if the mother returns to a career, and the father shares in the care of the infant, these more nearly equal activities will make them both more vulnerable to the loss. The more a parent does in the way of daily acts with the infant, the greater the loss he or she will suffer. The loss of a one-year-old infant will be more disruptive than that of a newborn. A woman in the traditional role will be more devastated by an infant death than a father. He will suffer bereavement too, but will feel it more intellectually, more through the mother's loss than his own direct experience.

When mother and father share equally in the daily tasks of caring for the infant, premature death will also be experienced equally. In the more modern division of parental labor, some men are staying home caring for infants while their wives pursue the role of breadwinner. The degree of distress either one will suffer following an infant death is related to the amount of daily time and effort spent. In turn the role of father or mother and the social playing of these roles influence which one engages in the grief work.

In current life, both parents will not feel the same degree of mourning. To discover this discrepancy is in itself often distressing to one or the other spouse. The degree of grief work is influenced by observable factors, and its absence doesn't mean a lack of heart, sensitivity, or morality. Some spouses take the absence of distress to reflect on their relation as lacking love, involvement, and so forth.

Conversely, some women need more time and opportunity to develop deep feelings and this includes their children. Typically, these women may be engaged in a career or full-time work. The death of a child, say at nine months, may not excite the same kind of emotion as observed in other women. Such mothers understand perfectly the tragedy of their situation, but just don't feel or express their emotions in a recognizable way. Unfortunately, if they don't pretend, they will suffer secondary distress from friends, relatives, or even spouses for not being normal. If they do go along with expectations, they will suffer from the survival gap of pretending grief. In trying to behave properly, they will experience frustration and hypocrisy.

Regardless of sex-role division in the parents, the loss of a child during the first year of life has impact. In addition to the mixed feelings about wanting or not wanting the child and the confusion between guilt and relief, there are other conflicts. Prominent is the idea that the infant continues life whether in heaven or in more secular fantasies. Surviving parents often give an identity to the developed infant, fantasize activities, and occasionally project their own wishes. All of this occurs in the privacy of an interior dialogue. It is not pathological although literally irrational. Most of the time it is harmless.

The insidious danger comes later when other children are born. Maternal fears are fed by the image of the last child. The phobias verbalized by a mother about a live child have been criticized by Philip Wylie in a *Generation of Vipers* and characterized by Philip Roth in *Portnoy's Complaint*. Children whose oldest sibling died prematurely usually experience a more compensatory protectiveness from both parents. When challenged or discussed, the real motives become apparent as the fear of another loss.

Marital conflict and divorce occur so frequently these days that everything becomes a likely cause. However, death of children, even stillborn, can predispose for divorce by insufficient mourning and grief work. The attention needed is minimal. Whether a religious service or a private discussion, some occasion marked as a memorial provides an opportunity. Frank acceptance of all unique, albeit mixed feelings is an absolute prerequisite. Successful carrying on after an infant death is long-range preparation for larger losses, when older children or adult family members die. More immediately the parents are helped to accept their own feelings and learn to grow from this universal hazard.

Death in Childhood

Children do die. This assertion is a necessary prerequisite in today's denial systems. About 3 percent of all annual deaths occur to infants during the first year of life. A lesser number die between the ages of one and fourteen. Children surviving beyond the first year are more vulnerable to accidents and homicides than to natural causes of death. However infrequent, parents occasionally find themselves bereft when a child older than one year dies. The survival gaps mentioned earlier also occur.

The suggestions offered earlier are relevant. However, the role of the child imposes special qualifications. The expectations for children are different than for adults. In the context of death, parents or older siblings are expected to react more strongly, show their grief more vividly, and alter their lives more dramatically. These expectations are implicitly held, and derive from the special poignancy of death prematurely stopping the life of a child. It is irrational, unrealistic, and injurious to survivors, but nonetheless encountered.

The excessive expectations for bereavement by the loss of a child come from the convergence of death avoidance and protective expectations for children. Parents are expected to care for and protect their young. American culture expects everyone to avoid death. When both stereotypes are broken, the survivors are expected to grieve excessively—regardless of how they really feel. They are also expected to forget quickly.

Needless to say, the survivors of a dead child need to

accept the loss. They can only arrive at this state of equanimity if they go through some grieving process, unique to their relation. In addition to the usual public or religious observances, some additional suggestions can be made. Start with the clothes, toys, personal effects. Go into the child's room or space where these are kept. Memories will be evoked, sorrow and tears will ensue. These are not bad. They are to be expected, even welcomed as signs of struggle leading to more growth. Many survivors will feel nothing. This is also acceptable and they will find it easier to follow these suggestions.

By deliberately sorting each item—some for removal, some for gifts, others for saving, the survivor goes through a personal separation process—in privacy, at his own pace, and in a manner unique to the lost relationship. Some items should have been thrown out long before. Others are sentimentally endowed and stir poignant, even happy recollections. Save them. Others can be special gifts to special people. Convey them with the appropriate sentiment. It is a way of memorializing the dead child in the hearts of those who survived and loved him. Many items will stir mixed emotions and indecision. Save these for another day. Go back as often as the need and the satisfactions prompt. A useful rule of thumb: repeat this until tears stop. For those who felt little at first, continue until some emotion occurs. Some survivors need more opportunities to grieve.

Death in Adolescence

After twelve, the major cause of death in adolescents occurs with automobile accidents. Fatal illnesses also occur, as do suicide, homicide and other kinds of accidents. Parents suffering the loss of a teen-ager have the additional burden of an unpredicted death, with the associated factors of careless, provocative and risk-taking behaviors. In addition to loss and grief, survivors suffer that special pain of regret over a young life nipped in the bud or the anguished soul-searching after a sudden death.

The death of a young person is tragic no matter what the

circumstances, because it blights promise and the eternal hope for improvement. In addition to the American hang-up about death, survivors also suffer the addition of frustrated hopes. If neglect factors are present, there is the continuing survival gap of guilt for failing to prevent or having contributed to the unpredicted death of the teen-ager.

Accidents are never completely random events although they occur suddenly. In hindsight, survivors can detect a variety of circumstances whose alteration might have prevented death. Unfortunately, there is usually an implicit witch hunt at least in the unspoken thoughts of participants. Who is there to blame? Whose fault is it? Typically, the one perceived as guilty is prejudged by other circumstances such as dress, previous rivals, or enemies. The reasons can become obscure. In addition to grief, the survivors struggle with feelings of revenge, hatred, and frequently guilt.

Accidental death is never fully due to one person. The victim, even if a provocative risk-taker, usually has help from many others. Psychological autopsies in cases of accident, suicide, or homicide demonstrate that margin for error, pre-disposing circumstances, and the decision to act are complexly interwoven. In short, it is impossible to isolate the sole cause, or the single responsible agent.

This rational statement is useful as background to a helper. However, survivors suffering from the loss of a recent adolescent death by accident will not be able to respond affirmatively. Instead they will continue to doubt, to search for scapegoats, to suffer guilt for clearly trivial or irrelevant acts. Psychological first aid is the same for these survivors as for others, with the exception that guilt is present.

The survivor who acknowledges his guilt is easier to approach. He or she needs acceptance and a chance to express self-doubts. Help occurs by nonjudgmental demeanor, and eventually, some approval. At the least, their role can be defined as neutral or inadvertent in leading to the death of a victim. The survivor who defensively denies any part in caus-ing the unpredicted death of another is more difficult. This person can be assumed to be in the same boat as the one who blames himself excessively. Both represent overreactions. No one person is ever fully or totally responsible for the death of another.

The problem of helping the defensive survivor who blames others, and denies excessively his or her role, is made complex by this hostile reaction. Acceptance and approval cannot start because this aid implies guilt. The helper is in a double bind. The source of the distress comes from the survivor's mixed feelings of guilt and denial for the unpredicted death of the victim. Perhaps the safest starting place is to listen, to hear out, and to wait. During this passive process opportunities may occur by events or through moments of self-doubt and insight. Whatever the source, the helper can acknowledge that everyone feels guilty about this unnecessary death. The helper can express guilt for neutral or inadvertent actions. He or she should do so only when these feelings seem natural. This move signals that others are willing to share the blame and reduces the compulsion to defend, or otherwise deny imagined guilt.

The helper needs to maintain a time perspective in which the person recognizes that immediate reactions after loss are mixed with irrationality. In the context of accidental teen-age death, the survivors' feelings will tend toward extremes of ugly emotions. In the hours and days after loss, the responses will reach a peak. Correspondingly they are easier to identify and leave faster. Irrationality occurring later will require longer effort.

Young Adults

The death of adults twenty to thirty is also tragic, but the special poignancy of death of the very young and helpless is diminished. The most typical cause of death in this age group is sudden and violent, most frequently by accident. Men are, in addition, more likely candidates for murder or a combat death.

In aggressive death, the victim is truly a victim in that another has killed a person who wished to live. The sur-

vivors' impulse is to seek revenge. In the past this has precipitated feuds, wars, and vigilante committees. To deny the
response is more civilized. However, the survivors still must
struggle with proper expectations, and the pain in their hearts.
This kind of survival gap is made worse by the implicit consensus of more remote survivors who validate the same feelings. Because of their lesser intimacy, they are more able to
verbalize sentiments of revenge and hatred towards the
enemy. In recent times this has been oriented toward the North
Vietnamese and other Communist groups in Southeast Asia.

Survivors are left with an element of hatred in their bereavement, focused on a remote enemy and unavailable for
direct expression. These residual feelings tend to blame the
system, fellow travelers, freaks, drop-outs, eggheads, and any
other identifiable substitute in America. The survivors are the
victims of this process. No crime is ever committed because
of such bitterness. Instead the grief work begins to corrode the
quality of life remaining to the survivors. Their purpose in life
becomes unstable.

The survivor faced with sudden aggressive loss has no
publicly acceptable way of seeking revenge. This response
was adaptive up till recent times, and represents another way
in which death has changed. Sigmund Freud touched on this
contradiction in *Civilization and Its Discontents.* He elevated
this conflict to the source of neuroses in that all natural impulses were blocked from direct expression by the needs of a
civilized society. In his day, he perceived sexual gratification
and aggressiveness as the basic instincts for survival. His solution was an intellectual one. The more a person understood the
dilemma, the more he could accept and resolve his conflicts.
There are many limitations to Freud's thoughts, which may
seem naive or inconclusive a half-century later. However, in
the context of death by homicide, his point of view still seems
the best.

The pain of bereavement, especially for a young victim, cut
down by the impersonal forces of war and politics, or a random
killer, puts the survivor in an emotional box—to seek revenge
or to stop living, because continuation of life seems virtually

impossible. At this point in the survivor's life, the idea of suicide or sudden cessation becomes tempting. Lesser escapes are movement, noise, or intoxication. The insightful solution requires time for preparation before, and much thought after a death. The Biblical solution is probably more immediate if a survivor can accept the trials of Job and maintain faith in God's will. For many Americans, the increasing secularization of traditional religions dilutes their daily practices, which in turn weakens the faith that yields comfort in a crisis.

A serial solution or tactic may be the best. The immediate reaction is always temporary and forgivable, short of violence to others or self. Even insanity can pass. As with all grief, the first few hours and days call for indulgence, accepting the survivor's unique way of grieving regardless of how irrational or improper it may seem. Later comes the working through: picking up the pieces of a disrupted relationship and trying to make sense out of the aggressive acts that caused combat or homicidal death. Later still comes the philosophical struggle. Where is God, if He allows these things to happen? What is the sense of life if death comes randomly? These questions are universal and recur with every death, but the special poignancy of innocent blood raises these questions in almost all people. Religious leaders have had more practice than others in coping with this special and formerly common source of grief, but their good offices are not used as often as in the past.

In Maturity

Death at the ages of thirty to fifty is most disruptive. The mature years, when adults are in their prime and responsibilities are at a maximum, carry the most complicated and burdensome problems: young children, debts, unfulfilled promises. Life insurance for the breadwinner tends to minimize financial burdens, but the emotional ones are uninsurable. Children who suffer a loss before the age of sixteen are more likely to become long-term inmates in prisons or mental hospitals. They are more likely to die violently.

Typically death in mature years strikes more men than women. The surviving wives and children need help in coping with the loss. The survival gap for the widow or widower is first the sheer shock of loss. Numbness is often reported. Where death is sudden, the immediate crisis usually brings temporary help. Where death is slow, the numbness is already present. Either way the presence of children old enough to need explanations forces the surviving partner to carry on—distracted by daily chores. The grieving gets postponed. Everyone hopes this is for the good and often it is. Sometimes it is not and the kinds of difficulties described previously begin to develop.

The immediate problem is when to tell the children. Some explanation is absolutely essential. Anything will work to some degree except telling them nothing, a lie, or a pious euphemism quickly contradicted by their peers. Again religious leaders in the past have had more experience and traditions to fall back on. They make useful consultants. However, no parent can ever delegate this choice, without creating more problems in its stead.

The perspective here, of course, is to have prepared for this eventuality by having a family point of view about death that makes it a part of daily existence. This whole book is about preparation for death. However, for those who come to this painful task without preparation, the advice is to start where the survivor is—bereft, upset, anxious, and with other heavy emotions. The children should be told how badly the surviving parent feels. This helps them to define their own feelings. Children don't always know what they feel. They look to adult definitions, but quite often are told only what they ought to feel rather than receiving help with identifying their emotions.

The initial discussion is prophylactic and represents psychological first aid to all immediate survivors. These acts put them in emotional rapport with each other and even more importantly keep them in touch with their own unique feelings about the disrupted relationship. This suggestion may not appear dramatic or earth-shaking, and is, indeed, quite pedestrian. It is used intuitively and often, even today. However, for those who are most vulnerable to trouble around bereavement with surviving children the obvious reflex tends to be halted. Its simplicity is deceptive. Parents who are most uptight about death are least able to follow this advice. Asserting it in this context may facilitate others in their helpful efforts.

Death in Senior Years

If normal death exists, it should occur in the years after fifty-five. While most people would argue that the fifties are early, death in these years is not tragically premature. Individual differences occur with respect to age and normal death. Just as measured intelligence is distributed around the average, the age of death also follows a normal curve of statistical occurrence. Average life expectancy for all Americans is about seventy. However, an equal number die before, as well as after. There is the same absolute number of deaths from natural causes at eighty-five as at fifty-five. If that statement seems startling, it is only because life expectancy is always related to the future. At age fifty-five, most men look forward to another fifteen or more years of life. At age eighty-five, the prospect is about five. However, among all male deaths in any one year, the proportion or frequency at age fifty-five or eighty-five is approximately equal.

Usually statisticians and the public media look at the death rate per 100,000 live people. These rates go up with age while life expectancy goes down. However, individual survivors are seduced into discounting the occurrence of normal death in the fifties and sixties. This introduction is intended as a perspective on death, which gives a rational basis for accepting cessation at some proximate time rather than "later."

It is impossible to offer comfort to the bereaved without some point of view about normal death. Where death comes slowly, as it does in the overwhelming majority, the survivors can be helped to accept the dying process more appropriately if they can conceive that normal death occurs to everyone. In turn they can perceive this particular time as an individual's unique readiness to cease. The value of this perspective lies in the license survivors receive to respond positively and appropriately to someone who is neither dead nor alive, but dying. In short, the problems for the survivors of victims past fifty-five is that of helping them to achieve a seemly death. The starting place is for the survivors to recognize that fatal diseases after the age of fifty-five may simply be that unique individual's special time of dying. The premise here is that effective medical interventions have been exhausted for this particular victim and his fatal disease.

The overall message to the survivor is that effective carrying on is easier to achieve if normal death is accepted as a reality rather than a statistical possibility for others. Survival gaps are diminished and grief work possible if a place for death is found in daily life.

12

The Life You Save May Be Your Own

Staying alive or postponing death is important. This aspect has been neglected because it always gets over-emphasized to the detriment of the equally important issue of how to die gracefully. This book attempts to redress the balance. Nevertheless, continuation and the worthwhile life are obviously dominant goals for everybody. This chapter is concerned with practical suggestions organized into four segments—general self-preservation, normal risk-taking, continuation with impairment, and prevention of self-injuries.

Self-Preservation

Earlier self-examination is the basic way of preserving life, since the failure to anticipate long-range end points makes continuation unnecessarily distressing. Methods of self-examination will be described now. These are merely ways of looking at the problems and relevant kinds of questions to ask that lead to better understanding of the issues. Essentially these suggestions are in the form of exercises that any reader can practice at his convenience throughout his life.

In this period of increased opportunities and reduced restraints, the range of behavior possible to everyone is greater than that which was available to the ruling classes in prior society. The long-range danger of complete freedom is that common practices will emerge that appear harmless, are immediately pleasurable, but may block future choices, or lead to unforeseen consequences. Cigarette smoking illustrates the former, and dropping-out the latter.

Any freedom carries a price tag. The more these can be anticipated, the more optimal the effective choices will become. The prospect of death enhances decision-making by shaping daily existence. Does the daily habit facilitate the kind of ending the survivor prefers? The exercises that follow sharpen personal awareness of the connections between daily practices and the kind of dying likely to occur.

If you had unlimited time, what would you do with it?

The conventional answers are travel, reading, fishing, resting, entertainment, watching TV, sports, movies, theater, music, art, and so forth. There is nothing wrong with such answers. They are to be recommended to some degree for everybody. But all of them are insufficient, because at some point they become boring. Judicious alternatives and timing can extend interest for a long interval, but like an unbalanced diet, these alone produce psychological malnutrition. The missing ingredient is something important, a value around which the survivor organizes his or her whole life. The usual answers are merely distractions, recreations, but only rarely *values* that give a life purpose.

The traditional answers of serving God, one's country, family, and perhaps employer are even less effective as goals for a lifetime commitment. While the importance of these diminishes in relevance or impact, the need for their replacement increases. Individuals must seek less abstract or remote goals to give their lives purpose. The suggestion here is to pay attention to the need. While all answers will be incomplete or only temporary, a continuing search for values will help to give life purpose.

Dealing with spare time as a resource, to be spent, saved, or distributed for whatever purpose deemed essential, is one way of continuously attending to values. Treating time as if it were money, is not a call for materialism, but merely a means of building in an exercise in daily self-examination. Actually more and more people are spending their money, credit, and assets the same way they spend time—thoughtlessly. Questioning the use of spare time is difficult, and the failure to achieve immediate answers will be frustrating. Equally disappointing will be the pseudo-answer that allays doubt for a day or two and turns out to be more frustrating exactly because it promised satisfaction. The essential advantage of this exercise will come from the continuous attention to the problem of how spare time is spent, the values that influence the choices, and ultimately the pursuit of a meaningful life.

If you had a million dollars in cash how would you spend it? The conventional answers here are: invest it, pay off bills, give some away, quit work, buy things. These answers are also self-limiting in that they either avoid a decision on how to use the money or are insufficient answers. For example, how many cars can one person actually drive? Similarly with clothes or even homes. The sad truth is that a sudden large acquisition of cash is impossible to assimilate into daily life in any satisfying way.

The immediate reaction is some form of panic, followed by efforts to delay choices, three, six, nine months, even a year or longer, before major decisions are made. The more foolish, but quite understandable reactions are from individuals who inherit large sums of money suddenly, and shortly thereafter have spent them. They react impulsively with an easy-come, easy-go manner. In the end, they express no regrets, and proclaim their willingness to do the same thing all over again. No criticism is intended, but this pattern is predetermined by the daily habits of these individuals. They really had no effective choice in how they spent their newfound wealth. The freedom to choose is always limited by the prior habits of individuals so that they are unable to shift gears radically even when circumstances change.

It is a common observation that where compulsions dominate, many victims will assert their freedom to choose the most. The best example occurs among drug addicts who argue that will power dominates their continued drug abuse, selectively ignoring all the determining influences which predispose them to the act. The examples of individuals who dissipate any sudden wealth illustrate the need for self-examination with respect to all resources and the kind of hazards they may encounter. Trying to anticipate a choice with large sums of money is a good exercise whether or not the cash ever appears. Actually, the use of sudden, unlimited money is a variation on spare time. The two go together in a complementary fashion. It's good practice to try one and then the other. Going back and forth from the one to the other creates a spiralling progress of sharpened awareness of one's values and personal limitations. The total process is a life-time one, but with increasing satisfactions all along the way.

How can you make your present life worse?

List three events or circumstances that represent the absolute worst things you can imagine happening to yourself. There are no conventional answers. Even superficial ones reflect some dominant motives in your life. The value of this question comes in the form of perspective. Knowing what you don't want somehow helps you judge how close you are to the things you do want.

For those who seek the old verities embodied in the American values of hard work, thrift, achievement, recognition, monogamy, and fidelity, this exercise will be helpful. Not abandoning or even changing old values, but being able to consider and accept deviations is the key. In the context of future shock, this exercise may be a preparation for a sudden trauma such as illness or accident. As an example, consider the value of work. A previous generation regarded the ability to work as a sign of virtue and morality. If the worst thing that could happen to a person is the loss of his or her ability to work, what options are left? Poor health and accident may often impair a person's ability to work. How does that person find a place after this loss? How does he or she retain self-respect? Answers are obviously personal, unique to the individual, but the ability to achieve adequate answers requires an appreciation for non-work, or the value of the non-worker in the present world.

Ironically, the ones who hold the work ethic closest are the ones who suffer the greatest distress when they lose their ability to work. Retirement and disability produce psychological casualties as well as the more obvious economic ones. Tolerance for those who do not accept the work ethic helps to prepare for the day when one will no longer be able to hold a job.

Considering the absolute worst circumstances permits the individual to gain sufficient understanding of the values he or she holds.

Can you go crazy on purpose?

Most people can pass for normal, but in American society everybody seems to harbor grave doubts. "Normal" usually implies perfection, average, or typical. Nobody is happy with criteria that prove he or she is less than perfect, mediocre, or predictable. Everyone has a secret desire to be different even while pretending to be ordinary. One of the great American, culturally-imposed conflicts is the wish to be different and the fear of the consequences.

Going crazy on purpose, choosing when to go, and more importantly, when to come back, is the ultimate measure of sanity. The reason is simply that symptoms of mental illness often lie in the eyes of the beholder. Additionally, these are often induced by the reactions of others. If mental patients are anything, they are sensitive to feelings and responses of others; especially those closest to them. Their psychotic reactions are often an adaptive compromise between what they need and what they sense others want from them.

The ability of anyone to go crazy on purpose becomes an exercise of increasing sensitivity to self and others. It provides practice in opening up blocked communications. Most people usually need a special license to attempt this exercise the first time. It certainly tests the acceptance of others as well as the subject's own capacity for new ideas. The better part of valor may well be verbal trial and error. However, this will already show the reader where he lacks control. Knowledge is power to grow and one does not always have to learn the hard way; hence even intellectualization about problems has its place.

The exercise of going crazy is also a variation on "making

things worse." The pair can be used in tandem, one complementing the other. Indeed, when subjects are asked to go crazy on purpose, their notion of crazy and worse are often equivalent.

Imagine you know with absolute certainty that death will strike within thirty days. What would you do with the time remaining?

Make a list right now before going on. Name at least three activities you would pursue if death were very close, assuming all the usual last things have been chosen. If you are like most people, you ignored the suggestion and are already reading this. Go back now and write down your responses. If you are negativistic about cooperating that is all right too, but it makes your task more difficult. Last chance to follow the advice given here.

The degree to which the list of your changed activities departs from ordinary practices is a measure of the discrepancy between your stated beliefs and actual existence. Everyone gets pressured into white lies, or doing things they don't believe. Most of the time these are small inconsequential things. Their importance comes from a practice that generalizes and spreads to larger and larger issues. Sooner or later, each person gets caught in a double-bind where dishonesty, manipulation, or cynical deals are necessary. Like New Year's resolutions, if the good practices are not incorporated into daily life on New Year's Eve, the odds are that they will never be.

If the prospect of death in the near future makes the reader aware of many things never done, this exercise will be distressing. However, the saving grace will be the fact that it is only an exercise, a make-believe. This suggestion will provide daily "last chances" to introduce behavior which has been postponed too long.

People who are actually confronted with imminent death have great trouble changing anything. If dying takes long enough, however, great changes are possible. The example of Caryl Chessman, who spent twelve years on death row, illustrates how the threat of imminent death can be used constructively. The Chessman who died in a California gas chamber was a very different person from the one who committed the horrendous crimes for which he was found guilty.

Selecting the most suitable mate

Love and marriage are highly esteemed by both sides of the generation gap. Ironically, both old and young are each skeptical of others' arrangements for lifelong partners. There is growing evidence that the institution of marriage as it has been known in Western civilization is changing fast, while the need for lovers to seek greater public commitment continues unabated. The problem for all lovers is how to make a lasting commitment when the only criterion is love, which by definition comes and goes whimsically.

The present exercise is a way of seeking, examining, and assuring the partners that the one selected is really compatible. The suggestion is based on the premise that faults cause all separations while virtues never prevent them. Therefore one should select prospective mates on the basis of faults. The kind of failings considered essential will depend on the person seeking a compatible lover.

First list the three most offensive faults imaginable and give them in order of priority. If the partner is available and can be induced to participate also, the exercise becomes far more effective. Keep the two lists separate, and avoid discussion until after each has completed the exercise suggested. When the list is completed, concede one fault to human imperfection. Allow the mate that one frailty.

For each fault listed, indicate your own response when the lover exhibits this failing during the course of being together. Anticipating the reaction to these worst of all faults helps prospective partners prepare for the inevitable letdowns after the honeymoon. Later, during the heat of some confrontation, this preliminary preview will provide a safety valve that enhances tolerance for human error.

Each fault named, and the reaction anticipated, suggests a reciprocal fault in the person engaging in this exercise. Complementary faults are always present in any close relation, especially that between lovers. Any couple can be described as deserving each other richly, with respect to their mutual faults. Recognizing this balance of faults permits the partners to struggle along a little longer before abandoning each other. In this willingness to stay with a significant other person lies the greatest self-preservation possible in current life. All death rates are known to increase with loss of spouses. Even natural death is more likely to strike partners recently bereft by terminal illness or divorce. The ability to stay with a lover is the best possible prophylactic against sudden death from accident, or suicide. The ability to communicate with a hostile spouse is equally good insurance against homicide.

Normal Risk-Taking

The completely safe life is impossible to achieve. Familiar dangers are accepted and overlooked most of the time, while harmless novelties arouse undue caution. Routine practices like freeway driving or entering a bathroom at home are familiar experiences, but the majority of fatal accidents occur in these familiar places. The young die more frequently in automobiles while the older succumb to household accidents. This generation gap reflects a difference in age, but a similarity in the way of death. Men are more vulnerable to accidental deaths than women. In part this may be due to greater risk-taking in the culture of masculinity. Women, at least of the pre-liberation type, didn't express this interest, but women in their twenties today are more likely to engage in the same sorts of risk-taking as men and their accident and suicide rates reflect this change.

Men are forever trying out new sports and new kinds of equipment. Recent examples are scuba-diving gear, skiing and ski touring, sky diving, parachute jumping, motorcycling, dune buggies, private flying. All of these activities share a common quality of novelty, controlled risk, and the manipulation of equipment. Most participants approach these sports with caution and careful preparation. The compensatory prudence in the face of small margin for errors makes these activities examples of safe danger and the sport a pursuit of normal risk-taking.

In an era of increasing leisure, added life expectancy, and medical technology that literally postpones death interminably, risk-taking appears as a strangely perverse motivation. However, not if it is noted that this is probably the first generation ever to be completely free of the daily threat to life and limb. The quality of death in America has literally changed.

All humans seem to need some minimal degree of excitement, change, danger, which is sought by real, symbolic, or substitute risks. Symbolic dangers are the more civilized kinds of hazards such as provocative questions, sexual encounters, a business deal, a professional achievement. All of these have in common an element of excitement in which there is psychological danger to values, self-image, or desire, but it is a symbolic one because no physical threat to life is immediately present.

Real dangers, on the other hand, are the usual and familiar ways of getting killed or maimed. A substitute danger refers to new ways of dying. All of these spare-time activities require great effort to carry out. The residual need for such excitement is difficult to explain, except to note its universality among men.

The adaptation suggested here is to accept this need but to minimize the risk by some deliberate planning. Always build in margin for error. The specifics are peculiar to each activity but the principles are to provide extra safety in quality of equipment, training, attention, time, energy or whatever else can become critical.

Clearly a sport like skiing is rewarding, voluntary, and associated with risks. To reduce risks, only ski when healthy, avoid fatigue, and set aside extra time to prevent overload. The very mundane quality of these suggestions shows how easy it is to put oneself in a vulnerable position. Since skiing tends to attract the young and the healthy, the problem of vitality, time, and fatigue may appear superfluous. However, the very abundance of these resources is seductive and predisposing to accidents. Most skiing mishaps come early in the season, the first day out, or the last run of the day. The clues here are lack of preparation in terms of conditioning and endurance. Toward the end of the day, fatigue accumulates, reflexes and control become poorer. Add to these circumstances some other predispositions, such as middle-aged skiers, skiing at higher altitudes with less oxygen content, causing more vulnerability to fatigue. Thus the danger of accidents increases. An insidious condition not often noticed also impairs good judgment. Typically, arranging for a skiing expedition requires juggling time, money, equipment, weather, traffic, accommodations for sleeping, and eating. Equally important are the other people in the ski parties. Skiers very rarely travel, ski, or sleep alone. Social overload occurs on every ski trip, especially if children and friends are involved. Typically the father scoots out of work at the gong, picks up the family, and drives to the ski resort. The trip is usually three to six hours long with lots of other people doing the same. The situation invites fatigue, distraction, and impaired responsiveness. Once there, other overloads accumulate in terms of sheer crowding of lift lines, poor service at restaurants, congested ski shops and bathrooms. There is the additional search for *après ski* life, food, wine and song to the wee hours. These do contribute to sensory overload. Each of these factors functions to reduce margin for error and predisposes for the eventual accident on the slope or the road.

Even the common cold robs the skier of some margin of safety even though they continue to ski with antihistamines, antibiotic medication, or simple running noses. Quitting earlier, or skiing less vigorously is a prudent compensation for any ailment, including the emotional or mental stresses. Divorce, job change, a major illness in the family or death are all typical examples of stress that tax the mental health of anyone. Survivors do not need to stop their major activities or interests, but do need to pay more attention to the ordinary hazards. This principle is true in any activity, but especially those characterized here as normal risk-taking. It is always desirable to slow down and think twice. It may even help to get away and rest during periods of stress. However, trying anything new or beyond ordinary limits is especially hazardous during these periods of transition.

Conversely there are many activities whose dangers are overlooked because of familiarity. An example of unsafe danger is crash diets, or anything that promises quick weight reduction. Even when these or special medications do produce weight loss, the survivors become vulnerable to infections, fatigue, and breakdown of predisposed organs. It's sort of a future shock for the body comparable to the stress of sudden time zone changes when traveling. Another example is promiscuous medication with or without medical supervision. Diet, sleep, birth, nerve, and pain pills have some effectiveness and that is why they are recommended or used. However, they all are self-limiting; either by increased tolerance or by undesirable side effects. In a less obvious way, all these converge to alter the internal environment, and through the circulatory systems, combine with ordinary foods and beverages to produce exaggerated effects or unanticipated complications. As long as these possibilities exist, and are engaged in, the victim is exposed to unnecessary hazards.

Nobody deliberately drives recklessly, yet competent drivers with good reflexes are the ones most vulnerable to auto fatalities precisely because they fail to provide a margin for road conditions, fatigue, or social circumstances. Young men on dates, on the run with one or two beers or a marijuana joint behind them, are the most vulnerable not because they are drunk or high, but because these activities reduce margin of safety.

These examples can be multiplied in current life. On-the-job or at-home types of accidents are further illustrations of unsafe dangers whose very familiarity seduces victims into insufficient prudence.

Continuation with Impairment

Physical loss can be more devastating than death to some victims, but for everyone it poses psychological threats to continuation. While most victims adapt, there are always some who have a special psychological vulnerability touched off by the specific impairment. Those people become crippled in their self-image. Many of these go on to self-injury and unpredicted death. The last are typically a very small minority, made all the more enigmatic because the majority do manage to get along. The essential difference, the difference that makes a difference, is the meaning given to the physical loss, and in turn to the values assigned to it. Some people value physical wholeness more than others. A successful athlete, for example, will suffer a greater sense of loss or impairment than a practicing accountant. While both can recover to the same level of psychological well-being, the obstacles facing the athlete are potentially greater. Even when the two victims are equally motivated, the one who has invested more of his or her prior efforts in a self-image of wholeness, fitness, and prowess with the consequent evaluations, will face greater obstacles to adaptation following a loss of limb.

There are several dimensions to this situation. The first relates to group expectations. These will be dominated by age, sex, social class, occupation, and education. The loss of a leg in an adult is a tragic event. In a child, it is pathetic. In an older man, it is sad, but part of the hazards of survival. Age alters the perception and expectations associated with physical loss. A similar variation occurs with sex. Loss of a limb is an insult to a woman's appearance, and to her traditional ideas of marriagability. To a man, it's a loss of his virility and the ability to fight or earn. These stereotyped social expectancies are always present as a force in the reference groups of any one victim. One must deal with the perceptions and reactions of others in addition to personal feelings about loss. The greatest need the victim of loss has at the start of his adjustment process is the recognition that this social pressure exists; to identify its quality and to note especially how this social influence can impede efforts to adjust.

In these situations, a starting point is to ask oneself, "Is this the worst possible thing that can ever happen to me?"

If the answer is no, a person is further along to successful adaptation than might meet the eye. If the answer is yes, the victim needs help with self-acceptance.

Anyone attempting to offer help needs to start acknowledging the victim's loss. The trauma of such a loss *is* upsetting. The victim has a right to feel badly, even extremely. The reaction may persist. The enormity of the loss may take several weeks, months or longer for full realization. The associated loss of vitality, fatigue, or depression may ensue directly from physical traumas or treatment. The early efforts to adapt are frustrating. Learning to walk again is extremely tiring. All of these experiences are to be expected, and discouragement is not uncommon. The would-be helper needs to be able to accept these reactions as temporary but essential phases in the victim's eventual adaptation. By accepting the initially bad feelings, a helper gives the victim a chance to start over realistically. Pretending to be optimistic is the worst behavior precisely because it hides real attitudes. Starting with the victim's tragedy is not indulgence or pity. It shares emotionally how that person is probably feeling about the loss. The net effect is to open a door to positive change.

Granting that this particular loss, say of a leg, is the worst, can anything more go wrong? Is there anything good still left in life? The purpose of these questions is to help the victim regain his self-respect by gaining some perspective about the future. Timing is important in the sense that he or she may be unable to respond positively when first asked. No one asking these questions of another or even of himself should expect greatly positive answers. Simple-minded optimism is out. If the victim is open, there is no harm in asking the questions stated above. They will register and perhaps months later a response will occur. The main value is to focus attention on the relative importance of the personal loss and the remaining possibilities for a worthwhile continuation.

No one can be cheerful about a physical loss, but some damage is not as devastating as others. Knowledge of the person's prior activities and history provides some sense of relative importance. Illustrations are a former athlete who loses a limb; the intellectual who suffers a stroke with prominent symptoms of aphasia, or the physician with a sensory loss.

Blindness in the sensory context, is probably the impairment that threatens most people. To some degree, a victim never recovers complete self-sufficiency. Even with seeing-eye dogs, tape recorders, and other gadgets, a blind person has lost an important sensory input. However, some continuation of activity is always possible. The solution lies in starting with a stark evaluation of the loss, then seeking compensatory skills or aids, and finally accepting some of the limitations. Compensating for loss, accepting limits of change, and knowing the difference, are ways of adjusting. The loss due to physical damage or sensory impairment does impose heavy burdens on the victim. But any sensory impairment also offers the potential for a worthwhile life, fully equivalent, although different.

Another area of sensory loss is in genital functioning. The problem occurs in several contexts. First in a man's life, it may be the contemplation of having a vasectomy to prevent unnecessary pregnancies. Biologically this surgery produces no consequences other than the blocking of sperm from the ejaculation. However, most men are uncomfortable with the idea, some regard it as literal castration, others feel themselves impotent. In the last analysis, these feelings represent a symbol of male chauvinism. Most men, for whatever irrational reasons, prefer an alternative contraceptive, which brings the ladies into the picture.

Women invest their bodies with far more value than men. If femininity can be localized in the body it probably is in the face and breasts, although clearly different women will pick different regions. The analogous areas of loss for women are not in the ovaries, womb, or associated organs, but rather in facial features. The prevalence of face-lifts is comparable to the male interest in monkey glands and testosterones as sexual restoratives. A better example may be the mastectomy required by certain kinds of tumors. The loss of a breast in a woman may be psychologically equal to the loss of potency in a man.

Of course, there are diseases that attack the male gonads. Cancer of the prostate is one. Treatment includes female hormones and removal of the testicles. Most victims are past the childbearing ages and the functional loss hurts no one. However, again, the victim's own perception of loss to his self-image is the most common danger. The psychological problem is the same as for the blind, the impaired, and the amputee. The reality is different but the sense of damage and tragedy is similar. Precisely because it is psychological, some rather straightforward discussion in acceptance of these feelings helps to overcome these things relatively fast. But conversely, if ignored, they become dominant phobias.

In old age, strokes, memory loss, even aphasia and speech impairment can be expected. These are not experiences to be sought or cheered about. However, they are not as devastating as they may appear. First the paralysis and loss of sensation occurring in strokes are reversible in the first few weeks. The sooner more functions come back, the less the residual damage to be expected. Physiotherapy and systematic efforts to exercise help to facilitate recovery, or more importantly, compensate for loss. In the end, some limitations will exist. Psychologically, the victim needs to shift his orientation, start where he is, and move on to what he can do. In the process, he recovers his self-respect and stops being a victim.

Memory loss, especially of recent events, happens to everyone, and much earlier in life than most people admit. Traditionally neurologists regard these as symptoms of brain damage. Psychologists, as a group, are rather threatened by the prospect of organic deterioration to the central nervous system. When I began noticing my diminishing recall of new names and occasionally words, I re-examined the prospect of my increasing symptoms of brain damage. My resolution is that with increasing seniority, experience, or wisdom, all the circuits get filled, and in order to add new information, prior facts get displaced. Naturally, the stuff near the top is more easily dumped than the older facts.

Aside from that optimistic statement, the limitation of memory is simply another restriction to which individuals must adapt.

Aphasia, some inability to use words, is more upsetting than memory deficits. However, there are points of similarity. There are several different kinds of aphasia. First is the inability to give the word but the ability to recognize the object or purpose. Second is the opposite, an inability to get the sense of a word actually used. Third is a motor aphasia in which verbal meaning for an action is known but the appropriate activity is not connected to the name. For example, a patient may know what "scratch" means, but when asked to scratch he doesn't know what to do or conversely he may be able to scratch but not know the word for scratching. The victim may understand the instruction but does everything except scratch. These impairments are known to be related to brain damage of specific areas. The aphasias are most apparent soon after a trauma to the brain and tend to diminish spontaneously. The individual struggling to cope with the loss may actually stimulate alternate channels, but even where some aphasia continues, it's rarely the total deficit that the naive observer expects. The patient can develop other ways of communicating even with these losses. Regardless of the impairment, each victim can hope for a continued existence with some worthy potential, according to his or her own prior values.

Self-Injury Behavior

Suicide prevention today consists of twenty-four-hour supervision and medication for depression, anxiety or thinking disorders. Both approaches are emergency responses, increasingly limited by time. If used alone, the ultimate moment of reckoning gets postponed. Eventually, supervision is reduced and the formerly suicidal patient gets the opportunity to hurt himself again. The majority of deaths from self-injury among the mentally ill occur after release from the hospital. The basic error in current practice is the failure to distinguish between "acutely" suicidal, when a person is identified as in immediate danger, and high-risk, in between acute episodes. About half of all mental patients are high risk, or in between suicidal episodes. Yet nothing is specifically offered these people to prevent a future suicide attempt.

Long-range answers for preventing suicide are totally absent at this writing. Several specific answers are suggested in this book. These are described shortly as good practices in suicide prevention. Implicit to all of these is the license to discuss death and self-injury with the same candor, acceptance, and moral neutrality that now occurs with sex, profanity, or other formerly taboo topics. Effectively, individuals are blocked from gaining usable knowledge about self-injury and its prevention by the shame and penalties that are imposed on victims labeled "suicidal." Patients rightfully expect any preoccupation or verbalizations about suicide to precipitate unwanted medications, surveillance, and continued hospitalization.

The professional faced with the care of a "suicidal" patient is under a compulsion to act preventively. He runs scared because of malpractice suits. The net effect is a double standard in which the kind of care that is employed with all sorts of mental illness is less available for self-injurious patients. By opening the subject up to legitimate discussion, professionals can elicit information that facilitates better clinical management.

Mental hospitals in America neglect the problem posed by suicidal patients. Fortunately, this avoidance does not lead to self-injury and death while in the hospital, because high-risk victims tend to kill themselves in the community; in between hospitalizations. However, the failure to act prophylactically while in the hospital represents a default in care of the self-injurious person when he is most amenable to influence. To do a more adequate job of dealing with the problem, every hospital should adopt a series of good practices that cumulatively create a systematic attention to self-injurious patients before, during, and long after their problems get identified. The list of good practices can always be expanded. The following list describes minimal good practices. What is tragic to contemplate is the universal lack of these procedures in all American hospitals.

Recommended Practices

1. How to report *the facts of a suicidal event.* The present medical entries are incomplete, mainly because of the breakdown in communications between the staff members observing the event and those writing the report. Telephone reports tend to get garbled or lost for those self-injuries that occur outside of the hospital. However, even when professionals are present, or have access to all the facts, they fail to ask relevant questions and to note significant details. A suicide event report listing the necessary information is shown below:

SUICIDE EVENT REPORT

Date_____

Name of Hospital _____

Name of Patient _____ Social Security No. _____

Address _____

Age _____ Sex _____ Race _____ Marital Status _____

Informant's Name _____ Relation _____

Significant Other's Name _____ Relation _____

Name of person
discovering body _____ Relation _____

Details of suicide incident*   ICDA Category (E 950-959)**

Time___ Date of Incident___ Suicide Note: Yes ( )*** No ( )

Place of Incident _____

Method _____Part(s) of body injured_____

Instrument used (if applicable) _____

Drugs ingested (names and amounts) _____

Alcohol (percent found in blood) _____

Other persons present
or participating? _____

Precipitating cause for suicidal event.

Intention to die:

Familiarity with Method
(hunter using gun, etc.) _____

Prior planning for act _____

Provisions to be rescued _____

Was patient hospitalized as a result
of suicidal act? (Name & address of hospital) _____

_____
(Name of Staff Member preparing this Report)

_____
(Title)

*   Attach copy of police report, if available.
**   International classification of diseases adapted.
*** Attach copy or write text of note on other side of page,
       if available.

2. *Evaluation of Risk.* Such information as above provides
a basis for evaluating suicide intent, the degree of the wish to
die. By stressing that all high-risk patients have some potential
wish to die, the clinical problem becomes one of assigning
appropriate prevention procedures to those with high risk.
Clinical management can be vastly improved by using specified criteria for degrees of risk. Even when self-injury occurs,

the professional team will have a better rationale for their decisions than current whimsical judgment. Where the admitting physician must discriminate between those threatening self-injury for an admission and those who are in greater danger of death, these criteria help to identify the appropriate treatment strategy. The low-risk person may not need emergency care but certainly requires prophylactic attention and education. They may be several years away from an eventual death by suicide, even though they can be threatening self-injury at a particular moment. The high-risk life cycle is shown in the table below as a resource in identifying a particular victim.

The High-Risk Life Cycle and Suggested Prophylaxis

EARLY

1. Bereavement before age 16 (parent or surrogate)
2. Parental or surrogate suicide at any time
3. Premature death of parent or surrogate after 16
4. Parental psychopathology at any age of subject
5. Emotional problems before age 16
6. Maladjustment at work, education, or military after 16
7. Marital problems at any age, divorced and widowed
8. Prior psychiatric hospitalization or treatment
9. Age, sex, race: 60, white, male
10. 30, male, Vietnam service, student status

a. Public Health Education, e.g., suicide lecture

b. Desensitization Groups

c. Brochures with facts

d. Local media: underground press, telephone, TV, movies

e. Existing gatekeepers alerted

f. Reference group mutual aid

MIDDLE

11. Self-defeating behavior, failures
12. Alcohol or drug abuse histories; legal dependency
13. Two or more serious accidents— include overdose
14. Uncooperativeness noted by clinicians in therapy regimes for prolonged illness

a. Referral to self-help groups, AA, Synanon

b. Outpatient therapy

c. Brochures, films, exhibits

15. Dependent, dissatisfied behavior,   d. Combat desensitization
    about care
16. Suicidal preoccupation; elevated to   e. Encounter group approach
    a "right"
17. Institutionalizations, prison, hospital,   f. Suicide prevention classes
    etc.
18. Suicidal threats, one superficial attempt
19. Death experiences
20. No meaning to life—drifting

END STAGES

21 Depression   a. Survivors Anonymous,
22. Aimlessness; many hospitalizations   discussion groups
    and contacts with psychiatric service
23. Several low to moderate attempts   b. Staff-led therapy
24. Significant others aggravation
25. Physical impairments including   c. Halfway House-live in
    cancer, heart disease, etc.
26. Overdoses accidental   d. Newspaper ads for help
27. One or more high-intent attempts
28. Criteria for heroic suicide approached
29. Gives up on life, world; pessimistic
    about society
30. Precipitating losses, failures, or
    rejections

3. *Routine interview with a survivor.* Whether or not a death has occurred, the hospital staff has an obligation to the next of kin or survivors. First, part of good care includes an adequate service to the relatives so that some effort to assuage guilt, shame, anxiety, or anger is accomplished. This represents psychological first aid. Failure to render this service approaches neglect: it is neither Christian nor nice to neglect survivors. Prophylactically, attention to relatives is potentially a deterrent of future self-injury not only for the survivors but for those in the next generation. Children of people who die by suicide tend to kill themselves, too. A second reason is the incompleteness of the clinical record for the facts about self-injury where staff fail to interview survivors.

4. *Suicide prevention plan for each victim.* On the basis of the preceding information, when the patient is still alive, the staff can formulate a suicide prevention plan that is appropriate to that unique individual. Thus a patient who has used pills need not be given excessive scrutiny for hanging, or gunshot wounds. By personalizing the effort, nursing care can be given economically. For a patient returning to the community who prefers guns, prevention can take the form of creating obstacles to attaining access, even though total elimination of guns may be impossible. By frequent, even daily, evaluations the prevention plan can be updated to reflect the patient's changing wishes and capabilities.

5. *Regular psychological autopsies.* Every suicidal event, whether it ends in death or not, should be reviewed by all participants. Typically, this includes the natural working group that has cared for the patient. However, it can and should also include all participants in the death such as friends, relatives, volunteers. This procedure was originally developed to reconstruct the victim's lifestyle and to explain the mode and cause of death. A larger value is to examine communication patterns in the treatment team. Suicide events imply some impairments. Regular autopsies following self-injury events give the staff a chance to practice, much like is done in fire drills. There are approximately ten self-injury attempts for every death, and thus ample opportunity for running into examples.

6. *Exit interviewing.* More attention is needed for the high-risk patient as he prepares to go home. The last week or two of hospitalization provides an opportunity to assess the degree of risk for the future. The patient can be placed somewhere on the high-risk life cycle and a tentative prevention plan formulated. Knowing the first three to six months constitutes the period of greatest risk requires the arrangement of fail-safe communications and appointment patterns. Future contacts should be assured by requiring regular return visits for renewed medications, clinical attention, or other services.

7. *Survivors Anonymous.* Patients with histories of suicide attempts, but no longer needing hospitalization, can be recruited for self-help patient clubs modeled after Recovery Inc. or Alcoholics Anonymous. These groups permit self-help, long-range follow-up and new social reference groups that accept the patients wihout stigmatizing them. To date this particular approach has not received much support or acceptance from the community.

Other practices suggested are the appointment of a suicide-prevention committee to recommend policy or procedural changes that improve prevention and communications concerning self-injury behavior. Part of this is to encourage better training of staff in prevention and to encourage research into the occurrence of suicide. Whether supported by money or not, any kind of research effort improves prevention by drawing attention to what is not being done. Along with these good practices is the general recognition that suicide prevention is everybody's responsibility. This can be done by giving annual awards for outstanding acts by employees. The very absence of this gesture demonstrates the neglect of elementary suicide prevention by most hospital administrations.

Suicide prevention classes for high-risk patients in between self-injury behavior have been offered by the author to hospitalized psychiatric patients. Since about half of all patients have histories of prior efforts to kill themselves, there is always a residual group considered high-risk. By simply inviting these patients to attend a twice-weekly class focused on self-help suicide prevention principles, a regular course can be organized. In a short time, the ward atmosphere relaxes and the topic as well as the acknowledgment becomes routine. Patients often prefer attending the class to going outside for recreational programs. One particular class was given at the Fresno Veterans Administration Hospital. The content was organized as a first aid course with six basic principles of suicide prevention taught. Each session permitted the members adequate opportunity to discuss topics and attitudes around which individuals had preoccupations or distress. The members are not currently suicidal or depressed. The approach was matter of fact and open-ended, clinical much as drug abuse, or sexual conflicts are examined in a group therapy session. The principles of suicide prevention are described next.

1. There is a difference between the wish to die, the act of self-injury, and the outcome. The wish is harmless in itself, occurs to everyone at one time or another, and is obscured by the more obvious wish to live. The act of self-injury expresses the wish to die, but occurs quite rarely in the population at large. In the high-risk individual, the isolated effort to hurt himself receives a great deal of attention to the detriment of suicide prevention in between attempts. The outcome, life or death, tends to be random in the sense that highly effective self-injuries are blocked by heroic preventions or accidents. Conversely, minimal efforts to die produce death when the victim misjudges his method or the movements of others. Confusions in the minds of the victim and his rescuers lump the three concepts into one hodgepodge of "suicide."

2. There is a conflict between the usual wish to live and the sporadically recurring wish to die that produces ambivalence, conflicts with respect to self-injury behavior. This contradiction of motives gets resolved by a temporary decision to seek death. As with all conflict behavior, any action toward one goal often induces opposite motions. This phenomenon permits victims to change their minds before, during, and after a self-injury event. Many live effective lives for years before another self-injury recurs. Ambivalence in the victim permits others to save him. This gratuitous aspect of suicide prevention is often used to justify the lack of professional effort with the often-heard rationalization, "If he really wants to kill himself, no one can stop him." Often overlooked is the equally possible notion that the victim can change his mind.

3. Death is an unknown, which is usually equated with sleep or other lapses of awareness. All have in common a later reawakening usually under benign circumstances. Most people expect to feel better after a self-injury produces death. The implication is that they will be around somehow to enjoy the change. The victim cannot imagine a world without himself in it. He can therefore contemplate his own death with some equanimity since his awareness appears to go on forever. This expectation makes death seductive as a release from present distress.

4. Every victim of self-injury has or develops a non-random plan to achieve his or her own death. The victim selects the method of injury that fits his personality. It is only secondarily a question of availability. Orientations to specific methods often include an association of specific attitudes in the minds of the victims. Simple inquiry is often sufficient to link a preferred method to some personal expectation. The unique meaning and pattern can usually be elicited. Once externalized, this information permits the development of a unique suicide prevention plan, suitable for the specific victim. Both the would-be suicide and concerned parties can focus their efforts on the preferred method rather than a shot-gun attempt to block all methods. Further efficiency can be achieved by mobilizing prevention efforts during the circumscribed time interval of greatest risk. Discovering the unique perception of meaning and method permits prevention to be focused on a specific time, place, and pattern of self-injury. Most dramatic of all is the conversion of a potential victim into a regular life-saver who cooperates in preventing his own death in between acute phases.

Some illustrations of the preceding can be given by the following examples. These associations of meaning are not meant to be universal, but apply instead to unique individuals. One victim who preferred death by gun shot did so because it was fast and efficient! Another liked pills because it was easy. This last association occurs often with heroin addicts when they discuss their favorite methods of self-injury. Hanging is often associated with guilt and expiation. Self-contempt occurs frequently when domestic poisons are used such as rat or roach powder.

5. *"You die the way you live."* The non-random suicide plan expresses the victim's orientation to life, personality, and motives. Policemen tend to use revolvers; doctors use medical paraphernalia; nurses use medications. Men use violent or physically destructive methods more often than women. The final choice of method expresses a person's whole way of life. Very often the previous self-injury behavior represents rehearsal phenomena in which the victim tries several different methods of increasing effectiveness for him.

6. *Impact on others and previous examples.* The victim
looks to the examples of others with respect to his own plan
for self-injury. Parent, ego ideal, peer or others set expectations both for methods and reasons. The innocent bull session
topic of "I'd rather be dead than . . ." often teaches potential
victims that certain conditions justify suicide. The source of
these expectations and the ego ideal's role in conveying them
are presented and discussed in order to provide maximum
choice to the patients in their present planning. Otherwise the
implicit standards of others covertly slant potential victims
toward a readiness to seek self-injury behavior.

A frequent theme in the suicide prevention class is the idea
that "No one loves me," or "I am better off dead, and no one
will miss me." Whenever this theme is elicited, the other
patients are always unanimous in asserting their own distress
at this idea. There are usually enough victims present who
remember the effect of other suicides, and can assert the nature
of the impact.

For the majority of future victims the last, and all too
often, only prophylactic currently available is simply some
persuasive argument against the right to commit suicide. The
time for this approach is always now better than later; when
individuals feel good rather than bad; and before the wish to
die emerges, rather than after. One example of this is a letter
to a potential suicide victim:

Dear Victim of Self-Injury,

There is always time to change your mind, and that is the
biggest argument against suicide. After you are dead, you
cannot correct the mistake. You have to be very right and very
sure that you want to die. Most people who injure themselves,
whether or not they survive afterwards, are not fully intent on
dying. A part of them still wants to continue on. Typically,
those who survive a first attempt live normal lives for many
years after.

We are all amateurs when it comes to dying. Our knowledge of death is based on going to sleep, getting drunk, "wiped
out," or anesthetized. From these, we always wake up with

more or less pleasant memories. These experiences make suicide tempting. The worse you feel, the more seductive death becomes.

Aside from yourself, you are hurting a lot of other people. The ones who respect and admire you the most not only regret your death, they may even follow your example. Would you want your best friend to kill himself because his girl friend left him? You are setting an example for him, your family, friends, and neighbors.

You have no family? Have you thought about your buddies? Would you want them to hurt themselves? You mean you wouldn't try to stop one of them from killing himself? Of course you would! Wouldn't they feel the same about you? Doesn't that mean they care and wouldn't they feel badly if they failed?

Are you thinking that it's none of their business or ours? Do you figure you have a right to kill yourself, when you have no reason left to live? When you feel badly, any answer looks good—even suicide. That is the seduction angle; but any right requires a free choice.

Are you thinking that you made up your own mind and used free will? Not that simple, friend. It turns out that you have been rehearsing for this suicide just about all your life. The odds are that you have often thought about when and how you would do it. You may even have tried before. Because you now have some experience, you will be more effective next time. Isn't that rehearsal? You don't think so? Well, how about trying some other method? The odds are you can't switch, at least not instantly, like a free choice implies. You will need to get used to the new method if the preferred one isn't handy. People die the way they live and especially when it comes to suicide.

The life you save may be your own.

This chapter has suggested ways to preserve the life of survivors, in four life-threatening situations. The good life and the good death are achieved by the same means. One is a preparation for the other. A book devoted to the goal of dying gracefully has to deal with both sides of the life-death perspective. Ending a book is like getting ready to die. The earlier is a preparation for the later. People die the way they live. If you started this book by reading the last page, you have defaulted. You cannot achieve a dignified death by waiting until you are dying. Start preparing now! Go to the first page of this book!

Last Letters about Last Things

Dear Friends:

I am going to die shortly. I don't know exactly when, but I am certain it will be within thirty days. Most of you have an opposite belief. You act as though you will live forever. No matter what dire mortal circumstance you encounter, some escape from death will be possible; and even when you do concede that death will someday come, you still expect to continue your awareness of human existence. Yours is the normal delusion; mine is merely atypical. By persisting in the belief that my death is imminent, I can reexamine the choices I have made so far, and perhaps live the rest of my life more prudently.

Nobody reading this letter has ever experienced death. Dead people don't read or do other things we alive people do. Because we have never died before, our notions of death are intellectual or the products of fantasy. The nearest experiences to death are interruption states such as going to sleep and awakening, fainting and recovering, being anesthetized and revived. From these we get the notion that death is a transition or a temporary cessation of our awareness. We expect to continue in some other form. Thus we anticipate immortality. As a result, our own death is something we deny and which always comes as a surprise. Indeed, most Americans prefer not to know the exact time of their approaching death. It's more comforting to make believe that our own death will never come and to deny that anything could kill us, make us really dead.

So what's the harm in a benign self-delusion that helps make life more bearable, especially one that so many people share? For most people there is no harm, and if you wish to retain your delusion, please stop reading at once. Of course, you might be one of those exceptions I have in mind. Yes, there are people whose denial of their own death predisposes them to use bad judgment. Their presumption of immortality permits them to act imprudently in dangerous situations. Examples? The woman with the new lump in her breast who thinks it's merely the change; the man who drives sixty-five miles per hour every day on the freeway as casually as he gets out of bed; the middle-aged executive who doesn't intend to start exercising now; smokers who won't give up cigarettes; patients who forget to follow diets or take their medicines; diabetics who stopped taking their insulin because "they felt better." If you deny the prospect of your imminent death, you are also vulnerable to denial of the circumstances that may threaten your life, because you have traded the apprehension that fosters caution for the comfort that comes from avoiding threats.

I am going to die shortly and I want to prepare for it. Prepare what? Me!? If I really am going to die shortly, I don't have much time left. I'll never be able to get all those things done that I have been putting off. And indeed I never did have time for everything. Only immortals have infinite time. I should have made these choices long ago, when I had more time. Ah, but in those days I thought I had infinite time. Of all the things I want to do, which three do I value most, which are the least expedient, and which must I act on today? The very idea that I must choose requires examination of alternatives, which alone can yield the satisfaction of a meaningful life. Of course I can avoid choice and not examine my courses of action, which is likely to occur when I deny my imminent death. Such a default means in effect that I have surrendered to the absurd life, where my best efforts yield only random consequences rather than the positive results I anticipate. Connections between present choices and future consequences imply meaning and therefore offer the satisfaction of having prepared myself.

I am going to die shortly. I am talking about the very real possibility that I am mortal and many forces operative today can lead to my unpredicted death. So what else is new? Rather than shrugging my shoulders and surrendering to the various possible kinds of evasion, I want to face the prospect of my death without denial, euphemism, or begging the question of my personal continuation.

Okay, so I am going to die. The only real question is when, and for most of us time becomes an issue only after a physical crisis reminds us of our mortality. The healthy man has little stimulus to consider the issue of his death. He can function secure in his delusion of infinite time. Others less fortunate with imperfect physiology have increasingly frequent and intense reminders of temporal limitations. There isn't much to be done for or with these sensations. Traditionally, we deny their significance by stereotyped thoughts about aging, lack of exercise, or diet. We use analgesics, intoxicants, and psychedelics so long as we can deny the threat of imminent death. Many people keep this denial up even after their first cardiac, surgery, stroke, or sudden catastrophe. This lack of cooperation with medical regime or acceptance of impairment represents a suicidal equivalent, since there is a reduction of life expectancy beyond that of the specific illness precisely because the patient fails to act prudently.

While there is nothing new about irrational motivation such as the delusion of immortality, especially in the context of suicidal behavior, the connection between the specific denial of death and self-destructive activities offers a prophylactic angle. The universal inability to translate death into sensations we can experience predisposes all of us to use denial as a protection against the apprehension which the prospect of death tends to induce. But for some people this denial facilitates carelessness, disregard, or actual risk-taking that leads to a variety of self-destructive behaviors. A genuine acceptance of our vulnerability to imminent death can serve

preventive functions in terms of minimizing accident prone-
ness, risk-taking, or suicide. This can be applied to known
groups with high risk of suicide or accidental death. Policemen
and physicians are exposed to death frequently in our culture.
Both tend to handle this confrontation with denial, as do most
people. But the hazardous nature of police work demands more
caution, which an appropriate fear of death can foster. The
physician's work is hazardous psychologically, since the constant exposure to dying threatens his denial of death. When
this defense is pierced, the physician is more vulnerable to
depression and suicide than are most people. Similarly, a
policeman is also highly vulnerable, especially because of his
familiarity with firearms.

Another high-risk group is the driver with excessive
citations or accidents. They could be exposed to a sensitizing experience with the imminence of their own death. The
recent Forest Lawn radio commercials urging certain kinds of
reckless motorists to purchase their own undertaking first
before driving is a superficial illustration of what I mean.
Instead of exhortation to safety, the driver needs reminders
of how imminent and permanent his or her personal death
really is.

All right, I am going to die shortly. Now I feel changes
taking place that warn me of dire things to come. I awake at
5:00 a.m. with the fog horn measuring time and the redwood
boards creaking their deterioration. My back is stiff; I have a
pain in my chest, gas, aches; and I know death is closer. I
know I am going to die, and I want to face it now while I have
all my resources. Isn't this morbid? No. I am merely trying to
anticipate my death by the best choices I can make now. You
die the way you live, in that you can judge the quality of living
by the kind of death, and vice versa. I am interested in the
versa, even though most people judge a person by the kind of
death he suffers. Consider, if I do die before my expected sixty-
nine odd years, people will reinterpret my past behavior in
terms of the kind of death that takes me. If I die in a plane
crash, it might be said that I was clearly suicidal because I am
a private pilot; if I die in a skiing accident, I will be labeled

accident-prone (who else goes back to a sport in which he suffers repeated traumas?); if I die while under the influence of alcohol, I will be considered a suicide equivalent (too conflicted to attempt the deed directly); if I die in an auto accident, I will be called a murderer if my car strikes the other's first and merely a victim if it's the other way around. If I survive you all, I will get the last word and do the labeling myself. In that event I will be called a philosopher. The point in all these examples is that every known detail of my life might be used as documentation for the particular conclusion being asserted, which in itself will be derived from the quality of death I encounter.

It is equally possible to engage in the opposite process and judge the nature of a death by the quality of the life that was lived. It's also possible to influence the kind of death you have by choosing the kind of life you live. How?

Life consists of activities, usually aimed at achieving goals. In these we employ consistent approaches, methods, plans, and efforts to attain a job, a promotion, an education, a person, a prize, or some other end. In all these goal-seeking activities we can see evolving but consistent qualities. Your prior experiences are a preparation for your later ones and eventually for the kind of death you will die. The moment of death is an anticlimax to the thousands of little deaths you have suffered in your prior choices—those little crossroads where a turn to the left defaulted on all the things to the right.

I am going to die shortly, and I want to face my death in my own way. Isn't this really suicide? Many people kill themselves in the process of achieving significant goals. Our heroes, martyrs, and philosophers who chose to die in the course of seeking an end, imposing a belief, or expressing a value are admirable people. Their choices represent preferences at the cost of their lives. This kind of suicide has to be admired, cannot be prevented, and has little in common with clinical suicide. The psychiatric patients who kill themselves are pathetic and self-defeating people whose lifestyles represent a psychological self-murder many times over, before they incidentally happen to do away with themselves in an anticlimax to a lifetime of psychological suicide. They are indeed the appropriate objects of suicide prevention, sympathy, and psychological study. In hindsight their death is always avoidable, their intentions always increasingly less ambivalent, their goals compulsively more intrapersonal and paradoxically more alienating from significant others. These are people whose life or death serves no cause, no belief, no value.

There is another group of suicides whose number is increasing but the relative frequency of which was always high. Their self-termination is neither good nor bad. I am referring to suicide in those aged who are healthy, intelligent senior citizens. As medical science extends their life, suicide seems to become for them merely another way of dying. Among senior citizens suicide increases with age as a cause of death. These are not altruistic deaths. Nor do I mean to include the irrational self-elimination on the basis of depression, involution, or other clinical motives. I am discussing people whose advancing age induces a loss of vitality, whose significant others are gone, whose life work is meaningless or formally over, and who may be terminally ill. However, that last characteristic may be a red herring. Their suicide often provokes the romantic notion of a person's right to kill himself when a rational evaluation permits the conclusion that his life is absurd. But the ones who argue this case most successfully are the ones least likely to commit suicide under any circumstances, because their problem-solving capacity is so effective that the need for self-destruction as an alternative never becomes a real choice for them.

I make these three distinctions because our attitude towards suicide must necessarily be different in each. The altruistic suicide cannot be prevented. The clinical can, and must be stopped because it is so expressive of self-defeating lifestyles. The elderly is more obscure. Perhaps if social practices change enough to minimize clinical suicide, the self-destruction of senior citizens might also be minimized, because both reflect social deficiencies that maximize alienation, purposelessness, and denial of death.

If my contemplation of death is suicidal in any degree, I

hope it is in terms of the altruistic kind. Of all the ways to risk my life, I would prefer to do so in the cause of a value or belief rather than as a victim of my own efforts to secure goals by self-defeating choices. But the simple observation that I do take risks is not enough to support any conclusion, since all human choices expose one to risks. The riskless life doesn't exist, except as a reciprocal definition of death.

All of which reminds me of an old-fashioned idea. Whatever happened to natural death, or *mors ipse?* Well, the explosion in medical knowledge changed all that. Natural death is now regarded as a state of ignorance. Modern medicine has moved us to the point where death itself is a shame if not quite a crime. Correspondingly, the quality of death in the United States during the last twenty years has evolved from mainly random, impersonal, and external catastrophes to highly unique events in which the victim participates in his own demise (car accidents, homicide, suicide). Even heart disease, cancer, and circulatory fatalities permit the victims to influence the quality of dying by the ways in which they follow (or fail to follow) medical regimes. All of this allows the quality of dying to express our unique lifestyles.

But my original question still stands. Is there a kind of death that we could call natural, in which we could agree that a life had been lived and that to linger on would be less than a blessing? The extremes are easy. Clearly the prolonging of vegetative functioning without the recovery of consciousness is not a significant achievement, but what about less extreme examples? How about a man in his seventies who is alone, healthy, economically secure? At what point is his psychological life over, such that termination could be construed as natural regardless of the pathologist's findings? If all his activities are devoted only to the biological processes of existence, he can be described as killing time—and he is liable to do this until time kills him. If he no longer engages in activities that capture his imagination or call for his best efforts, he is ready to die. He will be a latent fatality waiting for a morbid process to terminate his life. In the days before modern medicine was able to intervene, a death at such a point would have been called natural. No stigma would have accrued to the memory of the man or to his survivors. Today the absence of natural death prolongs life promiscuously, often as a curse rather than as a blessing; and it is a factor in the increased percentage of suicidal deaths in the elderly. All of this demonstrates the harmful consequences of a little immortality.

I am going to die shortly, and I want to die naturally and positively. What can I say about the end of everything I like? My first thoughts are regret, not only for the things I do but for the ones I care about. I am sorry to be leaving, and sorrier for the distress my absence will cause. These sentiments are universal and inevitable. They are even desirable, since they force those who survive to reconcile themselves to loss, grief, and the inevitability of their own deaths. But beyond this immediate feeling I want to find positive aspects of dying.

I now know that I will die in a month. I want to give my last thirty days the best I have and make them as meaningful as the first 15,695. What can I do that will be special? Absolutely nothing! At least nothing different from what went before. To reach for something special during these last days makes a lie out of the preceding life. If there are special things I want to do before I die, they must be started long before the end is in sight.

Our last days do not permit any process that has not been experienced earlier. We are all victims of the habits we live by, and crisis freezes these even more rigidly. Imminent death, especially if denied, is too traumatic a crisis to allow for creative innovations such as the special act implies. And so to the degree that your approaching death evokes special things to do, to that same degree you have failed to live the full or meaningful life, even on your own terms.

If a positive death is choosing to die the way you have lived, what is the value of knowing when death is imminent? What's so good about deciding to do nothing different? Why not maintain the delusion of immortality and the comfort of being surprised by your own demise? Either way, you die the way you live. But the difference comes from the element of choice. Facing the prospect of your imminent end permits you to start making the choices now that you truly value because you can anticipate the consequences more vividly. By making these choices before termination is in sight, you are choosing how you will die by the manner in which you elect to live. And choice is what saves your existence from becoming absurd. You either choose alternatives that make for a meaningful life or absurdities get you by default. To have a choice and fail to make it is the ultimate absurdity.

With best wishes,

F. C.

Last Letters

A person's family are the ones touched most poignantly by death and the ones who elicit the most concern as separation and cessation occur. No final word can ever be written on those feelings. I have selected a letter addressed to my immediate family expressing my concerns for them as individuals in the event of my death at the time I wrote it. Ten years later I would probably say different things. Still these do represent much of my latest, if not my absolute last, thoughts. If I were to die today, this letter would express my farewells and best wishes. Implicit is some form of blessing intended to help them carry on.

Dear Family,

These are my last wishes with respect to my own dying. They represent an extension of the "living will" suggested by the Euthanasia Foundation. The ideas written here are efforts to achieve a good death when my time comes. They are stated after careful thought and with optimal intellectual functioning. Unless I signal otherwise, I intend these to be binding on all persons who care for me as I approach a timely end.

1. I will be ready to die when I can no longer dream, imagine, and act upon intellectual ideas. Action includes writing and public speaking. These activities happen to be embodied in my professional duties. Even so they are my lifestyle rather than a purely isolated occupational skill.

A second criterion of readiness is the loss of my spouse,

whose replacement is impossible and whose absence would be intolerable. There would be a net increase in my readiness to cease immediately following her loss. I would attempt to adapt and carry on. Several years later I might even be able to remarry. But the period following the death of my present wife would be a hazardous interval in which there would be wishes to die and subsequent probabilities of accidents, or self-injury.

The loss of health and sensory functions might make my continuation more difficult and increase my readiness to cease, but they are not in themselves insurmountable obstacles. While such impairments might increase the wish to die if they occur when I am enfeebled, they are less threatening to me at this time.

2. From an external frame of reference, I will be objectively ready to cease when my daily behavior permits no surplus time or energy for the pursuit of play or professional activities, which have given me so much satisfaction in the past. These help to give my life a meaning and purpose. The specific examples vary with my age and stage of development. At this point I am physically able to enjoy skiing. When I lose interest or the ability to continue, I will replace skiing with a sport that I am capable of practicing. Eventually I will turn to sedentary or spectator sports. The sudden loss of interest in any kind of recreation without replacement will be one sign of increasing readiness to cease. A similar progression should be apparent with respect to more intellectual or professional skills and activities.

3. After termination, the part of me called "self," the recognizable identity that has continued from earliest recollection to this point, ceases. I do not anticipate any degree of continuation either in the traditional sense of immortality of the soul or in the Eastern idea of reincarnation. Neither do I expect the more mystical continuation in the form of ghosts, spirits, or other such substances. I do not anticipate a possible resurrection of my body and soul on Judgment Day. I also find deficient the neoscientific equivalent of resurrection summarized

by the slogan, "Freeze, wait, reanimate." It may eventually be technologically possible to thaw a frozen body and to revive the mind which formerly inhabited it, but the social and psychological complications of attempting to carry on impress me as too grim for my taste.

On the affirmative side, I believe in a graceful old age. I see it as a continuation of growth in which adaptation to increasing limitations is required. I expect to terminate within the three or four score years the Bible says is given to man and which modern life expectancies set as probable limits. In round numbers and with average luck I may reach seventy. Anything beyond will be fortuitous, lucky. This means I should make all the decisions about last things I have been recommending to others. At this writing I have not yet accomplished my own goals. Partly this is because I am still young enough to find the prospect of death difficult to make relevant—which documents how difficult it is to really prepare. Despite a sudden flurry of decisions concerning last things, I will attempt to make each day count in achieving the values I carry and thereby to earn an appropriate cessation.

I anticipate a degree of immortality in the memorials of my family, friends, and admirers. The people who have learned from me will provide a living externalization of my values for at least a period of time, and they will represent living achievements of which I am proudest. My children are included; they are the ones I have tried hardest to teach by my own example.

4. Circumstances optimal for termination occur next to mind. Granting a condition when death is preferable, when a psychological readiness to cease is recognized, with an explicit orientation understood about the meaning of cessation, the circumstances which represent optimal dying for me are as follows:

    a. In bed, preferably at home.

    b. As comfortable as physical health and environmental resources permit.

    c. With my wife and survivors present for typical but last encounters.

d. With capacity for imaginative associations undamaged.

e. With other intellectual faculties intact.

f. With pathological processes running their course and medical intervention restricted by my own evaluation of anticipated effects. I reject procedures that impede any of the preceding or the vitality to enjoy the end.

g. Given the array of terminal diseases that cause death in adult males, I prefer number four on the National Institutes of Health list—viral pneumonia with prominent symptoms of fever. As a former victim of wartime malaria, I anticipate the ultimate intoxication—getting high on fevers associated with my own termination.

h. If dying should take some form other than what I prefer, due to circumstances beyond everyone's control, I will find some way to reconcile myself to that necessity, even if only in my fantasies.

I write these statements with a great deal of confidence, which I derive from habit. We are born and we eventually die. In between, the life we lead is a rehearsal for subsequent events including death. The end I foresee for myself is based on the ways I have accommodated to past traumas and crises. My cessation will punctuate my life and serve as some kind of milestone in yours. This letter will become part of that event.

With much love,

F. C.

Local Resources

Providing Information or Service to Clients in
Life Threatening Situations

Assistance with problems of dying, death, and carrying on in the context of fatal diseases can be secured through one or more of the listed organizations. All of them will provide information and referral to other resources in your community. Local resources are usually the most effective because they are most convenient to use. Telephone directories are the greatest single source of potential aid. Local assistance can be sought from the following general listings in the yellow pages of your directory: Alano Club, Alcoholics Anonymous, American Cancer Society, Chamber of Commerce, Clinics, Clubs, Community Chest, Family Service Agencies, Fraternal Organizations, Health Departments (city, county, state), Memorial Societies, Mental Health Associations, Ministerial Associations, Senior Citizen Groups, Welfare Departments (city, county, state).

Life Events Scale

Dr. Thomas H. Holmes and his colleagues at the University of Washington have developed a life-events scale to measure the psychological stress resulting from changes in life circumstances. There is an association between one's total score and subsequent medical problems, including death.

An accumulation of 200 or more "life-change" units in a single year may represent more disruption than an individual can tolerate. Vulnerable people should attempt compensatory measures to make up for the losses or stresses implied in each life event. Note that the last three items occur to everybody, so that each year, thirty-six points are earned just by surviving. Conclusion? Build in periods of no change for the three months following any event with scores greater than twenty-five. Also attempt to follow suggestions given in the accompanying table. Chapter references are also indicated for further reading in the text of this book.

Life Change	Scale of Impact	Date	Accumulation
1. Death of Spouse	100		
2. Divorce	73		
3. Marital separation	65		
4. Jail term	63		
5. Death of close family member	63		
6. Personal injury or illness	53		
7. Marriage	50		
8. Fired at work	47		
9. Marital reconciliation	45		
10. Retirement	45		
11. Change in health of family member	44		
12. Pregnancy	40		
13. Sex difficulties	39		
14. New family member	39		
15. Business readjustment	39		
16. Change in financial status	38		
17. Death of close friend	37		
18. Change to different line of work	36		
19. Change in number of arguments with spouse	35		
20. Mortgage over $10,000	31		
21. Foreclosure of mortgage or loan	30		
22. Change in responsibilities at work	29		

No. of Item	Suggestion	Reread Chapter
1.	Adequate grieving, delay re-marriage	10, 11
2.	Replace services, delay re-marriage	12
3.	Replace services, delay re-marriage, join self-help groups	12
4.	Join Alcoholics Anonymous, Synanon, Recovery Inc., avoid old friends	4, 5
5.	Adequate grieving	10, 11
6.	Shorten hospitalization, lengthen convalescence, increase visitations, return to duty gradually	5, 6
7.	Prolong courtship, delay divorce plans equally: expect fights and incompatibility	1
8.	Find another job, preferably before termination	2
9.	Unpack! Try separate rooms next time	12
10.	Look for another job, doing what you like, this time	6
11.	Pray, visit, be grateful for small recoveries	5, 7
12.	Nine months to get ready	7
13.	Wait awhile, try digital manipulation	12
14.	Beware of sensory overload	12
15.	You are still the boss	12
16.	You are still in debt, like everyone else	3
17.	Adequate grieving; preparation for loss of spouse	7, 8
18.	Avoid additional changes for three months	1
19.	Spouses deserve each other's faults	12
20.	Postpone payment indefinitely; avoid other job changes	1
21.	Bankrupts have better credit than the over-extended	7, 8
22.	Seek fewer responsibilities and more duties you like	8, 9

Life Change	Scale of Impact	Date	Accumulation
23. Son or daughter leaving home	29		
24. Trouble with in-laws	29		
25. Outstanding personal achievement	28		
26. Wife begins or stops work	26		
27. Begin or end school	26		
28. Change in living conditions	25		
29. Revision of personal habits	24		
30. Trouble with boss	23		
31. Change in work hours or conditions	20		
32. Change in residence	20		
33. Change in schools	20		
34. Change in recreation	19		
35. Change in church activities	19		
36. Change in social activities	18		
37. Mortgage or loan less than $10,000	17		
38. Change in sleeping habits	16		
39. Change in number of family reunions	15		
40. Change in eating habits	15		
41. Vacation	13		
42. Christmas	12		
43. Minor violations of the law	11		

No. of Item	Suggestion	Reread Chapter
23.	Over twenty-five, what took them so long? Over sixteen, rehearsal for later separations	9, 10
24.	It's easier to move, buy a lock, or say no	10, 11
25.	Accept certificates, money, and trophies. Avoid publicity	11, 12
26.	Prepare for new demands—indulge half of them	1, 12
27.	Try status quo at home	2
28.	Allow three months adjustment before other changes	2, 3
29.	Alternate with other kinds of changes listed	2, 3
30.	He's got trouble with you, trade him for peace of mind	1
31.	Allow three months between above changes and the ones that follow No. 30. These can be delayed	8, 9
32.	Ditto	
33.	Ditto	
34.	Ditto	
35.	Ditto	
36.	Ditto	
37.	Another optional item; delay three months after above items	9
38.	Aim for eight hours sleep without medication; combine with three balanced meals and regular exercise	3
39.	Avoid increased eating, drinking, and backbiting	2
40.	Increase intake of fruits and vegetables; try walking or climbing stairs	3
41.	Any change of pace is a vacation; try daily meditation	12
42.	Cut down on gifts for everybody; try tokens	1
43.	Drive more in the country; pay your bills regularly; accept conventional restrictions	4

Service Organizations

The following national organizations will provide aid through a central office at the address indicated. Generally these offer information and referral through printed matter. Names and addresses are given alphabetically. Services and other comments are added where appropriate.

NAME/ADDRESS	SERVICE/COMMENT
Administration on Aging Department of Health, Education, and Welfare Washington, D. C. 20201	Information on continuing education
National Council on Aging 1828 L Street, NW Washington, D. C. 20036	Specific aspects of aging
State Office on Aging (Capital city, your state)	Services and employment opportunities
American Association of Retired Persons 1225 Connecticut Avenue, NW Washington, D. C. 20036	Information and group services to the elderly

NAME/ADDRESS	SERVICE/COMMENT
National Office of Arthritis Foundation 166 Geary Street San Francisco, Ca. 94108	Information
National Cancer Program Office of Public Affairs Bethesda, Md. 20014	Information on different body sites for cancer, explanation, therapy
Cryonics Society of California 216 Pico Boulevard Santa Monica, Ca. 90405	"Freeze-Wait-Reanimate" information, newsletter
Center for Death Education and Research Robert Fulton, Director Department of Sociology University of Minnesota Minneapolis, Minn. 55455	Cassette tape programs on death, grief, and bereavement. Listing on request
The Medical Secretary Society of Compassionate Friends 27 A Street Columbus Close Coventry CV1, 4BX Warwickshire, England	Care for bereaved parents with fatally ill children
Foundation of Thanatology 630 West 168th Street NYC 10032	Information and services for the bereaved
Ars Moriendi 3601 Locust Walk Philadelphia, Pa. 19083	Information and membership: "the art of dying," health and human values
Equinox Institute Melvin J. Krant	Information and consultation in care for the dying and their

NAME/ADDRESS	SERVICE/COMMENT

11 Clinton Street
Brookline, Mass. 02146

survivors

Widow to Widow Program
Mary Pettipas
Laboratory of Community
   Psychiatry
58 Fernwood Road
Boston, Mass. 02115

Report of mutual help efforts
by survivors and how to develop
local programs. Cost $2.50 for
printed matter

Epilepsy Foundation of
   America, Suite 1116
733 15th Street, NW
Washington, D. C. 20005

Information and brochures

Eye Bank Association of
   America
110 Irving, NW
Washington, D. C.

Condensed list for posthumous
donations

E. Doheny Eye Foundation
228 Lake Street
Los Angeles, Ca.

Presbyterian Medical Center
2018 Webster Street
San Francisco, Ca.

Lions Eye Bank
420 E. 9th Street
Denver, Colo.

Boston Eye Bank
243 Charles Street
Boston, Mass.

Euthanasia Foundation

Information on dignified dying

NAME/ADDRESS	SERVICE/COMMENT
250 W. 57th Street NYC 10019	
The Deafness Research Foundation 310 Lexington Avenue NYC	Information and local cooperating laboratories
National Drug and Safety League 3146 Francis Street Jackson, Mich. 49201	Information on drug abuse and other hazards to life
Muscular Dystrophy 810 7th Street NYC 10019	Education and information
Family Service Association of America 44 E. 33rd Street NYC 10010	
Family Life Bureau National Catholic Welfare Conference 1312 Massachusetts Avenue, NW Washington, D. C. 20025	
Department of Family Life National Council of Churches of Christ of USA 475 Riverside Drive NYC 10027	
National Council of Family Relations	

NAME/ADDRESS	SERVICE/COMMENT
1219 University Avenue, SE Minneapolis, Minn. 55414	
Continental Association of Funeral and Memorial Societies 50 E. Van Buren Street Chicago, Ill.	Also see Jessica Mitford's book *The American Way of Death* for suggestions and list of memorial societies
Gerontological Society One Dupont Circle Washington, D. C. 20036	Information and membership
American Heart Association 44 E. 23rd Street NYC 10010	Information and education
American Lung Association 1740 N. Broadway NYC 10019	Public health education in respiratory illness
National Foundation March of Dimes 1275 Mamaroneck White Plains, N.Y. 10605	Birth defects, education
National Society for Medical Research 111 Fourth Street, SE Rochester, Minn.	Donation of body organs, information and referral
National Association of Mental Health 10 Columbus Circle NYC 10019	Mental health information for aid in mourning and dying

NAME/ADDRESS	SERVICE/COMMENT
United Ostomy Association 1111 Wilshire Boulevard Los Angeles, Ca. 90017	Information and self-help for ostomy patients (ileostomy and colostomy)
Institute of Physical Medicine and Rehabilitation New York University Bellevue Medical Center 400 E. 34th Street NYC	Self-help devices for rehabilitation of seriously impaired patients
National Multiple Sclerosis Society 257 Park Avenue South NYC 10010	Information and counseling for the disease and referral
Public Affairs Pamphlets 381 Park Avenue South NYC 10016	Explanations for various public health problems with suggestions for self-help
American National Red Cross National Office Washington, D. C. 20006	Information and referral services
American Speech and Hearing Association Wayne State University Detroit, Mich.	Information and education
American Association of Suicidology c/o Charlotte Ross, Secretary Suicide Prevention Center 220 W. 26th Avenue San Mateo, Ca. 94403	Information, referral and membership

Recommended Reading

Abraham, H. S. 1969. The psychology of terminal illness as portrayed in Solzhenitsyn's *The Cancer Ward*. *Archives of Internal Medicine*. 125:758-60.

Abrams, H. S. 1969. The patient with cancer—his changing pattern of communication. *Annual of the New York Academy of Science*. 164:881-96.

Agee, J. 1963. *A death in the family*. New York: Avon Publishers.

Alvarez, A. 1972. *The savage god*. New York: Random House.

Anthony, S. 1940. *A child's discovery of death*. New York: Harcourt Brace.

Appel, J. Z. 1968. Advances in medicine. *Journal of the American Medical Association*. 205:513-16.

Bateson, G. 1972. *Steps to an ecology of the mind*. New York: Ballantine Books.

Baudry, W. A. 1969. Initiation of a psychiatric teaching program for surgeons. *American Journal of Psychiatry*. 125:1192-7.

Benjamin, A. F., and Benjamin, B. *New facts of life for women*. Englewood Cliffs, New Jersey: Prentice Hall.

Benoliel, J. D. 1970. Talking to patients about death. *Nursing Forum*. 9:254-68.

Birtchmell, J. 1970. Recent parent death and mental illness. *British Journal of Psychiatry*. 116:289-97.

Blachy, P. H. 1971. Can organ transplantation provide an altruistic-expiatory alternative to suicide? *Life Threatening Behavior*. 1:5-9.

Brim, O. A. et al. 1970. *The dying patient*. New York: Russell Sage Foundation.

Capote, T. 1965. *In cold blood*. New York: Signet.

Choron, J. 1972. *Death and modern man*. New York: Macmillan.

Cramond, W. A. 1968. Psychotherapy of the dying patient. *British Medical Journal*. 3:389-93.

Cutter, F. 1971. Suicide: the wish, the act and the outcome. *Life Threatening Behavior*. 1(2):125-37.

DeVries, P. 1961. *Blood of the lamb*. Boston: Little Brown.

Diaz, E. 1969. A death on the ward. *Hospital Topics*. 47:83-87.

Downey, G. W. 1970. Dying patients still have human needs. *Modern Hospital*. 114:78-81.

Engel, G. L. 1968. A life setting conducive to illness: the giving up—give-up complex. *Annual of Internal Medicine*. 69: 293-300.

Evanswentz, W. Y. 1960. *The Tibetan book of the dead*. Oxford University Press.

Farberow, N. L. 1963. *Taboo topics*. New York: Atherton Press.

———. 1971. *Bibliography on suicide and suicide prevention*. Washington D. C.: U.S. Printing Office.

Farberow, N. L., Stein, K., Darbonne, A. B., and Hirsch, S. 1970. Indirect self-destructive behavior in diabetic patients. *Hospital Medicine*. 6:5, 123-33.

Farberow, N. L., Ganzler, F., Cutter, F., and Reynolds, D. K. 1971. An eight-year survey of hospital suicide. *Life Threatening Behavior* 1(3), 184-202.

Gebhard, P. H., et al. 1958. *Pregnancy, birth and abortion*. New York: J. Wiley and Sons.

Glazer, B. G., Strauss, A. C. 1965. *Awareness of dying*. Chicago: Aldine Publishing.

Gorer, G. 1965. *Death, grief and mourning*. New York: Doubleday and Company.

Green, J. S. 1969. *Laughing souls: the days of the dead in Oaxca, Mexico*. Balboa Park: San Diego Museum of Man.

Grollman, E. A. 1967. *Explaining death to children*. Boston: Beacon.

———. 1970. *Talking about death*. Boston: Beacon.

Group for the Advancement of Psychiatry. 1965. *Death and dying: attitude of patient and doctor*. New York: GAP.

Gunther, J. 1949. *Death be not proud.* New York: Harper.

Hendlin, H. 1969. *Black suicide.* New York: Basic Books.

Hinton, J. 1968. *Dying.* Baltimore: Penguin Books.

Hollingshead, A. B., and Redlich, F. C. 1958. *Social class and mental illness.* New York: J. Wiley and Sons.

Hughes, R. 1968. *Heaven and hell in western art.* New York: Stein and Day.

Hulzer, H. 1971. *The psychic world of Bishop Pike.* New York: Pyramid Books.

Hurwood, B. J. 1971. *Life, the unknown.* New York: Ace Books.

Jackson, E. N. 1957. *Understanding grief.* Nashville, Tennessee: Abingdon Press.

Jones, B. 1967. *Design for death.* Indianapolis: Bobbs-Merrill.

Kalish, R. A. 1968. Life and death: dividing the indivisible. *Social Science and Medicine.* 2:249-59.

Kennell, J. H. Slyter, and Klaus, M. H. 1970. The mourning response of patients to the death of a new-born infant. *New England Journal of Medicine.* 283:344-9.

Kneisl, C. R. 1967. Dying patients and their families: how staff can give support. *Hospital Topics.* 45:35-6.

Kubler-Ross, E. 1969. *On death and dying.* New York: Macmillan.

Landsberg, P. 1953. *The experience of death.* New York: Philosophical Library.

Langer, M. 1957. *Learning to live as a widow.* New York: Julian Messner.

Legler, H. 1970. *How to make the rest of your life the best of your life.* New York: Simon and Schuster.

Lerner, J. 1969. The centenarians: some findings and concepts regarding the aged. *Journal of the American Geriatric Society.* 17:429-32.

Lowenberg, J. S. 1970. The coping behaviors of fatally ill adolescents and their parents. *Nursing Forum.* 9:269-87.

Lifton, R. J. 1967. *Death in life.* New York: Random House.

Marshall, J. G., and Victor, W. 1971. Treatment of death in children's books. *Omega.* 2(1):36-45.

McGuffey, W. H. 1962. *McGuffey's fifth eclectic reader.* New York: New American Library.

Mitford, J. 1963. *The American way of death.* New York: Fawcett World Library.

Nably, M. H. 1959. The child's view of death. In H. Feifel (Ed.), *The meaning of death.* New York: McGraw-Hill.

National Center for Health Statistics. 1971. *Vital statistics of the U.S.,* vol. 2, sec. 5. New York: NCHS.

National Home Study Council. 1972. *Directory of accredited home study schools,* pamphlet. Washington D.C.: NHSC.

New York State Department of Labor. 1971. *Are you a woman looking for a job?* pamphlet. New York: NYDL.

O'Connell, W. E. 1968. Humor and death. *Psychology Rep.* 22:391-02.

Pike, E. R. 1970. *The strange ways of man.* New York: Pocket Books.

Pollock, G. H. 1971. Anniversary reactions, trauma and mourning. *Psychoanalytic Quarterly.* 39:347-71.

Pomeroy, M. R. 1969. Sudden death syndrome. *American Journal of Nursing.* 69:1886-90.

Quint, J. C. 1967. The dying patient: a difficult nursing problem. *Nursing Clinic of North America.* 2:763-73.

Reich, C. 1971. *The greening of America.* New York: Bantam Books.

Riley, C. G. 1967. A doctor's moral obligation to his patient. *New Zealand Medical Journal.* 66:666-86.

Roazen, P. 1971. *Brother animal: the story of Freud and Tausk.* New York: Random House.

Roberts, J. L., et al. 1970. How aged in nursing homes view dying and death. *Geriatrics.* 25:115.

Rosecrans, C. J. 1970. Is acceptance of non-being possible? *Alabama Journal of Medical Science.* 7:32-7.

Rosenblatt, B. 1969. A young boy's reaction to the death of his sister. A report based on brief psychotherapy. *Journal of the American Academy of Child Psychiatry.* 8:321-35.

Russell, B. 1950. *Unpopular essays.* New York: Simon and Schuster.

Senescu, R. 1969. The problem of establishing communication with the seriously ill patient. *Annual of the New York Academy of Science.* 164:696-706.

Schuman, R. E. 1970. *Death, property and lawyers.* New York: Dunellen.

Sharp, D. 1968. Lessons for a dying patient. *American Journal of Nursing.* 68:1517-20.

Shneidman, E. S., ed. 1970. *Essays in self-destruction.* New York: Science House.

———. Perturbation and lethality as precursors of suicide in a gifted group. *L.T.B.* 1(1): 23-45.

Silverman, P. R. 1969. The widow-to-widow program. An experiment in preventive intervention with other widows. *Mental Hygiene.* 53:333-7.

———. 1970. The widow as a care giver in a program of preventive intervention with other widows. *Mental Hygiene.* 54:540-7.

Smith, A. G., and Schneider, L. T. 1969. The dying child. Helping the family cope with impending death. *Clinical Pediatrics.* 8:131-4.

Stengel, E. 1967. *Suicide and attempted suicide.* Baltimore: Pelican.

Strauss, A. C., and Glazer, B. G. 1970. *Anguish: a case history of a dying trajectory.* Mill Valley, California: Sociology Press.

Sumner, W. G. 1967. *Folkways.* New York: Mentor Books. 1967.

Sudnow, D. 1967. *Passing on: the social organization of dying.* Englewood Cliffs, New Jersey: Prentice Hall.

Toffler, A. 1970. *Future Shock.* New York: Random House.

Toynbee, A., et al. 1969. *Man's concern with death.* New York: McGraw-Hill.

U.S. Department of Labor. 1971. *Continuing education programs and services for women.* Washington D. C.: USDI.

Weisman, A. 1973. *Dying and Denying.* New York: Behavioral Publications.

Wertenbaker, L. 1970. *Death of a man.* New York: Alfred Knopf.

Williams, G. L. 1957. *The sanctity of life and criminal law.* New York: Alfred Knopf.

Wolf, A.W.M. 1958. *Helping your child to understand death.* New York: Child Study Association.

Wolfgang, M. E. 1966. *Patterns in criminal homicide.* New York: J. Wiley and Sons.

Index

About the Author

Fred Cutter is a research psychologist with the Veterans Administration Central Research Unit in Los Angeles, California, and also serves as consultant to the Suicide Prevention Center. He has helped to develop new approaches to understanding and assessment of suicidal risk by the use of ratings of self-injury behavior, the consensus Rorschach with families of victims, self-help groups with high risk people, and the use of visual art and cartoons in education for suicide prevention. He is currently leading an effort to use communication media in a national campaign to reduce death taboos that impair "the cry for help."

Dr. Cutter received his Ph.D. from Catholic University of America in Washington, D.C., in 1955 and has worked since with sex offenders, drug and alcohol abusers, and currently in suicide prevention. He is married to the Carmel painter, Dorothy Cutter, who works in her Morro Bay Studio. They have two children, David, 13, and Amy, 10.